THE JEWISH COMMUNITY

ITS HISTORY AND STRUCTURE TO THE
AMERICAN REVOLUTION

In Three Volumes

VOLUME ONE

Professor Morris Loeb, of New York, the distinguished chemist, scholar and public worker, who died on October 8, 1912, by his last Will and Testament, created a Fund under the following terms: "I give and bequeath to The Jewish Publication Society of America the sum of Ten Thousand Dollars as a permanent fund, the income of which alone shall, from time to time, be utilized for and applied to the preparation and publication of a scholarly work devoted to the interests of Judaism."

The present work, published in 1942, is the fourth issued under this Fund. The first, SAADIA GAON—His Life and Works, by Henry Malter, was published in 1921. The second, THE PHARISEES—The Sociological Background of Their Faith, by Louis Finkelstein, was published in 1938. The third, THE JEWS IN SPAIN—Their Social, Political and Cultural Life During the Middle Ages, by Abraham A. Neuman, was published in 1942.

THE MORRIS LOEB SERIES

THE JEWISH COMMUNITY

ITS HISTORY AND STRUCTURE TO THE AMERICAN REVOLUTION

BY

SALO WITTMAYER BARON

Jur. D., Ph. D., Pol. Sc. D., Rabbi

PROFESSOR OF JEWISH HISTORY, LITERATURE AND INSTITUTIONS
ON THE MILLER FOUNDATION, COLUMBIA UNIVERSITY

VOLUME ONE

GREENWOOD PRESS, PUBLISHERS
WESTPORT, CONNECTICUT

The Library of Congress has catalogued this publication as follows:

Library of Congress Cataloging in Publication Data

Baron, Salo Wittmayer, 1895–
    The Jewish community.

    Original ed. issued in series: The Morris Loeb series.
    Bibliography: p.
    1. Jews--Politics and government. 2. Jews--Biblio-
graphy. I. Title. II. Series: The Morris Loeb series.
DS124.B29 1972   917.3'06'924   74-97269
ISBN 0-8371-3274-6

121072

Copyright 1942 by The Jewish Publication Society of America

Originally published in 1942
by The Jewish Publication Society of America, Philadelphia

Reprinted with the permission
of The Jewish Publication Society of America

First Greenwood Reprinting 1972

Library of Congress Catalogue Card Number 74-97269

ISBN 0-8371-3274-6 (Set)
ISBN 0-8371-3889-2 (Vol. I)

Printed in the United States of America

TO

MY PARENTS

ON THE COMPLETION OF MORE THAN HALF A
CENTURY OF TIRELESS COMMUNAL ENDEAVOR

PREFACE

JEWISH communal history throughout the millennia of diaspora life has long been the subject of considerable scholarly attention. The European community of the pre-Emancipation era, especially, has for decades attracted modern investigators by its numerous extraordinary features. Its remarkable combination of religious and secular authority, its almost "extraterritorial" status and "sovereign" political powers and its overwhelming control over its members have flattered the political ambitions of nationally-minded modern Jews, but antagonized many reformers and anti-segregationists. Philo-Semites and anti-Semites among the non-Jews, too, have often held definite opinions about the "ghetto" community. Like their Jewish confreres, however, they, too, have frequently substituted one or another bias for reliable information and sound reasoning. It is hoped that this first attempt at a comprehensive historical and sociological analysis of the entire communal evolution to the Emancipation era will help to promote clarity, if not unanimity of appraisal.

Apart from the usual embarrassment in defining the highly ambiguous term "community" — it is used here in the prevailing, organizational sense which is even narrower than that of the German *Gemeinde* — students of communal aspects of Jewish history are beset by two opposing difficulties: an extreme dearth of material for certain areas and periods and a plethora of extant information on other regions and epochs. Modern literature on the subject, too, is unevenly distributed and much repetition in one field is aggravated by nearly total silence in others. The present author has made an effort to maintain the relative proportions of the various phases of his ramified topic regardless of this quantitative disparity. In the use of the vast and significant literature of rabbinic responsa, for example, he has been guided principally by the importance of the countries or centuries of their provenance. Representative samples from diverse areas and periods were considered more promising than mere concentration on works of a few outstanding masters, however great an influence the latter may have wielded on the subsequent evolution of Jewish law.

The focus of this entire work is centered on the European community of the Middle Ages and early modern times, both because of the great richness and variety of its historic accomplishments and, genetically, because of its intimate linkage to Jewish community life throughout the world today. At the same time its deep moorings in the ancient and contemporaneous eastern communities have come to the fore ever more insistently. In fact, while trying to detect the hidden springs of this phenomenally tenacious evolution, the writer found himself delving deeper and deeper not only into the obscure realms of the First Exile and the Persian and Hellenistic dispersion, but also into the early manifestations of ancient Palestinian municipal life. Many rather unexpected relationships have laid bare some of the most autochthonous roots of the diaspora community securely ensconced in the ever fertile soil of ancient Israel. It has been found necessary, therefore, to devote the first two chapters to a general outline of both the modern foreground and the ancient background of the community in dispersion in its extraordinary historic career from the Babylonian Exile to the American and French Revolutions.

It is with real pleasure that I take this occasion to express my gratitude to those who made possible the early completion of this book. During the final revision of the manuscript I have had the assistance of my pupil Mr. Herbert F. Hahn, who has verified numerous entries and carefully read all proofs. My wife has compiled the bibliography from the scattered references in text and notes and has been of constant assistance throughout the preparation of this work. My secretary, Miss Miriam Antler, has taken excellent care of all technical details and has also assisted me in the various stages of writing and proof reading. All three of them have also intensively collaborated with me in the arduous compilation of the Index. Mr. Herbert Solow proved extremely helpful in the editorial revision of the manuscript, while Dr. Solomon Grayzel and Mr. Maurice Jacobs have competently steered its course through the press. I am also grateful to Prof. Alexander Marx for a few suggestions given me after he had read two of the early chapters. These expressions of gratitude, of course, do not involve any delegation of responsibility.

S. W. B.

Yifat Shalom
Canaan, Conn.
May 6, 1942

CONTENTS

VOLUME ONE

VOLUME TWO

xi

VOLUME THREE

Notes, Bibliography, and Index to this work will be found in Volume Three.

THE JEWISH COMMUNITY

CHAPTER I

QUEST FOR NEW FORMS

"JEWISH community" has become an equivocal concept. It embodies the wide variety of meanings generally attached in sociological and juristic literature to the term community.[1] The complexity of connotations has moreover been increased by uncertainties associated with the adjective "Jewish." To the controversy of the recent decades concerning the primacy of the religious or national element in the Jewish people have been added the effects of Nazi policy, which includes in the Jewish community all "racial" Jews, i. e. persons whose "blood" is at least one-quarter Jewish. While both religious and nationalist Jews have always agreed as to the meaning of the Jewish community of descent, destiny and culture, they have also insisted on the preponderance of a subjective criterion, i. e. voluntary allegiance of an individual whether to his religious denomination or to his ethnic group. According to the Nazi doctrine, however, subjectivity is entirely eliminated, and membership in the Jewish community is immutable and wholly independent of individual will. Even persons born and bred in the Christian religion, who throughout their life participated in some European national culture without ever having known that they had Jewish parentage, become, immediately upon discovery of such parentage, members of the Jewish community.

3

Such a type of community is, of course, entirely new and unprecedented. Its major weakness consists not only in the obvious untruth of its underlying philosophy based on illusory pseudo-scientific assumptions concerning race — many an historic illusion has proved a powerful vehicle of progress or reaction — but also in its thorough repudiation by the members themselves. Certainly no human organization can long endure unless it meets with the approval of those whose needs it is supposed to serve. In any case, the experience of the Jewish community under the Nazi regime has been too brief, its work too much handicapped by antagonistic legislation, its functions so candidly transitional to complete annihilation that no far-reaching conclusions may be drawn as to its nature, durability and workability under less extreme conditions.

1. Religious or Ethnic Community?

Long before the rise of Hitler to power, a lively debate on the essential nature of the Jewish community and its corresponding organizational forms was carried on inside and outside the Jewish camp. The indubitable effect of the general secularization of the western world, concomitant with the rise of capitalism, democracy, Jewish emancipation and scientific rationalism, has so deeply transformed all phases of Jewish individual and group life that the Jewish community, organizational reflection of that life, has become the subject of burning controversy.

In western Europe and America, the religious factor has retained its preëminent position in the scale of communal values. Even where communities have been divided, officially or unofficially, among adherents of old-time orthodoxy or neo-orthodoxy, of conservative Judaism and of a variety of Reform trends, the religious congregation has been the mainstay of all organized Jewish life. In some countries, such as the United States, attempts have been made organizationally to overcome this religious disparity through concentration upon relief and defense activities uniting all Jews, but the religious congregation has continued to attract the relatively most constant and active participation of a large membership. Various Jewish federations of charities (especially through their nation-wide Council of Federations) and national defense organizations may have attained the position of super-communal entities, transcending the bounds of both the individual congregation and their national unions, but it has always been the religious element which has lent them their peculiar coloring. The federations themselves are frankly denominational and profess to serve their constituents in line with similar Catholic and Protestant charities. In our period of ever-increasing government responsibilities for relief and social welfare they adhere to the ancient historic tradition of church-administered charities, and see therein a major justification for their separate existence. As a matter of fact management of these charitable institutions rests predominantly with a class and individuals opposed to Jewish nationalism and professing to view Judaism as a religion only.

Their work, moreover, can never hope to attract the same intensity of allegiance or even the same extensity of effort as has so long been the case with the Synagogue. Despite our highly agnostic age it must be remembered that total congregational membership in the United States vastly exceeds, numerically, Jewish membership in purely philanthropic undertakings. Discounting the large floating population of casual synagogue visitors and of those attending High Holiday services in makeshift congregations, it seems reasonable to assume that, despite religious laxity prevalent in metropolitan areas, perhaps one-half of New York Jewry is affiliated with one or another of 1,300 permanent congregations. In many Jewish settlements numbering but a few families each, the lack of a regular congregation bars permanent affiliation. But these numerical losses are counterbalanced by hundreds of small communities which offer congregational facilities and in which enrolment is almost complete. The last decade, moreover, has shown none of the oft-predicted manifestations of further decline in congregational vitality. On the contrary, if the figures of the most authoritative recent census are to be trusted, the number of Jewish congregations in the United States has increased by 19 per cent in the years 1928–37, as contrasted with an increase of but 13 per cent for the Jewish population. While New York City Jewry increased some 16 per cent, its congregations increased by some 28 per cent. All this despite the severe depression and congregational mortality during the years 1930–33.[2] As to intensity of effort, the attendance of synagogue members at divine services ranging from one (Day of Atonement) to 365 days a year, and their participation in various synagogue activities of a social or cultural nature — however superficial, indeed futile many of these activities may appear to truly religious persons — far outdistance the active cooperation of members of federations, and other charitable associations, the bulk of whom perform only one act annually, viz. the signing of a check.[3]

In contrast to such trends, new socio-religious realities in eastern Europe and Palestine have given rise to secularist trends which have threatened to submerge the religious aspect of the Jewish community. Having maintained relatively intact the pre-emancipation communal heritage, the East European masses, especially those professing a nationalist or socialist credo, see in their community a complex entity satisfying an enormous variety of needs, secular as well as religious.. Hence they have tended to view their communal organization as merely a debased residuum of an ancient, cherished institution. Recognizing, however, the great transformations in modern life, their leaders attempted to translate the old, religious into a modern, secular nomenclature. Concomitant with the rise of Jewish nationalism in the last decades of the nineteenth century, was a rising movement to remodel the accepted Jewish *Religionsgenossenschaft* into an all-embracing *Volksgemeinde*. Such a "people's community" was to be a strictly secular organization of nationally rather than religiously oriented Jews, and would include even professed atheists or agnostics. A few extremist spokesmen demanded even the inclusion of such nationally-minded converts to other religious faiths as would elect to join. The community was to provide a multiplicity of cultural, educational and charitable services, many akin to those usually rendered by a municipality. Religious needs, while not necessarily beyond its scope were to be relegated to a special department whose relative significance would not exceed that of a contemporary European ministry of cults.

Usually combined with a program of national minority rights, this movement also demanded that all states of multiple nationality delegate important cultural responsibilities to national minority communities under the management of officers freely elected by members of the minority nationalities. Extremists envisaged supreme elective bodies, "people's parliaments," as the main legislatures for these reserved areas of public and cultural life. The state, without giving up its sovereignty in international or domestic affairs, would forego intervention in the autonomous functions of the minority communities and would restrict itself to supervision or the occasional convocation of a super-parliamentary body consisting of delegates of all sub-parliaments to reach decisions on questions of common concern to all nationalities.[4]

These ideological controversies merely reflected the stage of dissolution reached by the ghetto community under the impact of Emancipation. With the disappearance of corporative organization from western society, little room was left for the old, segregated Jewish corporate body. Leaders of the emancipatory movement, Jewish and non-Jewish, long agreed that the establishment of a general equality of rights and the incorporation of Jewish citizens into the national majorities was to be accompanied by the destruction of the former Jewish "state within the state."

To be sure, the principle of liberty of conscience, emerging from the centuries-old wars of religion as an indispensable prerequisite to peace and mutual toleration, presupposed freedom for professing Jews to adhere to their religion without loss of citizenship rights. Such disparity was to be reduced to the root essentials of religious non-conformity, however. Since the Christian denominations, especially in Protestant countries, had in the course of centuries divested themselves of many political features characteristic of the medieval Church, many champions of Emancipation expected the Jewish religion, too, to be purified of secular ingredients and to see its organized activities confined to the narrow range of worship, religious education and denominational charity. The more these liberal champions insisted on the humanitarian principle of equality, the more likely they were to extend political liberalism into the religious domain as well. Political liberals, indeed, often became the prime movers in Jewish religious Reform. The main difference between Christianity and Judaism, at least in practice, had consisted in the adherence of Jews to their traditional ceremonial law and ritual, but many Reformers were quite ready to embrace the prevalent antinomianism of the Protestant churches and to restrict Jewish ritual to a few bare essentials confined to synagogue precincts. A Reform Jew was expected to live fully the life of his Christian compatriot, to consume the same food, to work on the same days and to share in social undertakings with little reference to religious disparity. The synagogue itself was to be transformed into a pure house of worship which would preach to members and the world at large principles of ethical monotheism, foreswearing the nationalist hope of a physical restoration to Palestine in the messianic era and largely abandoning even the use of Hebrew as a medium of worship. A Jewish community so conceived was but a pale reflection of its former self.

Even some leading Reformers looked back to the established communal patterns of former ages for light and guidance, however. Aaron Chorin and Leopold Löw in Hungary, Abraham Geiger and Samuel Holdheim in Germany, often searched for precedents of older communities to justify innovations. The American Reformers, who more consistently repudiated the binding force of tradition and the need of justification by precedent, likewise professed interest in the historic continuity of communal evolution and a desire to maintain it where possible.[5]

Between these extremes of nationalism and Reform, of East European maximalism and German-American minimalism, hovered the mass of Jews who, whether or not truly orthodox in religious conviction, were tradition-minded. This mass, although relatively inert and inarticulate, as well as poorer in thinkers and writers who could successfully formulate its point of view, continued to adhere to an accustomed mode of life with greater or lesser consistency. In its communal efforts, too, it pursued roughly the line of tradition, making only such slow and gradual adjustments as were necessitated by changing environment, and novel legal situations.

2. Modern Experimentation

Each country was, of course, sovereign insofar as legal regulation of the communal destinies of its Jewry was concerned. Despite obvious world-wide interdependence and the many interterritorial features of Jewish community life, no attempt was ever made to consider its organizational aspects on an international scale. There was, instead, a multiplicity of national and local legislation and statutory or administrative regulation which, in the course of the nineteenth and twentieth centuries, gave rise to several new organizational forms. These were, as a rule, the resultant of a variety of environmental factors and of the consistent, though quasi-unconscious desire of the Jews to maintain at least a semblance of their previous organizational unity. Through the maze of detailed enactments and the chaos of contradictory legislation, judicial precedent and administrative practice, one may, nevertheless, detect basic forms which have dominated Jewish communal life in the course of the last century and a half.[6]

A new type, in many respects entirely unprecedented in the annals of Jewish history, has been developed in the Jewish "congregation" found in countries where prevails separation of State and Church. This type has been char-acteristic of the United States since its foundation, of France since 1905 and, to a certain extent, of many Latin American communities. It is based on the purely voluntary allegiance of members. Here the state disclaims all interest in the religious life of citizens, reserving to itself only a measure of supervision over the public administration of religious bodies so that they should not conflict with the accepted standard of morals and public order. Although such complete disinterestedness is often controverted by extensive tax immunities granted churches and synagogues and by state legislation requiring the observance of the Christian Sunday as a universal day of rest, it must be conceded that the government does not interfere with the selection of a congregation by an individual or with his abstention from joining any congregation. Beyond granting a charter to each congregation as to any other association, and exercising a rather perfunctory supervision over financial management and self-adopted statutes, the state claims no jurisdiction over congregational affairs. The long and checkered history of the American churches reveals state intervention to be close to an absolute minimum.

In some respects this condition is reminiscent of the ancient Graeco-Roman community. There, too, any ten adult Jews could organize a congregation of their own. If, as it appears, the new congregation did not require special

government approval of its charter, as did professional or
social corporations, this was due to a general dispensation
implied in the main privileges extended to the Jewish community throughout the Roman Empire. There, too, we
find an almost infinite variety of Jewish corporate bodies,
assuming statutory forms and adopting modes of worship
and ritual, according to their own decision, limited only by
the power of custom. There are, however, also many basic
differences between the modern and the ancient congregation. While the Roman imperial government before Constantine was extremely tolerant of mere religious disparity —
except for sporadic persecutions of Christians and an occasional outburst of anti-Jewish feeling — it did not disclaim
interest in religion. In fact, the Roman state religion was
still an integral part of the government structure, and
"atheism" was still prosecuted as a crime against the state.
The Jewish community, too, despite its kaleidoscopic variety
of patterns, had its unifying force in the vast control of
the Palestinian center, whose patriarch was recognized by
public law as the official leader of all imperial Jewry. On
the whole, one might say, the Graeco-Roman disparity in
Jewish communal life was due far more to religious creativity
and the intensity of sectarian feelings than to religious
indifference or superficial conservatism characteristic of most
Jewish communal endeavors during the present era.[7]

What may be designated as the Jewish "state church,"
created by some European dictatorial regimes since the
Napoleonic era, is entirely different. Although some examples survived under more democratic governments and found
means of adapting themselves to new liberal requirements,
they were basically conceived as tools of absolutism which
insisted on including organized religion within the scope of

an all-embracing state power. Some of these dictatorial regimes combined a certain anti-Jewish animus with their totalitarian ambitions. Others were free of anti-Jewish bias, but wished to control the synagogue as they did the Christian churches.

The outstanding examples of such state-controlled Jewish communities are the *consistoire*, organized by Napoleon in 1808, to last in France, with numerous modifications, until the separation of church and state in 1906, and in Belgium until the present; the "Jewish committees" which replaced the *kahal* of Czarist Russia from 1844 to 1917; Mussolini's fascist community, organized in 1930–31 but largely destroyed by the racial legislation of 1938; and, to a certain extent, the new community organizations instituted by Pilsudski in Poland, King Alexander in Yugoslavia, Kemal Pasha in Turkey, and so forth. Each has had peculiar features of its own, but all share the basic aim of serving the state purposes rather than those of the Jews.

The longest-lived, the Franco-Belgian consistory, revealed remarkable social adaptability and, especially under the more liberal Third Republic (1871–1906) and twentieth-century Belgium, succeeded in ridding itself of the more obnoxious features of state control. Its adaptibility, however, was largely conditioned on the Jews' forming but a slight minority in the overwhelmingly Catholic populations and on the understandable interest of both France and Belgium in closely supervising the activities of the inter-territorial Church. In view of the preponderance of both pro-Catholic and anti-Catholic biases in the general religious legislation of the two countries, its effects upon the Jewish community were decidedly secondary and derivative. From its inception, moreover, the consistorial system enjoyed more

whole-hearted support from the Jews than did similar organizations in other lands. Napoleon had rather successfully
concealed his absolutist aspirations behind a cloak of what
were alleged to be the freely expressed wishes of an assembly
of Jewish leaders. Before long, the new organization became
associated in the mind of French Jewry with the great
achievement of Emancipation, and was invested with some
of the emotional loyalty engendered by memories of Jewry's
progress from "serfdom" to equality. The compulsory features of the consistorial set-up, while vesting greater powers
in communal leadership and thus enabling it to perform
tasks of considerable magnitude, in the long run nurtured
religious indifference, however, and created superficial allegiance rather than deep-seated loyalties.

In Russia, on the other hand, the overtly anti-Jewish
aims of the government defeated their own purposes and
robbed the Jewish committees of effective influence on Jewish affairs. Combined with the staunch orthodoxy and the
powerful national feeling of the Russian Jewish masses,
these government measures merely stimulated the preservation of an extralegal communal organization along the lines
of the traditional *kahal*. Though devoid of government
support, this extralegal community organization successfully
weathered the storms of Jewish Enlightenment and of the
incipient social revolution until 1917.

From the brief, though varied, experiences under fascist
and semi-fascist legislation, on the other hand, little can
be concluded, since the communal groups there have not
passed the earliest stages of evolution and since their effectiveness has constantly been impeded both by the unbal-
anced state of European affairs and the tremendous expansion of anti-Semitism.

A third form is represented by more recent attempts to realize the nationalist demand for a people's community. The Soviet Union is thus far the only country which has made this attempt on a truly large scale. The opposition to all established religions and "godless" agitation fostered by the Soviet regime from its inception, combined with the recognition of the Jewish population as a national minority to which Lenin had been converted by the pressure of Soviet realities, necessitated the reorganization of Jewish communal life along some such new lines. The general safeguards for national minority rights proclaimed by the Council of People's Commissars in November 1917 were reinforced by the simultaneous outlawry of anti-Semitism, and led to the establishment of new secular Jewish communities in charge of the cultural life of a Yiddish-speaking constituency. In the Jewish colonies, especially in the autonomous Jewish regions of the Ukraine and Crimea, the Jewish communities have resembled small municipalities. In the Jewish mass settlements of White Russia and the Ukraine, too, local Soviets have helped administer their affairs by using Yiddish as their main medium of communication. Jewish people's courts have adjudicated litigations in Yiddish, and Jewish schools from grammar grades to sectors of universities and academies, have given extensive instruction in Yiddish. At one time the Yiddish speaking school population was estimated at over 250,000. To climax this Jewish autonomous structure there was finally conceived the idea of gradually establishing an independent Jewish republic in Birobidjan which would ultimately become a member of the federated republics of the Soviet Union.

At the same time, however, certain other hard realities of the Soviet evolution have greatly militated against the realization of the original postulates by protagonists of the *Volksgemeinde*. Due to a combination of a class-struggle heritage from the Czarist community and of the Soviets' early anti-British orientation, Zioni m has been outlawed and declared a counter-revolutionary movement. Together with it, Hebrew was banished from school curricula and reduced to a subject of instruction at universities on a par with other classical but dead languages. As a vehicle of both Zionism and religion, its use was likewise classified as counter-revolutionary, at least to the extent that teaching Hebrew to children below the age of eighteen became a crime punishable by a long prison term. Thus the Jewish community saw itself suddenly despoiled of the three main pillars of its traditional structure: the Jewish religion, Hebraic culture and the Zionist messianic ideal. While Yiddish letters have now begun to be cultivated with increasing vigor and full government support, the main emphasis was naturally laid on the Communist world outlook and, especially, the indoctrination of children. Many close observers of the Russian Jewish scene have expressed doubts as to the ultimate survival of the Jewish minority in the new clime of totalitarian assimilation and of the worship of what is practically a rival religion. Even those who do not share this extremely pessimistic view admit the gradual lessening of the vitality of Jewish communal endeavor during the last decade, a diminution in the enrolment of Jewish schools and a decreasing effectiveness of Yiddish education. Particularly sharp has been the decline in communal allegiance (emphasized by the high ratio of mixed marriages) of those hundreds of thousands of Jews who, through the processes of three Soviet five-year plans, have been transplanted from the Ukraine and White Russia to the metropolitan areas of Moscow and Leningrad or to the new industrial centers along the Volga and the Ural. No one can as yet foretell the extent to which this decline may have been checked, and possibly reversed, by the recent absorption of some two and a half million Jews in the newly incorporated Polish, Rumanian and Baltic areas and the subsequent Russo-German War.

Another distinct type of people's community has, in the meantime, been growing in Palestine. Constituting a much less definite break with the past, and being less exposed by the environment to forces of assimilation — indeed, being often excessively segregated from the majority by the flare-up of national animosities — the Palestinian community was never menaced by the same dangers affecting the Soviet community. If religion has lost preëminence, it was neither banished nor suppressed as a communal function. The old Hebraic culture has received new regenerative stimuli from an amazingly speedy and creative Hebrew renaissance in the country. Zionism, though suffering from the usual clash between ideal and reality, between exalted expectations and unavoidable compromises, has remained the dominant element of Palestinian culture, mutually fructifying all areas of communal endeavor.

In the all-Jewish towns of Tel-Aviv and Petach Tikvah, as well as in some two hundred Jewish colonies throughout the country, the Jewish community has become more or less identical with the municipality, embracing all the tasks appertaining to both municipal and religious bodies. Even among the Jewish populations of bi-national cities, Jerusalem, Haifa and their like, the edifice of religious congregations, labor unions, social and educational associations, crowned by the National Council of Palestine, has achieved a measure of success unrivaled, at least, since the days of the ghetto community. To be sure, the precariousness of the international position of Palestine, its dependence upon an influx of funds and manpower from abroad, certain threatening phenomena in the social and psychological evolution of the second generation, have cast many a shadow on the future and even on the actual efficacy of this remarkable communal structure. But it is this very sense of insecurity, incidentally felt much more widely in the Diaspora than among the Palestinian Jews themselves, which has stimulated the quest for new solutions and communal creativity of a high order. In any case, this large-scale experiment has injected a most significant new element into the composite picture of Jewish communal evolution during the Emancipation era.

A fourth type, representing the least radical break with historic continuity, has been in existence throughout the nineteenth and early twentieth centuries in most countries of central and east-central Europe, particularly in Germany and Austria-Hungary. Of course, there was no uniform German community. Certain areas in southwestern Germany, such as Württemberg and Baden, were deeply influenced by the Napoleonic consistorial system. The most important German country, however, Prussia, which embraced an increasing majority of German Jewry, tried in its basic community law of 1847 to reconcile the realities of the traditional pre-emancipation community with the demands of the new era. Despite modifications of detail, enacted particularly in the first years of the Weimar Republic, this combination of traditionalism with modernity proved an effective and workable answer to modern complexities.

The extreme anti-Semitic measures of the Nazi regime have naturally greatly undermined the economic strength of the Jewish constituency. Apart from ultimately withdrawing its early recognition of the community as an institution of public law, the government also forced it to concentrate solely on the speedy liquidation of German Jewish life and the facilitation of overseas emigration. By thus converting communal organs into reluctant agencies of oppression, the Nazi regime eliminated much of the ideological appeal which had underlain communal endeavors. Nevertheless, by forcing even the most recalcitrant Jews into the communal fold, by giving all the communities an organizational superstructure in the *Reichsvertretung der deutschen Juden*, by delegating to the Jewish community exclusive control over the cultural life of the remnant allowed to persist in Germany, and by concentrating much of the relief and emigration efforts in its hands, it has unwittingly given the Jewish communal organization a new lease on life.

The Austro-Hungarian Empire, too, long succeeded in maintaining an equilibrium between the traditional community and the needs of the Emancipation age. In the Jewish community law of 1890 Austria gave its Jewries considerable leeway for an autonomous evolution which went far beyond the strictly religious domain. Hungary, rent asunder by decades of struggle between militant Reform and equally militant orthodoxy, ended by permitting the organization of independent orthodox or "neolog" (Reform) communities, parallel to those which adhered to the *status quo*. Despite these divisions and conflicts, which after all were merely symptoms of pulsating life, the Austro-Hungarian communities were, like the German, powerful vehicles of Jewish self-government. Largely continuing, at first with but minor modifications, in the successor states of Austria, Czechoslovakia, Hungary, and the provinces in-

corporated in Poland, Rumania, etc., this communal organization survived the revolutions of 1918 and, to a certain
extent, still functions within the "new European order"
established by the Nazi war machine.

A fifth, rather intermediate type is represented by the Jewish communities of the British Empire, particularly the United
Kingdom. Due to a peculiar historic evolution in the period
of Resettlement, which will be sketched below,[8] the Jewish
communities on the British Isles long lived outside the framework of public law. With the bulk of Jewry long concentrated
in London, the Spanish-Portuguese congregation and the
German-Polish Great Synagogue respectively retained such
preëminence in the Sephardic and Ashkenazic communities as
to make a measure of centralization in the period of greater
populousness and geographic dispersion an almost automatic
necessity. The peculiar position of the Anglican Church in
Great Britain's governmental structure, on the other hand,
necessitating constant parliamentary legislation on religious
and ecclesiastical matters, ultimately brought about government recognition of the Jewish community and a modicum
of communal legislation. While far from converting the Jewish
community into a government organ of the consistorial type
or giving it those powers of taxation and law enforcement
provided for by the German, Austro-Hungarian and Polish
communal constitutions, the British government has given the
Anglo-Jewish community more legal recognition than is possible in countries where state and church are separated. With
its United Synagogue effectively controling the majority of
Ashkenazic congregations, with the Chief Rabbi serving as an
official ecclesiastical head of most congregations and as an
unofficial spokesman of almost all of the remainder, and
with its Board of Deputies uniting both Ashkenazim and

Sephardim, the Anglo-Jewish community has had far greater cohesive powers, at least organizationally, than is shown by the communities of the Western Hemisphere.

The above five major types of modern community are illustrative of the variety of solutions offered to the problem created for organized Jewish life by Emancipation and the modern state. They reveal extraordinary creativity in the effort to reconcile inner historic continuity with the constantly changing demands of a new era. Our cursory review shows also that the last three decades have been the period of the greatest fermentation and experimentation, and that the evolution which began in the areas of Resettlement even before the American and French Revolutions, but which received new stimuli on the official admission of Jews to full citizenship in the modern state, has not yet reached even a temporary point of rest.

3. Law Enforcement and Democracy

As can be seen from this brief, somewhat oversimplified survey of modern communal evolution, recognition of the Jewish community by public law played an enormous role in the diversification of the new communal types. Such recognition has, indeed, always been a vital factor in shaping the destinies of the Jewish community. Some modern writers, puzzled by the numerous extraordinary features of Jewish communal history, have often spoken vaguely of a "mystic urge" impelling Jews to create everywhere their own communal institutions in the face of the worst odds. Viewing historical developments less supernaturalistically, one may see in such an urge only a conscious or unconscious group desire to preserve its identity and to develop its life along accustomed lines. The adaptation of institutions to new and unprecedented situations may merely be the enforced modification of such a drive for continuity. One must, however, fail to understand the basic factors in Jewish communal history if one focuses exclusive attention upon such desires or, more generally, on the inner propelling forces of the community. As a matter of fact, it has become fashionable in recent years to swing to the other extreme and to speak of the Jewish people in the dispersion as the object of its history rather than a subject guiding and determining its own destiny. This assertion, entirely unjustified in its sweeping formulation even for the political and economic domain, is ludicrous when applied to the history of the Jewish community. Between the two extremes of mystic inner urge and outward political pressure, one must find one's road, recognizing the importance of both factors in varying degrees throughout the history of the dispersion.

There is little doubt that much of Jewish communal evolution can be explained only by the state's self-interest in the effective fiscal and ecclesiastical organization of Jewish subjects; the influence of political and economic struggles between the organized Jewish group and similar groups among their neighbors, especially the burghers; the general evolution of corporate bodies in a particular society; the forces of imitation of institutional and legal patterns developed by the non-Jewish nations; and, generally, by that subtle and often indiscernible interplay of social and cultural influences between the Jews and their environment. Recognition by public law undoubtedly was a major expression of the sum total of these environmental factors, which always affected even the inner life of the Jewish community. Recognition by public law, moreover, has always strengthened the hand of communal leadership, reinforced the peculiarly Jewish means of law enforcement by placing at the community's disposal the assistance of the state executive organs and giving it the full compulsory powers of taxation.

Such public law enforcement was not altogether indispensable, however. In two major historical instances the absence or withdrawal of such recognition seems to have produced no immediate dire results. In the Christian-Roman Empire the hostility of the dominant creed resulted in the removal of major state sanctions which had theretofore effectively supported Jewish communal control. By converting the Jewish courts of justice into mere courts of arbitration in 398 C. E. and by suppressing the Palestinian patriarchate about 425 C. E., the imperial administration clearly indicated its hostility towards Jewish group life. There is nevertheless no evidence of any ensuing breakdown of community organization, except for the general deterioration of Jewish status occasioned by the decline of Roman civilization, growing fiscal oppression and antagonistic political and economic administration. In most areas of modern Jewish Resettlement, especially in England and France during the seventeenth and eighteenth centuries, existing communal formations were either ignored or forbidden by statute. In both mother-countries and in British and French colonies there nevertheless sprang up numerous Jewish communities which, notwithstanding important modifications in detail, continued to maintain an undiminished hold upon their members.

It must be borne in mind, on the other hand, that in the Roman Empire the conservative force of a centuries-old tradition could not be swept away by a sudden outburst of legislative hostility. Again, many Jews came to Resettlement areas from countries with deeply rooted communal organizations. Almost automatically they continued on accustomed communal lines. Even Marranos, often the prime movers and early pioneers of western Jewish communities, sooner or later, upon settling in freer countries, attempted to organize communal groups along patterns familiar in pre-expulsion Spain and Portugal and in Italian, North African and Levantine communities established by refugee predecessors. Secondly, professing Jews living in Catholic or Protestant environments were shut out from all organized forms of religion unless they built their own synagogues, established their own cemeteries and formed closely-knit organizations which greatly resembled public law communities in other lands. Differences were considerable from the outset, however, to become ever sharper with time. When major changes in general society, especially a radical separation of state and church, loosened the ties of communal control within all religious bodies, they became fundamental. The Jewish community was set adrift, freed to shape its own destiny.

Support by public law, moreover, was not always an unmitigated blessing. Where it supplemented existing loyalties, it undoubtedly was a source of added strength. By tipping the scales in favor of a dominant leadership, however, it strengthened those economic, social and cultural forces which tended to create a communal oligarchy. In many cases it helped perpetuate an oligarchic rule which otherwise would have been forced to give way before popular discontent, and greatly contributed to the growth of inner dissensions and occasional outright class struggle. Wherever, as in most modern communities, communal loyalties were no longer powerful, public law enforcement was frequently resented by members as one more hostile manifestation of state police power. Many Jews chose to escape this power and, incidentally, also to save their share in communal taxation, by withdrawing from the

Jewish community. In many cases, especially among large taxpayers, the economic incentive was in itself sufficiently strong to motivate withdrawal. In many others, Jews retained communal membership and went through the motions required of members, paying annual dues, occasionally visiting the synagogue and generally securing religious rites at birth, marriage and death, but otherwise becoming profoundly estranged from a communal organization which, they felt, had been imposed by government fiat. Religious indifference, stimulated by modern trends toward individualism and scientific rationalism, was often reinforced by the compulsory aspect. The Franco-Belgian consistories and the German communities offer numerous instances of such adverse effects of public law recognition.[9]

Absence of public recognition, on the other hand, made communal organisms entirely optional, as in America. It may be true that about one half of American Jewry does not actively participate in any organized form of Jewish communal life, belonging neither to a synagogue nor to a charitable, fraternal, labor, defense or any other group. But those who do belong to an organization do so of choice, albeit, perhaps, a choice influenced by the examples of neighbors, by pressure of public opinion, or other external factors. The amazing record of achievement of the American Jewish community, despite its innumerable obvious shortcomings and weaknesses, testifies to the frequently superior vitality of such optional organizations as against those composed of largely indifferent or unwilling taxpayers.

Any consideration of the modern community, must bear in mind another sociological factor of prime significance, namely the tremendous urbanization and metropolitanization of Jewry during the last century. With the exception of

Constantinople and Amsterdam, there probably was no community in medieval and early modern Europe which had a
population of more than 10,000 Jews, while the vast majority
of Jewish settlements in eastern Europe as late as the nineteenth century were much smaller. Today probably over three
million Jews, or nearly one-fifth of all world Jewry, live within
one hundred miles of Times Square. There is an enormous
difference between a Jewish community counting a few hundred or a few thousand members and the new gigantic agglom-
erations of Jews found in New York City or even in Chicago,
Philadelphia, London, Moscow, Budapest and other great
cities. Even if the entire system of law enforcement characteristic of the ghetto community could have been maintained
with undiminished vigor in the New York area, its application to such a vast mass of Jewry would have created so many
unprecedented difficulties and produced so many modifications
of the general principle, as to generate an entirely novel communal type.[10] Without such enforcement, cross-currents
created by the multiple forces which have given all modern
community life an aspect of impermanence (rapidly changing
neighborhoods, high individual mobility, impersonality of
human relationships, absorption in economic struggle, competition of interests intensified by newspaper and radio stimuli,
etc.) have naturally played havoc with communal control in
the Jewish area. The New York *ḳehillah* movement of the
period of the First World War failed not only for accidental
and personal reasons; the failure was primarily a reflection of
real disorganizing forces. In any case, its operation, had it
begun to operate, would have required new methods, indeed
entirely new approaches, and its effectiveness would have
been limited at best. Little wonder that, confronted by a

majority of world Jewry settled in metropolitan areas of one million population and over, Jewish communal planning faces altogether unprecedented tasks and must embark on wholly unprecedented routes.

Another major difficulty in meeting the perplexing new conditions is the ancient dichotomy between communal authority and individual freedom. There has been a great deal of rhetoric concerning the "democratic" features of the old type of Jewish community. Even a cursory glance at Jewish communal history must persuade the unprejudiced observer that the term "democratic" as here applied has a meaning entirely different from that used for the political organisms of our day. The simple facts are that the bulk of world Jewry, even after the second fall of Jerusalem, was for several centuries subject to the control of the Palestinian patriarchate. Simultaneously, that part of Jewry which was under the Parthian and Persian empires was under the control of the Babylonian exilarch until the beginning of the second millennium C. E. After the suppression of the patriarchal office, all Jews lived under the exilarch. It is obvious that both the patriarchate and the exilarchate had all the basic features of hereditary monarchy. Although the prerogatives of the Jewish leaders, unlike those of other oriental potentates, were curtailed by competing powers of scholars and of individuals who wielded influence at various courts (the so-called *shtadlanim*), one can hardly speak of a democratic regime at any time in this long epoch. In medieval and early modern Europe, on the other hand, the frequent concentration of wealth gave a preponderant share in communal administration to a few families, which often determined communal affairs against the clear wishes of the majority. In early modern Holland, Germany and Poland, particularly, the steady growth of communal oligarchy had practically eliminated all vestiges of constitutional democracy which were retained in formal statutes.[11]

Democracy of a particular type, however, was an indubitable reality. Sociologically, the more or less permanent scholarly leadership, from that of the ancient academies down to that of the modern *yeshibot*, although it tended to become an "aristocracy of learning," was essentially democratic. Scholarship was never restricted to a particular class. Scholars themselves insisted on the educational obligations of the community and individuals, so that education was more widespread among Jews than in any other community down to the nineteenth century. This emphasis on study as a supreme value in itself, together with the great social and intellectual rewards of learning, created opportunities for most individuals, even those of the humblest origin, to rise to the highest rank in society. Combined with the absence of a hereditary nobility — the hereditary priesthood had practically long lost its importance — and the general insecurity and instability which prevented all but a tiny handful of Jewish families from remaining wealthy for more than one or two generations, the democracy of learning gave to the Jewish community a democracy in some respects more real than could have been achieved by any purely constitutional safeguards.

This is but one example of the inapplicability of general political categories to Jewish communal history. Long before the full evolution of its diaspora community the Jewish people had become a basically non-political entity. Indeed, in its long diaspora career it had demonstrated the independence of the essential ethnic and religious factors from the political principle. Through a concatenation of unique historical circumstances, it early learned to discard the general acceptance of state supremacy and to proclaim in theory, as well as to live in reality, the supremacy of religious, ethical and ethnic values. That is why a purely political interpretation, even of the constitutional life of the Jewish community, will do less than justice to the non-political core of the problem. This circumstance has often been overlooked by historians and publicists writing on the Jewish community, especially those who have preached its reorganization along the political lines of a people's community.

4. MILLENNIAL EXPERIENCE

The tremendous task of communal reorganization now confronting world Jewry requires, then, a closer understanding of the fundamental lines of the earlier historical evolution. Only through a deeper penetration of the essential trends in the millennial history of the Jewish community will we be able to comprehend the chaotic variations of the contemporary community, all of which go back to the same original structure and still reveal its indelible imprint. Interest in Jewish communal history, true enough, is fairly universal in Jewish circles. Reformers and Zionists, orthodox Jews and socialists, indeed, all wings of Jewish public opinion have for decades expressed intense interest in the past as well as the present of the Jewish community. An enormous monographic literature has grown up in recent decades, making available primary sources of information for many areas and centuries — although leaving others shrouded in darkness — and subjecting them to close juridical, sociological and historical scrutiny.

Thus far, however, no attempt has ever been made to describe in some detail the history of the Jewish community from its inception to the present. There is, in fact, no book in any language which seeks to synthesize the findings of specialized research, to achieve a general understanding of the whole evolution and thus to stimulate further investigation.[12] It is hoped that the present attempt at such an analysis for the period ending with the eighteenth century will, despite its obvious imperfections, help fill this widely-felt gap.

CHAPTER II

THE PALESTINIAN MUNICIPALITY

THE ancient Palestinian town differed in numerous respects from the average American or European town. With few exceptions, such as the industrial regions of Beit-Mirsim and Beth-Shan during the Bronze Age, the Palestinian township was, in a higher degree even than other ancient oriental cities, primarily a settlement of farmers, only secondarily a center of trade and industry. Geographic factors united with political insecurity and a growing historic tradition to create many very small settlements to which the terms city, town, hamlet or village could be equally well applied. Because of their autonomous municipal structure, however, almost all must be classified as townships in the political and organizational sense.

1. Physical Regionalism

Western Palestine (without Transjordan), with an area of but 9,000 square miles, has extraordinarily varied geographic features. Leaving Syria with its moderate climate, one reaches, after a few miles, the subtropical region of Tiberias. Surmounting the cooler plateau around Jerusalem, one suddenly drops to the almost tropical environs of the Dead Sea. A fast airplane can cover the entire distance from the high, snow-covered peaks of the Lebanon to the desolate, arid dunes south of Gaza in less than half an hour. Rain is scarce everywhere, but its distribution is even more inadequate. Sections

31

of the little land may have a temporary oversupply of water,
but in other parts man, cattle and plants thirst for a drop of
that regenerative fluid. The frequent excess of evaporation
over precipitation is further aggravated by the geological
formation. The prevalent limestone is conducive to the disappearance of the rainwater deep under ground, where it
forms caves and, occasionally, springs, but is otherwise of
little direct use to the farmer. In short, no less than forty
distinct geographic units have been detected within the area
of Palestine, each requiring special human adjustments and
nurturing a spirit of local independence as well as of tribal
separatism.

Even the early nomadic cattle-raisers needed a minimum
supply of water. For the farmer, Canaanite as well as Israelite,
the vicinity of a brook or spring became a matter of life or
death. From time immemorial settlements clustered around
every spring and around the few rivers and rivulets. First
in the valleys and then on mountain slopes, entire clans of
farmers built their houses, planted their orchards and vineyards, and cultivated their fields as closely as possible to the
source of water. In between there long remained many
"empty," uninhabited places, open to roving tribes of nomads,
whose swift appearance and disappearance in the neighborhood of the established settlements aroused but little resentment among the residents. We may thus understand the
slow, pacific penetration of the country by Israel's patriarchs,
so gloriously described in Genesis and largely confirmed in the
more matter-of-fact documents preserved in the archives of
Tell el-Amarna. With the gradual increase in population,
especially after Israel's conquest, more and more of these
empty spaces were filled by permanent new settlers. But
even then the original characteristic concentration of human

habitation around the main source of water supply remained the dominant feature of Palestinian civilization.

This concentration was further stimulated by the long prevailing political insecurity. Throughout its civilized history Palestine was exposed to frequent raids of the proud and warlike, but often famished, Bedouins to whom even the less fertile regions always appeared as lands flowing with milk and honey. To offer more effective resistance to such raiders, the Palestinian farmers preferred to erect their dwellings in close proximity to one another and, if possible, to surround them by a wall. The inconvenience of the walk to and from the family parcel of land, where most of the able-bodied gathered each day, was more than compensated for by the pooling of resources of the community for the repelling of sudden attacks. Since the walk, however, could not be unduly long, a fairly large number of small, concentrated settlements best corresponded to the needs of Palestine's growing agricultural population.

The historical developments of the second millennium B. C. E. added strength to these political and economic forces. Albrecht Alt has argued plausibly that in Egypt and Palestine many deserving warriors were rewarded by the Hyksos conquerors with grants of land. This semi-feudal practice led to the creation of many small, but largely independent, city-states. In the El-Amarna period, at any rate, the country was covered by such tiny political organisms. While acknowledging the overlordship of the king of Egypt, the rulers of these city-states engaged, of their own right, in negotiations and alliances, spun far-flung diplomatic intrigues and waged petty wars upon one another. With Egyptian control steadily declining, the petty rulers held sway over their respective cities and a few smaller townships and villages in the vicinity. This regional independence had lasting effects upon the political structure, even after the unification of most of the country under the Israelitic monarchs.

Little wonder, therefore, that a close comparison of the available records from Thutmes III's enumeration of the cities which he conquered during the fifteenth century with the list of cities allegedly occupied by Joshua — which, it now seems, was composed under Josiah only a few decades before the fall of Jerusalem — shows that no less than 400 localities inhabited by the ancient Israelites bear the distinctive name, town (*'ir*). The average distance between such towns was no more than about four miles, making it possible for the vast majority of their inhabitants to reach their places of work by walking two miles or less. Most of these towns were, of course, very small. Few exceeded a total of 1,000 inhabitants. From our western point of view, nearly all might be classified as villages, were it not for the fact that many were surrounded by walls and all possessed a large measure of political and economic self-sufficiency. Those which did not, usually styled *ḥaṣerim* (hamlets), consisted as a rule of but a few homesteads. Placed within the small orbit of the larger "city," these hamlets were under its complete economic and political control. They were, in biblical terms, the "daughters" of the respective cities in whose public life they fully participated. It is in such semi-rural "townships" that the large majority of Israelites lived and struggled, and their political and organizational make-up left an indelible imprint upon subsequent communal developments in Jewry.[1]

2. Provincial Supremacy

The weakness of the Israelitic monarchy, in part the effect of these separatist forces, enhanced local powers as opposed to the central state authorities. Arisen from a national emergency caused by the encroachments of the Philistines, the crown retained significance in the life of the people primarily in periods of war. For a time the military and economic expansion under David and Solomon, the splendor of the latter's royal court and Temple, and the prolonged period of widespread prosperity seemed to place the Israelitic monarchy on the road toward absolutism such as existed in the neighboring countries. The subsequent division into two kingdoms, however, followed by the speedy rise of the Aramean and the Assyrian Empires, soon reduced the Israelitic and Judean monarchs to a position of revered first officers of the state rather than its absolute masters.

Old traditions of the days of the semi-nomadic "patriarchs" and of the regional "judges," called upon to lead the army in a campaign and immediately thereafter to retire to private life, long persisted to nurture a free, "republican" spirit. In the vast steppes of Gilead and southern Judah, in particular, where the prevailing cattle-raising economy fostered a conservative adherence to accustomed ways, monarchy was increasingly regarded as the effect of Israel's sinful abandonment of its reliance upon the leadership of God, its only rightful monarch. The growing social unrest in the country from the ninth century on, brought about by the increasing economic inequality among the classes of theoretically equal citizens; the conflicting interests of the landed and urban aristocracy, the royal bureaucracy and the priesthood; the intellectual and religious clashes between the sophisticated, luxury-loving, often "corrupt" inhabitants of the two capitals and the large majority of provincials — all contributed to the weakening of royal authority and the rise of a decidedly anti-monarchical spirit among the masses and their leaders. From Hosea to the end of the two kingdoms, prophets and historians united in either overtly denouncing the monarchy as sinful degradation and blind assimilation of the most hateful ways of foreign nations, or in demanding that the kings mend their ways, stem the abuses of the ruling classes and of their own officials, and conduct a foreign policy based, not upon ordinary power-politics, but upon the deeper interests of the masses. The oldest messianic prophecy in the Bible (Gen. 49.10 ff.) seems overtly to have been directed against the powerful regime of Solomon. Every major revolt against the established order soon found a prophetic abettor. The successful rebellion of Jeroboam I was instigated by Ahijah the Shilonite, that of Jehu by Elisha. Unrest and agitation became so irresistible that finally, in the Deuteronomic Reformation, the youthful King Josiah himself had to proclaim a constitution which re-duced monarchy to a mere shadow of what it had been in the days of Solomon.

Before this Deuteronomic revolution there existed no legally defined delimitation of the royal power. Some exuberant poets and psalmists, especially those in royal employ, may have emulated their fellow songsters of Egypt or Babylon and exalted the kings of Israel as godlike creatures, as the "sons" of God, if not as gods in their own right. Even they had to admit, however, that their king was not above, but under the law, and that justice, the full and impartial administering of his due to each and every citizen, was the very core and justi-fication of royal power (Psalms 45.7–8; 72.1–4, etc.). For the others, monarchy, if not altogether an evil, had constantly to justify its existence by living up to the most far-reaching expectations of the people and by unreservedly subjecting it-self to the divine will as conveyed to each monarch by the "true" messengers of God. Apart from the difficulty of choos-ing between the "true" and the "false" prophets, few kings could fulfill the often extravagant prophetic demands without sacrificing what they personally regarded as the legitimate rights of royalty or the true interests of the nation. Wilful, strong individuals, such as Jeroboam II and Menasseh, often ruthlessly suppressed all opposition. They left behind them, however, merely the bitter aftertaste of tyranny. Such excesses not only failed to obtain the consent of the governed, but stimulated a determination to prevent recurrence.

In any case, the influence of the royal government upon the daily life of the people outside the two capitals was rather slight. Biblical records are neither extensive nor explicit enough to permit definitive conclusions, but it appears that in periods of peace the central government made itself little felt in the hundreds of provincial townships and their dependencies. If, as we have good reason for assuming, the combined population of Samaria and Jerusalem never exceeded a total of 80,000, it is readily seen that perhaps ninety-five percent of all Israel lived outside the immediate reach of the central government.

There is no evidence that royal taxation was a permanent feature under the First Commonwealth. Samuel may allegedly have sounded a warning concerning the evil fiscal effects of Israel's insistence upon the election of a king:

> And he will take your fields, and your vineyards, and your oliveyards, even the best of them, and give them to his servants. And he will take the tenth of your seed, and of your vineyards, and give to his officers, and to his servants . . . He will take the tenth of your flocks; and ye shall be his servants . . . (I Sam. 8.14–17).

But it cannot be proved that, as some scholars contend, this warning reflected the later practice in Israel rather than that among their neighbors. In periods of concentrated royal power, as under Solomon, the king doubtless taxed heavily the physical as well as pecuniary resources of his subjects. He drafted scores of thousands among them for *corvée* labor, imposed heavy customs duties and other tolls on merchandise shipped in or through the country, and exacted many "gifts" from seekers of favors. It was primarily from these sources that huge sums said to have totaled 666 talents in gold (the equivalent of some $220,000,000 at the present rate of $35 per ounce) could have come into Solomon's treasury in a single year. On the occasion of the payment of a very large tribute to Assyria, we learn that King Menahem of northern Israel taxed 60,000 of his leading citizens (*gibbore ha-hail*) 50 silver shekels each. The absence of further records of direct taxation, imposed upon the ordinary citizen year in and year out, would be difficult to explain were such taxation a regular feature of Israelitic life.

It seems probable, moreover, that, like the other ancient states, the two Israelitic kingdoms would have found the business of actually collecting the tithe of every crop in kind and disposing of it through the usual commercial channels too arduous to be dealt with directly. Like ancient ,Babylonia, Egypt or Rome, the Israelitic government would have employed tax-farmers who, for a lump sum, would obtain the right to collect all taxes. Apart from the inconclusive references to Solomon's twelve provincial governors whose duty it was to maintain the royal court and administration from the revenue of their respective provinces, and to Omri's and Jehoshaphat's similar administrative division, we hear neither about publicans nor about the manifold abuses inherent in this method of taxation. Even more harshly than the talmudic sages, the ancient prophets would have stigmatized such abuses among the social evils they so persistently denounced.

Under these circumstances one may, perhaps, venture the assumption that direct taxation for the benefit of the king was neither permanent nor universal. In any case, whatever taxes were imposed by the state, the task of collecting seems to have remained entirely to the local administration.[2]

Neither was military service a regular duty of the Israelitic citizen in peacetime. The standing army, chiefly the royal bodyguard, seems to have been recruited for the most part from among foreign mercenaries. David had pointed the way when he attached to his own person a number of Cretan and Philistine soldiers, uninterested in local party conflicts. Among the Israelites, it seems, only the wealthier landowners were called upon to equip themselves and participate in a regular military campaign. Other able-bodied citizens, too, helped to resist invaders, but their services seem to have been more intermittent and local. As soon as any war was over, both groups returned to ordinary tasks, in which they encountered but little governmental interference.

The position of the king in the administration of justice was more significant. The Israelite, like most other Semites, visualized law and justice as the very essence of his public and private, religious and secular life. God Himself was primarily "the Judge of all the earth," and his earthly king appeared but as a magnified sheikh dispensing justice to his flock. The king could adjudicate all litigations brought to his attention; he could serve as a court of appeal from all lower courts; he could establish legal precedents and, perhaps, even issue ordinances regulating certain matters of substantive and procedural law. Absalom's method of earning wide-spread popularity by sitting in judgment where there was "no man deputed of the king to hear" the litigants clearly demonstrates the importance of this royal prerogative. Nevertheless the

mere size of the country and its population as well as its growing commerce and social stratification, which undoubtedly led
to more frequent legal disputes, must have prevented the king
from taking an active part in any but a slight minority of
cases awaiting judicial decision. Neither do we possess conclusive records of any permanent royal judiciary, except perhaps in the capital. If we disregard Absalom's rather irregular
intervention, we learn from historians, prophets and psalmists
only about kings personally sitting in judgment. In the provinces, the administration of justice was entirely in the hands
of the local authorities. As far as the bulk of the population
was concerned the royal control of the judiciary was largely
nominal.[3]

The influence of the center upon provincial religious life
was likewise merely sporadic and restricted to a few major
issues. Even if we assume that, before the establishment of
the monarchy, the tribes of Israel organized a sort of "am-
phictyony," gathering at stated intervals at the amphic-
tyonic sanctuary at Shiloh,[4] it is still questionable how large
a group of representatives participated. Even after the
erection of the great Temple of Jerusalem and the central
sanctuaries of Dan and Bethel for the northern kingdom,
only a small minority, those living nearby, could avail itself of the opportunity of worship at these holy places.
Certainly the three relatively small sanctuaries could not
accomodate the hundreds of thousands of adult males of
the two kingdoms. Probably many of them never saw a
central sanctuary. At least until the Deuteronomic centralization of the Temple cult the local town-sanctuary supplied
for everybody all the necessary opportunities for both sacrificial and liturgical worship. It was also the function of

the local priesthood to provide necessary guidance for public and private religious conduct.

In short, the life of the average Israelite was far more determined by the events and institutions in his place of residence than by what happened in the central agencies of state or religion. He lived within his locality and under the guidance of his local elders. Unlike highly centralized and state-capitalistic Egypt, which effectively controlled all economic and political life, equally unlike militaristic Assyria which marshaled all physical and economic resources in the service of a utopian dream of world conquest by force, Palestine, through a concatenation of historic and geographic factors, failed to achieve even that measure of unity and centralization which characterized Babylonia in the expansive periods of Hammurabi and Nebuchadrezzar. On the whole, it resembled a loosely-knit federation of tribes and townships more than a unified centralized state.[5]

3. The Palestinian City

The average Palestinian "city" may be visualized as a small self-contained community of citizens largely equal before the law, if not in economic status. Few Palestinian cities, even after the Israelitic expansion, exceeded in size Canaanite Megiddo or Jerusalem which, as modern excavations have shown, covered an area of only twelve acres each. Apart from a few more imposing buildings, some of which had been taken over from the Canaanite city-kings, priests and patricians, most of the houses were small, one-story stone dwellings constructed by the owners from unhewn limestone amply available in many parts of the country.

These structures, consisting as a rule of two or three rooms with a total area of 150–300 square feet, served principally as a shelter for the generally large family at night or during the short rainy season. Adults and children alike spent most of their free time on the flat housetops in sight and speaking distance of neighbors, lingering on the narrow, crooked streets or congregating at the city gates. These gates, a necessary aspect of city walls,[6] served as a passage for farmers going to or returning from their fields — the psalmist speaks of the Lord guarding "thy going out and thy coming in" (121.8) — and for visiting merchants and travelers. They generally resembled in function the market place of a medieval town or the Main Street of an American hamlet. There the Israelites transacted business, adjudicated quarrels, debated public and private issues, proclaimed ordinances, "rehearsed the righteous acts of the Lord" (Judg. 5.11) and, when necessary, held public gatherings to discuss and act upon matters of common concern.

The townships were to a large extent economically self-sufficient. Most of them produced almost all the foodstuffs and industrial products used by their inhabitants. With vineyards, orchards and truck gardens in the immediate vicinity of the dwellings, with a substantial area in grain at a somewhat greater distance, and with a good deal of pasture preserved for sheep and cows, they had, except for years of regional or country-wide drought, a sufficient supply of food and essential raw materials for their moderate needs. As a matter of fact, they often produced an exportable surplus. Thus they could pay for those few articles which they were unable to manufacture, and make whatever contributions were imposed upon them by the state or foreign overlord. Private ownership of vineyards, orchards and fields had been well established in the Canaanite period and was undoubtedly maintained by the new settlers after the redistribution of land resulting from Israel's conquest. It is possible, however, that at least pastures remained communal property. The prevalence of such communal holdings among various Semitic groups and the traditions of the patriarchal semi-nomadic cattle-raising economy based upon clan ownership and management, would seem to favor such an assumption. In the period of conquest such communal property could easily have been established on the estates of subdued city kings, and on the no-man's land frequently available between cities. On the other hand, the almost total absence of literary and archeological evidence (except for a dubious passage, in Micah 2.5) seems to indicate that such communal holdings were neither significant nor widespread. They doubtless were overshadowed by the royal domain which, as early as King David, required twelve high state officers as "the rulers of the substance which was" the king's (I Chron. 27.25–31).

Whether or not communal property existed, the administration of the township played a vital role in the life of the Israelitic masses. The leaders of the city are called in the Old Testament, as in most other Semitic sources, "elders." In the early period of the Israelitic clans the elder usually was the oldest member, if not the progenitor of the entire clan. When, after the settlement in Palestine, the territorial organization of townships began displacing the family structure characteristic of clan life, a group of such elders, perhaps at first the chiefs of the respective clans or families, became a permanent council in charge of all major city affairs. It seems that the frequent references to seventy such elders in local as well as national councils[7] reflect reality

insofar as this number was found to represent a wide group
in the population. Very likely these seventy men delegated
certain specific functions to a smaller group or committee,
and at times appointed a special executive committee, the
members of which may have had the distinguishing title of
princes (*sarim*). One may perhaps explain the existence in
Succoth, in the days of Gideon, of 77 princes and elders as
referring to 70 elders and 7 princes. In any case the existence
of such a large council in a city of Succoth's size, which, in
that early period, could not possibly have had more than
several hundred inhabitants, indicates the representation on
it of almost all larger families in town. This impression is
fully born out by the picturesque and evidently authentic
description of communal action in the story of Ruth. It is
Boaz who "took ten men of the elders of the city"—obviously almost any ten men would do — and later addressed
himself "unto the elders and unto all the people" (4.2, 9).

As to how democratically the Israelitic municipality was
organized and governed in general, the evidence hitherto
available is contradictory. It has become fashionable
among modern scholars to speak of a city oligarchy in whose
hands rested control over all municipal life. Eduard Meyer,
for instance, has read in the old Song of Deborah evidence
for an extremely aristocratic constitution. The Song reflects,
in his opinion,

> the dominant position of the big landowners who have
> succeeded in reducing into a state of dependency all
> the middle-class and petty farmers, notwithstanding
> the legal equality granted to all members of the
> community by the old tribal organization. They
> [the big landowners] hold all public offices and, in
> many cases, assume the character of exempted fami-

lies of a nobility sharply differentiated from the rest of the people.[8]

A closer examination of these and other passages in the Bible does not bear out such a sweeping assumption, however. Of course, Deborah addressed herself to the recognized leaders of the old clans and the new townships, which at that time still seem to have existed side by side. This was as natural as addressing the President and Congress in the democratic United States. The process of concentration of wealth in ever fewer hands was then in its early beginnings, and it took several centuries before social inequality reached a state in which class conflicts began to have political repercussions. Even then the "constitutional" equality of all citizens was never publicly denied. In fact, it was reasserted and expanded in the Deuteronomic Reformation.

The few available biographical data of Israelitic leaders demonstrate the full operation of the egalitarian principle. According to tradition not only Moses and Aaron, but also the leading "judges," including the nearly royal Jephtah and Gideon, came from the small and less wealthy clans. It certainly was not distinguished parentage which accounted for the rise to power of Samuel, Saul (who was elected by lot!) or David. Most of the founders of the ever changing northern dynasties, from Jeroboam down, had been successful military chiefs, resembling the later Roman praetorian generals, but hardly ever of "patrician" rank. Omri, perhaps the most important among them, did not even have an Israelitic name. Among the great prophets, only Isaiah was a "noble" of royal blood. Jeremiah and Ezekiel were members of a small provincial priesthood, Amos, a poor sycamore grower in Judah, while Elijah and Hosea seem to have been altogether outsiders from the "Bedouin" fringe in Transjordan. Although some decisions were made by assemblies of representative "elders" from all over the country, the frequency of popular assemblies testifies to the vitality of the egalitarian system.[9]

To be sure, underprivileged groups always existed throughout Israel. Apart from women and minors, who had little or no share in the public life, most Israelitic townships included a number of slaves. Notwithstanding the humanitarian slave legislation of ancient Israel, the position of a "Canaanite," or even of a "Hebrew" slave during the six years of his bondage, was one of decided inferiority in theory and of considerable hardship in practice. This class, however, never was large. Rarely used in agriculture and industry, slaves were primarily employed in catering to the domestic needs and the desire for display of the few wealthy families. They were concentrated in the households of the leading aristocrats and priests in Jerusalem and Samaria, but were rather rare in provincial cities.[10]

Of far greater numerical importance were the various classes of aliens appearing in the Bible under the equivocal term *gerim*. To these belonged foreign merchants who, often more or less permanent residents, played a conspicuous role in local as well as in international trade. They included also innumerable natives who, never fully displaced in the period of conquest, were absorbed by the conquerors through a process slowed by the obvious racial heterogeneity of these natives, many of whom, as excavations have shown, bore Mitanni, Hittite and even Iranian and Indian names. Until their ultimate assimilation to the Israelites, long after the reign of Solomon, such groups of natives must gradually have sunk to a status of economic and legal inferiority in many Palestinian cities. Even Israelites who left their native hamlets — whether to escape the punishing hand of the Law, the wrath of an avenger in one of the perpetual family feuds, a hostile invader, famine or pestilence — as newcomers in a strange locality must for a time have swelled the ranks of the *gerim*. The same factors, which throughout ancient history, operated to force entire clans and tribes to seek food and shelter in distant and none-too-friendly Egypt, undoubtedly brought about frequent migrations of families and individuals in their own country. Whether or not impoverished farmers, who lost their hereditary parcel of land, automatically joined this inferior group of aliens in their native city cannot be definitely proved. Many probably preferred to abandon the native locality and go elsewhere in search of work and a new opportunity.[11]

One must bear in mind, on the other hand, that the Israelitic clans (the *mishpaḥot*) were not exclusively based upon blood relationship. Even in the conditions of patriarchal society, as among the primitive Arabs, a stranger could be adopted by a clan through the ritualistic ceremony of a "covenant." With the dissolution of the clans in the new Israelitic townships, such absorption of *gerim*, whatever their origin, must have become both more frequent and more informal. It was only from the eighth century on, when growing social inequalities forced large groups of landless farmers to move to the larger cities in search of employment and when the Assyrian invasions set in motion recurrent streams of refugees, that the *gerim* became a social issue of considerable significance. From that time on until after the First Commonwealth, prophets and legislators sought a just solution of this problem. These attempts, reaching a climax in the Deuteronomic legislation and the constitu-

tional projects of Ezekiel, reveal the difficulties which
eventually arose within the essentially egalitarian social and
legal structure of the Israelitic city.

Before the eighth century, however, these alien groups
(apart from the as yet unassimilated Canaanites) seem to
have been numerically insignificant, especially in the provincial townships. The bulk of the adult male inhabitants
of the typical locality took an active share in public life.
The average Israelite may not have *elected* his "elders" but,
since one or another of them was the recognized chief of his
own clan or family, he could feel that he was represented in
the council as well as or better than if he had cast a ballot.
The deliberations of these elders, usually conducted informally at the city gate in the presence of a large gathering
of interested persons, undoubtedly gave to every citizen
opportunity to express his views. A few country-wide public
gatherings have been recorded in which all adult Israelites
present, rich or poor, learned or illiterate, patrician or plebeian, participated in the election of a new king and in the
adoption of new basic laws. If these provide a clue, we may
surely assume that in major local decisions the entire town
citizenry was directly consulted.

The most important regular function of both council and
popular assembly was the administration of justice. Ludwig
Köhler has argued plausibly that the ancient Israelitic
courts were for the most part of the type of the modern
Swiss *Gassengerichte* — a survival of the early Teuton *Land-
teidinge.* From the story of Ruth, especially, we learn how
a man who required legal assistance appeared before the
city gate, approached ten elders of his own choice and applied
to them for recognition of his right of "redemption." The
ten, acting in the double capacity of judges and witnesses

in the presence of a crowd of none-too-silent onlookers, speedily and rather informally went through the procedure of fact-finding, adjudication and execution. Jeremiah's arrest, trial and vindication (26.8 ff.) may serve as another illustration of the proceedings in such people's courts. A constant repetition of this practice instilled in the mass of the population a certain familiarity with and reverence for the law, fostered a universal law-mindedness which was to become a powerful factor in the socio-religious development of the Jewish people, and strengthened the feeling of equality and fellowship among the bulk of the citizenry.[12]

Another center of communal life was the local altar, the *bamah*. If information concerning secular life in provincial communities is obscured by the central orientation of the sources, knowledge of the religious practices at the innumerable local shrines is altogether dependent on data supplied by outspoken enemies. Through the haze of constant denunciation we may still perceive a vigorous religious life centered around a Yahwism, which may have appeared adulterated to the lofty prophetic and priestly bearers of the Mosaic tradition, but which nevertheless met well the requirements of the unsophisticated masses. At local shrines the professional priest officiated along with the elder and other prominent laymen. Each individual offered his sacrifice personally (the exclusive sacrificial charisma of the levitical priesthood seems to date from a later period), made his vows, and recited prayers mostly of his own making and, together with his fellow townsmen, celebrated national and local festivals. In these *bamot*, it also appears, there long reigned, despite the presence of the professional priest, an egalitarian spirit inherited from the old days of common clan worship.

4. THE DEUTERONOMIC DEMOCRACY

With the rising social inequality, the exploitation of the poor by the wealthy in the last generations preceding the fall of Samaria, this type of political and religious democracy came to an abrupt end. Many established priests, as well as some of the equally hereditary elders, sided with the oppressors against the oppressed, frequently "alien" members of the community. As prophetic preachers coupled in their denunciations the social abuses of the dominant classes and the religious degeneration of the leading priests and laymen, they fostered the unholy alliance between the local "aristocracy" and the local priesthood. The conflicts were sharpened by the upheavals of the eighth century, the fall of Samaria and the invasion of Sennacherib which set in motion large masses of Israelitic and Judean refugees. To many localities, thoroughly depopulated by Sennacherib's deportations, came new settlers from widely separated regions. The old municipal organization, with its clan elders and its distinctions between the full-fledged native majority and the "alien" minority, now obviously became an instrument of perpetuating the rule of an "aristocratic" group. With the loss of the southern sections to Edomite settlers and the constant growth of the capital, moreover, Jerusalem entered a much more intimate relationship with the provincial cities than had been possible earlier. In the constant exchange of influences between the truly urban capital and the still predominantly rural provincial townships, were born those new social and religious forces which, inspiring what is now styled the Deuteronomic Reformation, vitally influenced the subsequent diaspora communities even more than they did

Judea, which for another generation retained its political independence.

After a covenant publicly concluded by the youthful King Josiah with the popular assembly of all citizens, the new "democratic" constitution greatly curtailed the prerogatives of the monarchy which had been found wanting both in its capacity to hold off foreign invasions and to check internal abuses. The local elders remained, but they seem to have lost their self-perpetuating status. In their most important function, the administration of justice, they were replaced by elective "judges." "Judges and officers shalt thou make thee in all thy gates," so read the new constitution, "and they shall judge the people with righteous judgment" (Deut. 16.18). While it is not altogether clear how functions were divided among the judges, elders and "officers" (*shoṭerim*), there is little doubt that the mass of each town's population was again to lay down fundamental policies and to entrust execution to men in its confidence.

The establishment of a supreme judiciary in Jerusalem did not at all conflict with these newly-won democratic liberties. The growing feeling of unity in the small kingdom with its large capital, fostered by the evident value of the united action which had led to the proclamation of the new constitution, made it appear desirable that there be a central agency which could unify local tendencies in a common legal structure. The growing intelligentsia demanded that a large body of the law be confined to writing — a practice recorded as early as Isaiah — which likewise tended to increase legal uniformity. Social abuses, often combined with miscarriage of justice, could be more effectively checked if an appeal against a local judgment could be carried to a

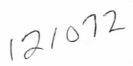

superior authority in the capital, more likely to be free of local entanglements. In certain cases (whether a teacher had spread heresies [*dibber sarah*] or not, for example) a single authoritative, national tribunal was indispensable for the newly expected religious conformity.[13]

Neither did the centralization of sacrificial worship at the Temple of Jerusalem seriously interfere with the self-governing life of the smaller communities. Whether or not the reform was fully carried into effect, the local shrines were all razed and the provincial priesthood prevented from offering sacrifices (neither likely in itself nor borne out by Jeremiah's and Ezekiel's continued fulminations against the *bamot*), new forms of ritual and congregational life gradually replaced the old ones, exercising an even profounder influence upon subsequent religious and communal evolution. Divine services were not discontinued. As before, provincial male citizens could be expected to visit the Temple at most only three times a year. The mass of women and children might, perhaps, be expected to fulfill that religious duty in connection with the general assembly of all during the Feast of Tabernacles of each Sabbatical year. Local congregations continued to worship their God on all traditional holidays, Sabbaths and New Moons. They merely adapted their worship to the new demands, increasing the number of prayers and liturgical songs and introducing the recitation of chapters from the growing body of ancient sagas and histories, prophetic letters originally collected in order to spread the new teachings among provincials, and codes of civil and ritual law. Hezekiah's prayers, whether or not historically authentic, clearly reflect a widespread pre-exilic practice. So do various prayers offered by Jeremiah and the characteristic recitations prescribed by Deuteronomy.

The tenor of this entire work, moreover, reproducing a sort of continuous exhortation by Moses, seems to indicate that some kind of sermon along similar historical and legal lines had also become a part of congregational worship.[14]

The disestablished local priests, too, found novel functions to perform. They became the main teachers of the Torah, led in prayers and recited from the accumulated literature of the ages. There is reason to assume that they early recognized that the recitation of legal maxims governing sacrifices, at first practiced only in schools for training priests, should entirely replace sacrifices. "So will we render for bullocks the offering of our lips" (Hos. 14.3) became the watchword of the age. What offering could be better than the recitation of laws governing the sacrifice of these bullocks? Out of these provincial gatherings, designed to replace the banished sacrificial altars, was soon afterwards born the exilic synagogue.

5. City and Community

We thus find in the peculiar features of the ancient Israelitic municipality many nuclei for the subsequent development of the exilic community. Geographic heterogeneity united with the weakness of the central agencies of state and religion to foster independence and self-reliance in the masses of provincial Israelites and Judeans. A large measure of economic self-sufficiency promoted concentration upon local rather than national affairs. Created to meet predominantly local or regional needs, the self-governing agencies of the local administration, judiciary, school and place of worship influenced the life of the people as a whole much more than did the monarchy and leading priesthood in Jerusalem. That is why, when the successive national catastrophies overtook

Israel and Judah, when scores of thousands were deported
and monarchy and Temple were destroyed, Jewish groups in
exile, by congregating in small self-governing communities,
could, on the whole, pursue their accustomed mode of social
and religious life. They had merely to make major or minor
adjustments required by their new and ever-changing environment and status.

Religious universalism was, even before the Exile, greatly
strengthened by the inner social conflicts, the weakness of
monarchy, the absence of a single dominant class, and the
very contrast between central and local political organs,
central and local sanctuaries. The leaders now proclaimed,
as a matter of principle, the superiority of the ethnic-
religious unity of Israel over Israel's state and territory, and
the possibility of survival in foreign lands in purely ethnic
and religious communities which, in all basic forms of communal life, could refer back to pre-exilic local evolution.

The Deuteronomic Reformation helped further to undermine central political control, without being able to substitute for it, in the few remaining decades of Judah's independence, a truly effective central religious control. By
largely disestablishing the provincial priesthood and outlawing local sacrificial worship, the new trend happened to
strengthen those forms of congregational life which proved
best adjustable to the new life in Exile. By such an extraordinary concatenation of various interdependent factors in
their national career the deported Judeans found themselves
in a position to embark upon a venture which was destined to
leave an indelible imprint upon the history of human group
life.

CHAPTER III

SYNAGOGUE

AFTER the fall of Jerusalem, the Jewish communities on Babylonian soil had more than one precedent to guide them in reconstructing their shattered national existence. National minorities transplanted to foreign soil had existed in the ancient Near East long before the Assyrians made it a practice to shift entire populations. As far back as the end of the third millenium we find, for example, in Kültepe (Asia Minor) a large colony of Assyrian merchants organized in an effective self-governing community, living under their own law and their own elected or appointed leaders. They retained for long a large measure of independence with respect to both the government of the country in which they lived and the central authorities at home. Later, Phoenician and Greek groups of merchants or mercenaries were to be found in many Mediterranean cities, even some in which the mother country had no political influence whatsoever.

Although at first distinguished from all these alien colonies by the lack of a powerful mother country, the Babylonian Jewish community could utilize a millennial experience in adapting itself to new situations and in evolving new organizational forms. That some of these combinations of old and new forms were altogether unique, and that they ultimately revealed an elasticity and adaptability to changing environment which far exceeded all those known to men before, was due to the general psychological and social make-up of the exilic community as much as to its peculiar communal antecedents.

1. Growing Dispersion

The Jewish people already had behind it a centuries-old, often painful experience of life in dispersion. The inextinguishable, increasingly cherished memories of their deliverance from Egypt must have included certain reminiscences of life in Goshen, where they seem to have enjoyed some sort of autonomy. However much the entire Egyptian ordeal came to be identified in national consciousness as one of relentless persecution, perhaps as a psychological compensation for contemporary miseries, the constant references must have reminded the exiles of the time when they had lived under the rule of their own elders in a hostile environment. It was, after all the Egyptian community which had reared the great leader, Moses, whose personality and work became ever more significant to the exiles.

Be this as it may, there is no doubt that soon after the Exodus and the occupation of Palestine, entire groups of Israelites were at least temporarily forced to settle in regions outside the country. Those Danites about whom Deborah sang that they used to sojourn "by the ships" (very likely a reference to a practice of hiring out to Phoenicians), must have followed their captains to Phoenician colonies throughout the Mediterranean. King Solomon's "royal merchants" and the Israelitic members of the crews on the combined fleets going to Ophir and, perhaps, to Tartessus in Spain, may easily have furnished a kernel of historical basis to the widespread medieval legends concerning the early settle-

ments of Jews in various parts of the ancient world. In any
case, it was for such merchants that King Ahab, by a treaty
with Ben-Hadad, obtained special "streets" in Damascus.
These Israelitic merchants in Damascus, and probably elsewhere, must have enjoyed a measure of autonomy similar
to that granted the Assyrians in Cappadocia. While we
possess no direct information concerning a Jewish *bit karun*
which "held court, fixed interest rates, participated in the
trade in cloth, received loans" and generally served as a
combination of bank and city hall, we must postulate the
existence also in the Jewish "streets" of some such communal
agency to correlate commercial activities, protect interests
against infringement by local powers and adjudicate internal quarrels.[1]

These sporadic lessons in the school of extraterritorial life
in a neighboring land were suddenly put to extensive use
in the tragic years before and after the fall of Samaria.
Although we possess the authentic records of only two large
deportations, that of 27,290 Israelites by Sargon in 719
B. C. E., and that of 200,150 Judeans by Sennacherib in
701 B. C. E., we have every reason to assume that they
were preceded by large scale deportations in 733, when the
Assyrians detached most of the provinces from the Israelitic
kingdom, and in 725, when they occupied the entire country-
side before laying siege to the city of Samaria. In addition
to the deported there must have been thousands of refugees
who fled to neighboring countries before the approaching
enemy. It was from such voluntary expatriates and, perhaps, from Jewish mercenaries sent to Egypt in return for
horses that were recruited the growing communities of ancient Egypt before the days of Jeremiah. From Tahpanhes-

Daphnae in the Delta region, through Noph-Memphis in central Egypt, to Pathros in the south, the once inhospitable land was dotted with Jewish communities. One, a soldiers' colony in Elephantine apparently founded in the seventh century, has left behind numerous invaluable papyri to tell the story of the social, political and religious adjustments of its members to life in exile. Other such refugees or voluntary emigrés must even then have reached the islands in the vicinity of the Phoenician cities to which Deutero-Isaiah was soon to refer in his prophecies extending comfort to the far-flung dispersion. Jeremiah and Ezekiel most likely had living remnants of the northern brethren in mind when they prophesięd the forthcoming reconciliation between Israel and Judah and insisted upon the common interests of "all Israel."[2]

A new and decisive turn came with the deportations from Judah in 597 and 587–6 and the flight of another group after the assassination of Gedaliah. The first of these events brought Ezekiel to Babylonia, the last led Jeremiah to conclude his life in Egypt. Archaeological evidence has largely confirmed the biblical view concerning the depopulation of Judah after the Babylonian invasions. The continued expansion of the diaspora was stimulated, in particular, by the establishment of the vast, well administered and tolerant Empire of Persia, reaching from India to Ethiopia. Before long a Jewish prophet could boastfully exclaim:

> For from the rising of the sun even unto the going down of the same My name is great among the nations; And in every place offerings are presented unto My name, even pure oblations; for My name is great among the nations, saith the Lord of hosts.[3]

2. The Congregation

Nebuchadrezzar had selected the leading citizens of Judah from the King down to the skilled craftsman for immediate deportation. With them the center of gravity of the whole people was suddenly transferred to the Euphrates valley. It now became the task of the Babylonian leaders to devise new methods of communal life to meet the great crisis of exile. In these colonies of aliens without a mother country, building on the foundations of the Palestinian township as well as of the older diaspora communities, was to be realized the national-universal program of the pre-exilic leaders and the people's will to survive without state or territory.

Largely recruited from previously wealthy and educated classes, the exilic leaders included a large number of former elders, priests and prophets — Jeremiah enumerates them in this order in his famous letter to the people in captivity (29.1) — whose experience and training stood them in good stead when they were suddenly confronted by new religious and administrative tasks. Following an apparently old custom (II Kings 4.23), some of these leaders began gathering on Sabbaths and holidays in the house of the leading prophet, Ezekiel, and, apart from listening to his discourses, took counsel in all matters of communal concern.

In one of these momentous gatherings it was decided to abstain from resurrecting on Babylonian soil the sacrificial worship of the Temple. The Deuteronomic centralization of worship had not definitely disposed of the issue for the diaspora communities. Apart from the obvious survival of not a few provincial *bamot* to the very end of Judah's independence, it seems that there was no clear-cut policy formulated with respect to Jewish temples abroad. At any rate, we know that even much later, leaders in Jerusalem did not altogether discourage the rebuilding of the destroyed Temple in Elephantine. They seem to have insisted upon the exclusion of animal sacrifices, but did not mind the "meal-offering and incense." Later, in the stormy years of the Maccabean revolt, even this limitation was dropped with respect to the newly erected Temple of Onias in Leontopolis. After some deliberation, however, the Babylonian leaders reserved the right of offering sacrifices to the central sanctuary in Jerusalem, the rebuilding of which in the near future they proclaimed as both a hope and a program. It was, in fact, the detailed blueprint for the forthcoming sanctuary prepared in exile by Ezekiel (or one of his disciples), which served as a model for the Temple of Zerubbabel. In foreign lands, however, God himself had become "to them as a little sanctuary."[4]

The main emphasis was now laid upon prayer and the recitation of the traditional or new psalms, sagas, historical records and collections of legal maxims. Side by side with the priests of the house of Zadok, who had dominated Temple worship at Jerusalem, there were numerous provincial priests whose pre-eminence was based upon their reputed descent from Aaron. Ezekiel still looked forward to the leadership of the Zadokite priests, to whom alone he wished to entrust the offering of sacrifices, religious instruction and the administration of justice. The "levites," whom he could not forgive their former ministering "before the idols" at the local shrines, he wanted to see limited to a few liturgical and menial tasks (44.9–31). At the same time the school of priestly lawgivers who, evidently from pre-exilic records and precedents but with new exilic emphases, reconstructed the old laws in terms of the Priestly Code and

compiled the entire traditional Torah along the lines of our
Pentateuch, wrote exclusively from the point of view of the
Aaronides, who were to be the main priests of the Sanctuary.
But whether Aaronides or Zadokites, whether followers of
Ezekiel or of the priestly legislators, the priests felt that, as
before at the desecrated shrines so now in Babylonia, the
best substitute for the forbidden sacrifices would be a recitation of the laws of sacrifice. With the general glorification
of the Sabbath in the Babylonian Exile, the weekly gatherings devoted to such commemorative, edifying and hope-
inspiring services became a central feature in the life of each
community.[5]

This new type of religious gathering came to be called
'edah, in contrast to the predominantly secular pre-exilic
assembly, the kahal. The former term, used with predilection by exilic writers of the Old Testament, is correctly
translated in the Septuagint by the word συναγωγή. Both
words, originally meaning simply a gathering, increasingly
came to be identified only with a worshipful gathering of
Jews. Neither 'edah, however, nor the closely related keneset
(Aramaic: kenishta) was ever reduced to the final and most
specific meaning of the synagogue as the house of worship.
The talmudic tradition was, indeed, correct, when it defined
'edah as any religious congregation of ten Jews regardless of
its locus or organizational form. These ten Jews could
assemble in any private house, whether that of a prophet or,
as in the story of Susannah, of an ordinary citizen. They
could follow the old tradition of congregating at the city
gate. The popular assembly under Ezra, which had all the
earmarks of a synagogue service with levites chanting and
a precentor reading from Scripture, met before the "water-
gate," not on the Temple mountain.[6]

Of course, any communal house could also be utilized for occasional or regular divine services. "The house of the people," which had existed in pre-exilic Jerusalem, evidently because the growing pressure of municipal affairs in the capital had made it desirable for the city elders to retire to somewhat more restricted quarters, and similar institutions of a later age, could also be used by worshipers. Centuries later the Palestinian populace, as well as the Mandean sectarians, still persisted in calling the synagogue "the house of the people." Only "houses" of worship, not the congregations as such, were within reach of enemies. Nebuchadrezzar may have destroyed that first "house of the people," Antiochus Epiphanes may "have burned up all the meeting-places of God in the land," but the congregations of the faithful could continue to worship their God in any locality.[7]

This was a truly epochal revolution. Building upon precedents forcibly established in the Judean provinces after the Deuteronomic Reformation, the exilic community thus completely shifted the emphasis from the place of worship, the sanctuary, to the gathering of worshipers, the congregation, assembled at any time and any place in God's wide world.

We must not believe, however, that these gatherings were exclusively devoted to worship and religious instruction. It was essential for the very survival of the Jewish people in the First Exile that religious doctrine and practice become more central in the life of every individual than is usually the case even in those religious-minded communities which are also territorially rooted and politically independent. The existence of a widespread, intense religious feeling and a new emphasis on traditional holidays and customs as unifying forces is not only asserted by the biblical sources —

which, written by the religious leaders of the exilic generations, may overstress religious issues — but is also attested
by incidental evidence emanating from contemporary Babylonian documents. The prominent Jewish merchants and
landowners, whose contracts with the Babylonian banking
house of Murashu in the fifth century B. C. E. came to light
in the early years of this century, named their children for
the most part in a manner clearly indicating their belief
in the one and only God, their yearning for the restoration
to Palestine, and their profound reverence for the Sabbath
and the other Jewish ceremonies.[8]

Nevertheless, there were many secular aspects of life
which required much attention from these congregations and
their leaders. Early sufferings under the harsh conquerors,
and the lot of the ever new waves of captives or individual
slaves, could be alleviated by the intervention of older and
more prosperous members. Political relations with local and
central authorities of the Babylonian Empire necessitated
frequent consultation and decision. The constant improve-
ment in these relations, which in 561 culminated in the
liberation of the captive king, Jehoiachin, and his elevation
to an influential position at the Babylonian court, suggests
a remarkably united and sagacious leadership.

3. The Leaders

An influential central agency became even more indispensable when the Jews sought to obtain from the kings of
Persia those great charters which established a Jewish homeland in Palestine and safeguarded the communal autonomy
of the far-flung imperial diaspora. Whatever one thinks of
the historicity of the book of Esther, there must have been
more than one person high in the ranks of Persian bureau-

cracy who resented the existence of "a certain people scattered abroad and dispersed among the peoples" whose laws were "diverse from those of every people" (3.8). The continued success of the Jews in averting the disastrous results of such hostile elements, whether through skillful court intrigue or, as appears more likely, through persistent efforts of Jewish courtiers and "scribes" in or out of the imperial administration, presupposes some sort of united leadership. These leaders undoubtedly argued the advantages accruing to the heterogeneous empire, ruled by a small minority of Persians, from such a scattered, non-political group. They succeeded in persuading the kings and their chief advisers that a religious autonomy and "theocratic" regime among Jewish subjects promoted, rather than obstructed, the interests of imperial Persia. They found attentive listeners in Cyrus and his successors, whose general policy was based on fostering local theocracies as the mainstay of imperial power and patriotic allegiance.

These Jewish leaders secured not only decrees of Temple restoration and imperial support from Cyrus and Darius I, but also a decree from Artaxerxes "unto Ezra the priest, the scribe of the Law of the God of heaven," giving him the right to "appoint magistrates and judges, who may judge' all the people that are beyond the River," far beyond the confines of the small Jewish homeland (the satrapy *Abar Nahara* included also Syria, Phoenicia and Cyprus). Through their efforts, Nehemiah was appointed governor of the entire province apparently from their own midst. A typical diplomatic memorandum, written in defense of Palestine Jewry and sent to the "King of Kings" by Tabeel and his associates, has been successfully reconstructed from the book of Ezra (4.7–6.15). Other such leaders must have been responsible for the memorable circular sent out by order of Darius II in 419, severely enjoining the Jewish garrison in Elephantine and probably all other Jewish communities in the Empire to

> count fourteen days of the month of Nisan and keep the Passover, and from the 15th day to the 21st day of Nisan (are) seven days of Unleavened Bread. Be clean and take heed. Do not work on the 15th day and on the 21st day. Also drink no beer and anything at all in which there is leaven do not eat from the 15th day from sunset till the 21st day of Nisan, seven days; let it not be seen among you; do not bring (it) into your dwellings, but seal (it) up during those days. Let this be done as Darius the King commanded.[9]

Who were these exilic leaders? From both Jeremiah and Ezekiel we learn that, almost immediately after their settlement in Babylonia, the Jews had a group of "elders" who, together with some priests and prophets, were in charge of all local and general Jewish affairs. Among these elders, apparently, were the "heads of fathers' houses" who led the returning exiles under Zerubbabel and Ezra (Ezra 1.5, 68; 8.1, etc.). Like their pre-exilic predecessors, they must also have had a share in the administration of justice among Jews, although the growing class of ritualistic and juristic experts, the priests and scribes, seems gradually to have crowded out the ordinary elders. Our information for Palestine in the post-exilic period is scanty; for Babylonia and the other exilic communities it is altogether in the realm of conjecture. We cannot even tell whether the recorded custom of convoking popular assemblies of all Jews, including women and children, under Ezra and Nehemiah in Palestine was the continuation of a Babylonian practice or merely a return to the pre-exilic assembly. The severe threat "that whosoever came not within three days . . . all his substance should be forfeited and himself separated from the congregation of the captivity" (Ezra 10.8) has, however, the earmarks of an exilic innovation. It appears likely, moreover, that while a general assembly of all exiles, scattered over a vast area from Egypt to the Iranian Plateau, was physically impossible, popular gatherings in individual communities were very frequent. It was in the very nature of the new unit, the 'edah, to have all male members readily available at each divine service. The membership thus could easily voice an opinion on any matter of importance to the congregation or to the community at large.

A most intriguing question is the composition and leadership of each individual congregation. While in small settlements all Jews undoubtedly congregated in one locality, in the larger communities, such as Nippur, more than one congregation must have existed. The congregations seem to have been founded along two lines. Exiles who had been deported *en masse* from single Palestinian townships, or members of particular ancient clans who had been exiled at various times and found one another on foreign soil, might now constitute themselves into new communal units. In the course of time, the dividing lines among the *Landsmannschaften* became more and more blurred, whereas the growing feeling of ethnic distinction stimulated the sense of family membership and the pride in descent from one of the better known clans of ancient Israel. While the exiles returning with Zerubbabel are divided into practically the same number of clan and city units, although the former are numerically much stronger, those in the days of Ezra seem to consist of clan units only. Since many exiles had been craftsmen in Palestine and many others had undoubtedly learned a craft from their industrially advanced Babylonian neighbors, organizations along occupational lines may have been found side by side with clan and city units. Such "guild" congregations perhaps best explain the presence of a group of goldsmiths, perfumers and merchants among the builders of the wall in the days of Nehemiah.[10]

The existence of such diverse units as late as a century and a half after the fall of Jerusalem, testifies to their vitality in Babylonia and to their capacity for cohesion in the face of overwhelming forces of assimilation either to the non-Jewish environment or to other groups of Jews. It may not be too venturesome to suggest that from their very inception many of these congregations possessed peculiar characteristics which helped maintain unity even after the original reason for their organization had disappeared. The persistence of ceremonies and other ritualistic peculiarities is well known. It is not unlikely, therefore, that after the Deuteronomic Reformation laid the foundations for non-sacrificial worship, particular groups of Judeans developed certain peculiar divine rites. Since there apparently existed no central agency to influence local gatherings, each locality or family or professional congregation within a larger city could choose its own prayers and passages for recitation and adopt a ritual grounded in local practices or family reminiscences. Upon arriving in Babylonia, people of the same original rite naturally preferred to congregate together and continue to worship in their accustomed way. Such congregations of peculiar ritualistic antecedents were to become familiar in all later countries of Jewish immigration. What happened to Jerusalem under Herod or to imperial Rome might well have occurred also in ancient Babel or Nippur. Hence also, perhaps, the fact that in the restoration

under Zerubbabel there were local groups hailing from
small Palestinian localities, while Jerusalem, which undoubtedly furnished the bulk of the deported in 587, seems to be
represented only by the numerically stronger family groups.[11]

A congregation of the family type was governed by its
natural elders. The local group, too, was easily dominated
by the respective "heads of fathers' houses." After all the
Palestinian city had long been governed by such a council
of heads of families. Since many of the local groups counted
only forty or fifty members and but few had as many as
six or seven hundred members, a council of all family heads,
perhaps occasionally reaching the traditional number of
seventy, would have been thoroughly representative. It is
impossible to tell, however, to what extent these congregational elders participated in the general affairs of the
exilic community. The elders who conferred with Ezekiel
may have been only the chiefs of the leading congregation
of Nippur.

There also existed permanent individual chiefs. Men like
Iddo and his brother, "who were set over the place Casiphia"
— a locality identified by Winckler with Ktesiphon — and
who furnished Ezra with ministers for the Temple (Ezra
8.17), must have had considerable influence over the affairs
of their respective communities. If we may take a clue from
Artaxerxes' decree empowering Ezra to appoint judges and
chiefs in and around Palestine, we may perhaps assume that
these northern chiefs were likewise appointed by some central Jewish authority. The claim of the later Jewish exilarchs
in Babylonia that they were direct descendants of King
David can neither be proved nor disproved on the basis of
the available sources. The acknowledgment of this claim
by their greatest rivals, the Palestinian patriarchs, is not

necessarily conclusive. In view of the great likelihood that some such central authority existed under both Babylonia and Achaemenide Persia, however, the silence of the sources concerning any outstanding leader after the death of Ezekiel is very puzzling. The answer may well lie in the new princely position of the Davidic house subsequent to the elevation of Jehoiachin by Amilmarduk (Evil-merodach). In describing the released captive as a Jewish leader living at the king's court and holding a high political position, the author of the second book of Kings paints a picture closely akin to what is known about the later exilarch in the neo-Persian Empire. When we also consider the recorded activities of his son Sheshbazzar (= Pedaiah?), "the prince of Judah," and of his grandson, Zerubbabel, we must admit that the old tradition connecting them with the beginnings of the Babylonian exilarchate is much less fantastic than it first appears.[12]

4. A MILITARY COLONY

While these Babylonian developments are highly conjectural and can only be reconstructed from a few extant, often chronologically dubious, biblical passages, we are fortunate in possessing, since 1904–1906, much first-hand information about another Jewish community in the Persian Empire, the soldiers' colony in Elephantine, Upper Egypt. Established by Psammetichus I or II to defend the Egyptian boundary against the inroads of the Ethiopians, it has left behind a large number of Aramaic papyri dating from 495 to about 300 B. C. E. The data supplied by these contemporary sources would be invaluable for our knowledge of the post-exilic diaspora community at large, were it not for the many peculiarities of the Elephantine colony which caution against rash generalizations.

Although probably established before the Babylonian Exile and showing greater religious affinities to northern Israel than to Judah, the colony consistently used in the Aramaic context the Hebrew term '*edah* for its assembled congregation. That here, too, the congregation performed functions other than worship is evidenced by the remarkable marriage contract concluded about 441 B. C. E. between Mibtaḥiah and her Egyptian husband, Ashor, possibly a convert to Judaism. They agreed that if "tomorrow or another day Mibtaḥiah should stand up in the congregation and say 'I divorce Ashor, my husband,'" such divorce should immediately take place. Ashor, too, by publicly declaring his wish to divorce his wife would escape the penalties of a private, informal divorce which Jewish law permitted to husbands. This important document[13] shows that, notwithstanding the "covenant" of Ezra and Nehemiah outlawing intermarriage, its legality seems not to have been questioned in Elephantine. The contract also reveals that the Elephantine woman could enter on business transactions without the concurrence of her husband or father. Perhaps this was the result of the males' exclusive concentration on military affairs. Most striking is the woman's capacity to take the initiative in divorce proceedings and to obtain a divorce even against her husband's will. Jewish law has never before or since granted women such a right. Finally, we see here a congregation acting in a semi-judicial capacity, reminiscent of the public gatherings at the city gates of pre-exilic Palestine. It is likely that a similar practice existed also in other congregations of the Persian Empire.

Unlike the other congregations, however, this colony had a military organization. Besides belonging to the congregation, which apparently embraced all Elephantine Jewry, each soldier was also a member of a company (*degel*). While we shall encounter a somewhat analogous organization, the Greek *phyle*, among civilian Jews and non-Jews in later Ptolemaic Egypt, the company communal unit seems peculiar to Elephantine Jewry in the Persian period.

It may also be owing to military discipline, and the obedience due their largely non-Jewish commanders, that the Elephantine Jews so frequently repaired to non-Jewish courts. The oldest of the papyri refers to a "share granted us by the king's judges and Ravaka the commander." The exclusive use in their deeds and records of a rather poor Aramaic, instead of Hebrew, with which the writers evidently were much more familiar, shows that these documents were primarily intended for evidence in Persian courts. Persia had long since adopted Aramaic as the official language for administrative and judicial dealings with subjects in the western provinces. There is no similar record of Babylonian Jews appealing to non-Jewish courts. The Murashu and other cuneiform tablets, in which at least one of the contracting parties was non-Jewish, prove nothing, of course, with respect to litigations involving Jewish parties exclusively.

Even in Elephantine, however, it was the communal leadership as a whole, and not the captains of the individual detachments, which administered religious affairs. The "heads" of the congregation as well as the priests were in charge of their temple, at which they continued to offer sacrifices as in the days of national independence. When the temple was destroyed by an Egyptian uprising, it was Yedoniah "and his colleagues the priests" who in 408 appealed to Bigvai (Bagohi), the Persian governor of Judea, and to the Jewish and Samaritan leaders in Palestine to intercede with the Persian authorities. Lay leaders, on the other hand, seem to have been in charge of all fund collections, to one of which, in 419, one hundred and thirty-five persons contributed.

More remarkable and, perhaps, warranting a conclusion for other Jewish communities, is the existence of a communal archive, where not only records of major religious developments, but also business deeds and other secular and private documents were deposited. The Babylonian leaders were also able to send copies of previous favorable decrees to the imperial government in Persia (Ezra 6.1). The great insistence upon the purity of lay as well as priestly families evidently imposed the duty upon each community to maintain exact records of births, marriages and deaths (Ezra 2.62). The genealogical scrolls (*megillot yuḥasin*) of Babylonian Jewry were held in high repute for centuries thereafter. The antiquity and frequency of local repositories, found also in most foreign merchant colonies of the ancient Near East, make it all the more plausible that many Jewish communities likewise had such archives. Once established and properly kept, such collections of documents enhanced the orderliness and continuity of communal management.

The existence of a professional notary in Elephantine should also be observed. One Nathan ben Ananiah, although neither particularly skillful in handwriting nor proficient in Aramaic, was employed to write at least three of the extant papyri in the years 456–441 B. C. E. With all its imperfections, his learning was undoubtedly superior to that of the majority of soldiers, who were either illiterate or unfamiliar with Aramaic. Another papyrus, of 425 B. C. E., seems to have been written by his son, Maʿuziah, perhaps indicating heredity in the profession. Unfortunately, we are not told whether he held an official position in the community, serving as "scribe" in court, or whether he plied his craft privately, being paid by a client for each service. It may be conjectured, however, that the greater the self-government enjoyed by the Jews, the more numerous and important the matters depending on communal or court action, the greater must have been the need to employ a professional "scribe" who could fulfill the functions of a recorder of transactions of public sessions, an archivist, a secretary for correspondence and an expert qualified in writing deeds meeting the ever more complicated requirements of formal law. Indeed, such "notaries of the province" appear among the signers of an official application written in 428 B. C. E. The Persian chancery likewise employed such scribes, one of whom, Ezra, became for the Jews the "ready scribe in the law of Moses" (7.6). Whether or not other Jewish scribes united a secretarial post with that expert knowledge of Scripture which came increasingly to be associated with the title, we probably have here the nucleus of a professional bureaucracy in the diaspora community.[14]

5. The New Ritual

Prepared by a long inner and outward career, the Jewish people thus emerged from the great crisis of Exile in possession of a new instrument for national survival. The new type of congregation, meeting in any locality, could easily be adapted to changing environments in the subsequent millennium of history. The synagogue, having early, underground roots in the crucial evolution of the last decades of Judean independence, now sprouted into the focal institution of an ethnic-religious group living outside its own land.

However much the Holy City and the Temple were idealized after both seemed lost for ever, the neighborhood meeting place became much more important to the average Jew for all practical purposes of worship, social relationship and communal action. It was this average Jew who, when he became established in the vast Persian Empire, furnished most of the manpower and funds necessary for the reconstruction of Palestine.

Later, strengthened by the new autonomous homeland in Palestine, diaspora Jewry could cherish and foster its epochal invention, with little outside interference. It laid the foundations for an increasingly uniform and standardized ritual through the recitation of the newly edited Pentateuch in a triennial (later annual) cycle, and of sections selected from the prophetic literature, the so-called *haftarot*. At the same time it constantly added more or less individualized devotional and commemorative psalms. Through this fine balance, Jewish leadership succeeded in making synagogue worship uniform enough to maintain the unity of Jewry and pliable enough to be easily adjusted to varying congregational needs. By orienting all prayerful assemblies in the direction of Jerusalem[15] it also focused world Jewry's attention on a single goal. The Jewish people could soon entertain the hope, so beautifully expressed by the Second (or Third) Isaiah, that ultimately the Jerusalem "house shall be called a house of prayer for all peoples" (56.7). Guided by an extraordinary combination of diaspora and Palestinian leadership, equipped with a unique form of worship and communal organization, Jewry was well prepared for its memorable expansion in the Graeco-Roman world.

CHAPTER IV

GRAECO-ROMAN ASSOCIATION

WHEN Alexander the Great's armies injected the new dynamic force of Hellenism into the Orient, the Jewish communities of the Persian diaspora had behind them a centuries-old religious, political and organizational history. Alexander and his successors, the Ptolemies in Egypt and the Seleucidae in Syria and Babylonia, at first backed only by a small minority of Macedonians, hesitated to interfere with the established mores, religious practices and organizational forms of the heterogeneous groups living under their rule. Only in the newly-founded cities, which waxed in numbers and affluence, did truly Hellenistic constitutional forms prevail.[1] Since the Jews were often found among their earliest settlers, however, these new emporia of trade and culture likewise preferred to respect the Jewish communities as autonomous units. Alexander's appeal to his subjects, for example, to populate the newly-founded Egyptian metropolis, Alexandria, undoubtedly found eager listeners among the Jews of his empire. One of the most dispersed of ethnic groups, they had for generations been inured to a minority status in the industrial and commercial centers of the entire Near East. Sometimes there occurred forcible mass deportations of Jews from province to province. But generally little persuasion was needed to induce them to settle in the new cities under favorable terms.

Among the numerous inducements were guarantees of

religious toleration and of a measure of ethnic and cultural self-government. Notwithstanding the frequent later opposition of the local Hellenistic majorities to Jewish privileges, the Jews succeeded in convincing the central governments that the maintenance of their favorable status was dictated by both age-old tradition and well-conceived imperial interests. When the Roman Empire superseded the Ptolemies and Seleucidae as ruler over the bulk of Jewry, most of the early emperors, impelled by similar considerations and by the memory of the early alliances of the Maccabees with Rome, maintained and even extended these privileges. The diaspora community, quickened rather than hindered by the vast expanse of the Empire, entered a new decisive stage in its historic career.

1. Egypt and Cyrenaica

It is for the countries of northeastern Africa that we possess the first definite literary and epigraphic records concerning Jewish communities and their synagogues. Although some of these records have been subjected to a variety of interpretations, their easily ascertainable authenticity and chronological setting give a sense of relief to the conscientious investigator disturbed over the highly conjectural nature of most biblical data.

Without prejudice to their repeated claims that their privileges included full equality of political and civil rights, most Egyptian Jewries appear to have been organized in separate *politeumata*. This term, usually connoting "an organization of men of the same political status outside their native habitat," was applied in Hellenistic Egypt to such alien groups as the Idumeans, the Cretans and the Phrygians. It carried with it no stigma of inferiority, since there existed also a Greek *politeuma* in Memphis. Other terms were applied with equal freedom here and elsewhere. The author of the so-called Letter of Aristeas (second century B. C. E.) used interchangeably the designations, "elders of the Jewish *politeuma*," and "leaders of the people."[2]

, In any case, the Jewish communities enjoyed full religious autonomy. Analogous, from the standpoint of public law, to the free Greek religious associations of *eranoi* and *thiasoi*, they governed themselves according to their own statutes which, in this case, were tantamount to the entire body of Jewish law insofar as it was accepted and practiced in Egypt. Thus having a more permanent and uniform organization, they were subject to less governmental supervision. The frequent dedication of synagogues to the kings and their families — most inscriptions hitherto unearthed are such dedications — apart from being forceful expressions of allegiance, placed the particular house of worship under the special protection of the royal family. They do not indicate any direct supervision on the part of the Crown or the royal authorities. Indeed, the Jews of Athribis in the second century B. C. E. wrote more circumspectly, "In honor of King Ptolemy and Queen Cleopatra, Ptolemy, son of Epikydos, chief of guards, [and] the Jews resident in Athribis [dedicate] this *proseuché* to God, the Most High." The use of the latter attribute, incidentally, was not only due to the increasing fear of taking the name of the Lord in vain, which induced Egyptian Jews to employ *kyrios*, the Greek equivalent of *Adonai*, as a circumlocution for the divine name, but also to the evident appeal exercised by such a designation upon the minds of henotheistic pagans. The Jewish leaders of Babylonia, Palestine and Elephantine preferred, in communications to the Persian authorities, to use the more neutral terms, "God of Heaven" and "Great God." Now the "Most High" God, the *hypsistos*, came to be worshiped, probably not without Jewish influence, by various groups throughout the Hellenistic world.[3]

In Cyrenaica, too, as far back as 85 B. C. E. extensive self-government must have complemented the peculiar intermediate status of the Jewish group, between the full-fledged citizens and the metics. The constant stream of immigration into both countries, which swelled the number of Egyptian Jews in the days of Philo to about 12 per cent of the population, although conducive to clashes and inner disparity, could not fail steadily to reinforce the communal structure. With the growing affluence and the political and cultural achievements of some of its members, Alexandria became the leading Jewish community in the dispersion, Jerusalem's "sister," as she was called in a message of a Palestinian rabbi. The great double-colonnaded synagogue in the Egyptian capital so impressed the Palestinians that, centuries after it had been torn down by Trajan, they marveled at its beauty. Heaping exaggeration upon exaggeration, various versions of the legend reported that the synagogue could accommodate twice the number of the Israelites who had left Egypt (i. e. 1,200,000 adult males), that seventy-one golden chairs, each costing 25 myriads of gold denars (according to one version they were adorned with precious stones and pearls) or even 25 myriads of gold talents (some $9,000,000,000), were prepared for the seventy-one elders, and that the multitude, unable to follow the recitation, had to be signalled from an elevated point by the *hazzan* to respond, *Amen*. The audience was divided according to trades; the gold, silver or ordinary smiths, the regular weavers, the carpet weavers and so forth, each seated in separate sections, so that any stranger arriving in the city knew how to find his fellow craftsmen and, through them, to secure employment.[4]

Egyptian Jewry possessed another great sanctuary. During the difficult years of the Maccabean revolt, Onias, a refugee priest from Jerusalem, secured a charter to erect a temple in Leontopolis. There, as previously in the Elephantine colony, he resumed the sacrificial worship which had been temporarily suspended in Palestine. In the light of conditions at home and the indubitable legitimacy of the founder (he was the son of Onias III, the legitimate high priest in Jerusalem), the Palestinian leaders did not object even to the sacrifice of animals, a privilege which the reconstructed Elephantine temple had no longer enjoyed. Onias' application, as reported by Josephus, referring to Jewish community life in Egypt, Syria and Phoenicia, states "that the greatest part of your [the King's] people had temples in an improper manner, and that on this account they bear ill-will against one another."[5] It is questionable, however, whether Onias succeeded in eradicating the ritualistic disparity in the Egyptian synagogues, which he evidently had in mind. The resumption of the Temple services in Jerusalem which, under the powerful leadership of the Maccabean dynasty, became increasingly the "metropolis" of world Jewry, relegated the new temple into obscurity. Long before it was shut down by Vespasian in 73 C. E., it had ceased to play a vital role in the consciousness even of Egyptian Jewish writers, such as Philo.[6]

2. ROME

The situation in the imperial capital was different and in many ways unique. The Jews, for the most part having come there as captives or slaves, remained for long members of the poorer classes residing in the unsanitary quarter on the right bank of the Tiber. There were no wealthy bankers among the Jews of the imperial city who could compare with Demetrios, the Egyptian alabarch. They were, indeed, derided in many a satire because of their poverty and their trade of peddling. Nevertheless, placed in the politically focal point in the Empire, their importance far exceeded their numerical or economic strength, and their leaders often were confronted with tasks of significance for all imperial Jewry. Due to the peculiarity of burial practices in the capital, numerous Jewish catacombs have been preserved which, yielding hundreds of funerary inscriptions, have shed much light on the peculiar organization of the Roman Jewish community.

The imperial city was not altogether tolerant of the many groups of foreigners who had been attracted to it by its economic opportunities, its glamor and amusements and its exceeding liberality toward the poor. In 65 B. C. E. a *lex Pappia* demanded the general expulsion of all non-citizens, "because they were too numerous and were unworthy to live with the Romans." One of these intolerant outbursts in the republican era seems to have affected the Jewish community of Rome at its very inception, about 140–139 B. C. E. In 19 C. E., Emperor Tiberius, under the instigation of his councilor, Sejanus, who, in the words of Eusebius, "insisted that the entire Jewish people be destroyed at one blow," severely suppressed the Jewish cult in the city. He revoked his decree twelve years later but, soon afterwards, the generally more benevolent Claudius forbade all Jewish gatherings in Rome or all of Italy. Neither this decree nor the similar Hadrianic prohibition, if it was extended to Rome at all, could wipe out a community which, under Augustus, had embraced some five per cent of the city's population. The persecutions, nevertheless, had a disrupting effect upon the continuity of communal life. They may also have stimulated the Jews to leave their original Transtiberian quarter and settle all over the city, thus contributing to the decentralization of worship into some thirteen synagogues apparently located in various parts of the city.[7] A large and magnificent structure resembling, within the means of the Roman community, the central synagogue of Alexandria would not only have increased Roman resentment, but would have become a target for attack and seizure during any of the hostile interludes.

The thirteen congregations clustering around their respective synagogues reveal a number of interesting features. Four are named after prominent individuals: Augustus, Agrippa, Herod and Volumnius, probably the procurator in Judaea. The Roman congregations, like those in Egypt, thus wished to place their houses of worship under the protection of powerful personages or to commemorate the names of benefactors. Two congregations of the Suburenses and Campenses are named after their respective quarters of residence or the location of their synagogues. The congregation of the Calcarenses seems to have been founded by a professional association of lime-kiln workers, for which the guild congregations of the Babylonian Exile and the professional subdivisions of the great Alexandrian synagogue may well have served as a prototype. The remaining six congregations, nearly half the total number, evidently belong to the *Landsmannschaften* type. They are the synagogues of the Hebrews, namely Aramaic-speaking Palestinians; of Vernaculi, or native Romans; of Elaians in Mysia; of Tripolitans; of Jews from Scina in North Africa; and of those hailing from Arca in the Lebanon. The latter may, however, have been so styled because of the wish to commemorate the birthplace of Alexander Severus, the patron of many a synagogue. We find, indeed, in the thirteenth-century commentary of David Ḳimḥi a reference to an ancient "synagogue of Severus."[8]

These Roman congregations seem to have attracted wider attention among non-Jewish contemporaries than did any of the numerous other foreign groups in Rome. Not only proselytes and semi-proselytes of various shades, then a more or less regular appendage of every large Jewish community, but also professing pagans often attended Jewish services which offered a combination of exotic ceremonies and fascinating, though puzzling, doctrines. Just as Alexandrian "Greeks," much as they disliked Jews, were attracted to the peculiar annual celebration on the neighboring island of Pharos in commemoration of the Greek translation of the Bible, so did heathen Romans often find a visit to the local synagogue of more than passing interest. Juvenal's interlocutor, to whom the poet addressed the ironical inquiry, "in which synagogue shall I search thee?"[9] was not alone in his quest for a more satisfactory type of worship than that offered him by the increasingly petrified ritual of the Roman temples.

3. European and Asiatic Provinces

The spread of the diaspora into all corners of the Empire, then the equivalent of western civilization, created an increasing number of Jewish communities. The Seleucide Empire had already harbored a multitude of Jews in its Babylonian and Syrian possessions. For a short time it included Palestinian Jewry as well, and about 200 B. C. E.

Antiochus III issued its great "charter." Although interrupted soon afterwards by the intolerant reign of Antiochus IV Epiphanes, under whom a combination of greed, power politics and cultural chauvinism led to forcible hellenization of the Jewish masses in Palestine and probably also in other provinces, liberty of conscience and ethnic-religious autonomy were fully restored by Demetrius I and II in 151 and 142 B. C. E., respectively. Both were also fully maintained by the Roman and Parthian successors of the Seleucide regime.[10]

Similar freedom of organization prevailed in the other communities of the Roman Empire. A compilation, prepared some twenty years ago, of all ancient towns in which Jewish communities or synagogues have definitely been established through literary, epigraphic or papyrological evidence has furnished the following statistical data: Syria, including Phoenicia, 12 localities; Asia Minor, including Cyprus, 31; the Balkan Peninsula, including Greece and the Aegean Islands, 19; Italy, including Sicily, 18; Spain, Gaul and Hungary, 5; Africa, including Egypt and Cyrenaica, 21. While the sources for some of these communities appear rather dubious, the omissions in this list due to oversight or subsequent discovery raise the certain known total above this figure. The officers of the Jewish community of Cologne, for example, are directly addressed by the imperial decree of 331 C. E. It is the oldest definitely proved Jewish community in Germany.[11]

The recent epochal discovery of the third-century synagogue in Dura-Europos on the Euphrates has opened new vistas on the history of the entire institution and of its art. Of great interest are also the synagogue inscriptions found in recent years in the territories of Yugoslavia, Bulgaria and

Hungary and referring to synagogues built there in the first centuries of the Christian era. The number of congregations, moreover, exceeds the number of localities, inasmuch as many a city had more than one synagogue. Rome, for instance, figuring in the above list as a single locality with 11 synagogues, is now known to have accommodated at least 13 congregations. Among the European synagogues that of Delos, dating back to the second pre-Christian century, is especially noteworthy. Doubts frequently voiced as to the Jewish character of the remains appear unfounded in view of the term *proseuché* used in an inscription, the location of the building outside the town and in the vicinity of water and the indubitable existence of a Jewish community in the city. The usual content of the synagogue epigraphy may perhaps best be illustrated by the following inscription, unearthed a few years ago in Stobi, Yugoslavia, and dating, according to palaeographic evidence, from about 165 C. E.:

[I], Claudios Tiberios Polycharmos, also named Achyrios, Father of the Congregation of Stobi, who conducted my whole life according to Judaism, [have], in fulfillment of a vow, [erected] the buildings for the Holy Place and the *triklinion* together with the *tetrastoon* with my own means without in the least touching the sacred [funds]. Howbeit, the right of disposal of all the upper chambers and the proprietorship [thereof] shall be vested in me, Claudios Tiberios Polycharmos, and my heirs for life; and whosoever shall seek in any way to altér any of these dispositions of mine shall pay unto the Patriarch two hundred and fifty thousand denarii. For thus have I resolved. But the repair of the tile-roof of the upper chambers shall be carried out by me and my heirs.[12]

4. Communal Institutions

The great divergences of socio-economic status, cultural outlook and local traditions in the Graeco-Roman communities were reflected in their organizational and institutional structure. That they did not differ even more widely and that, in certain fundamentals, they followed a common pattern reveals, more clearly than the few extant sources, the great advances in the communal evolution of the Persian diaspora. "The Jews," says Hecataeus of Abdera, "have greatly modified their ancient institutions because of their mixing with strangers."[13] Nonetheless ample room remained for creative innovation. Quickened by the dynamic force of Hellenism, permeated with a strong missionary spirit and profoundly confident that their religion and culture were destined to conquer the world, the individual groups of Jews settling in new countries vigorously adjusted their public and private life to changing requirements. The prevalent religious syncretism and sectarianism likewise had many repercussions within the Jewish community.

These outside influences were but slightly mitigated through the occasional close settlement of Jews in certain quarters. Such "ghettos," established without legal compulsion, were by no means exclusive and harbored numerous non-Jews while many Jews lived in other sections of the city. They are recorded in Alexandria (where the Jews first congregated in the fourth of the five districts, the so-called Delta, and later spread to another district), Apollinopolis Magna (Upper Egypt), Sardes and, possibly, Halicarnassus (Asia Minor). In Sardes, at the request of the first Jewish settlers, the city decided that "such a place be set apart for them by the praetors, for the building and inhabiting the same, as they shall esteem fit for that purpose." Josephus, in repudiating an anti-Semitic assertion of Apion, describes the Jewish quarter in Alexandria as placed on the seaboard which "is, by universal consent, its finest residential quarter," and declares that it had been presented to the Jews by Alexander himself. In another connection he emphasizes the importance of this grant to the Jews as given them "in order that, through mixing less with aliens, they might be free to observe their rules more strictly." This concentration did not prevent the Alexandrian Jews, however, from possessing synagogues in all the other districts and a necropolis at the other end of the city.[14]

True to their historic origin from non-sacrificial assemblies around the desecrated altars or near the city-gates, prayerful gatherings and processions in free open spaces long continued, particularly on special occasions such as invocations for rain or the celebration of fast days. Philo's description of the annual festival at Pharos clearly indicates that the prayers and thanksgivings were offered on the beach.[15] As a further survival of such open gatherings we find numerous "field synagogues" even in medieval Europe.

Nevertheless under the influence of progressive urbanization and of Greek models, the congregations became more and more attached to houses of worship. The word *synagogé*, to be sure, for centuries retained its original meaning of assembly, rather than place of worship. In classical Greek it had stood for any kind of collection, even of inanimate objects. In the Hellenistic papyri it increasingly became narrowed down to an assembly of men and, still more specifically, to a worshipful assembly of Jews. It appears in the Septuagint as the usual translation for *'edah*, and Philo feels induced to explain the term insofar as it refers to the "sacred places" of the Essenes. For the Egyptian Jewish houses of worship he as well as the authors of the numerous extant inscriptions and papyri prefer the name *proseuché*. At first widely used for pagan places of worship, this name increasingly came to be identified with the Jewish non-sacrificial temple. The *synagogé* followed suit. Before long it became the main term for a Jewish house of worship, just as *ecclesia* gradually came to connote a Christian church. Both words retained, however, also their original significance, inasmuch as the Synagogue and the Church continued to represent the aggregate of their respective communities. The Hebrew equivalent, *keneset*, beginning its career in a similar generic way and used for a storehouse of lumber or a congregation of Gentiles, soon became identified with the Jewish community as a whole. Usually it required the determining word, *bayyit*, to render the Jewish house of worship.[16]

From its inception, however, the synagogue was more than a mere sanctuary. Reminiscent of ancient informality when Jews used to gather on city squares, in private houses or in some sort of "house of the people," it served everywhere as the center for all communal and many private affairs. In Tiberias, during the great war, "there was a general assembly in the prayer-house, a huge building, capable of accommodating a large crowd," and the members of many other communities gathered in the synagogue to deliberate on political action. Here many Jewish tribunals sat to judge and mete out punishment. Paul regretfully reminisced as to how he had previously punished the Christians "in every synagogue." Here the communities kept funds and treasures, and temporarily deposited the annual collections of half-shekels and voluntary contributions for the upkeep of the Temple or the maintenance of the Palestinian patriarchate. Like the Graeco-Roman temples and that of Jerusalem, the synagogues served as depositaries for communal and, presumably, private funds. The desecration of any sanctuary was severely censured by public opinion and appropriately punished by the courts. Exposed to the hostility of Hellenistic neighbors and the rapacity of imperial or local officials, the Jews had reason to place property under the protection of a sanctuary. The safeguard did not always prove effective. Just as Antiochus Epiphanes and Crassus brazenly despoiled the Temple treasury, so did L. Valerius Flaccus, Roman governor of Asia Minor, "confiscate," with a flimsy excuse, the contributions of Jews of four districts which were awaiting shipment to Jerusalem. But the unfavorable reaction of most of the civilized world to Antiochus' violence — which explains his subsequent defensive fabrication of tales about the Temple ritual — and the prosecution of the derelict Roman official by the Roman courts, reveal the extent of security vouchsafed by any sanctuary. This legal and popular recognition may, in fact, have influenced many an informal community to erect a house of worship, thus adding impetus to the transformation of the synagogue. Following the example of their neighbors, moreover, many diaspora synagogues extended the right of asylum to certain groups of accused. In others, likewise following a Hellenistic practice, Jews manumitted slaves by public oral declaration and commemorated the event by an appropriate inscription. Still others, emulating the example set by the great synagogue of Alexandria, served as a sort of labor exchange. Finally, we learn from Ovid that young men, Gentile as well as Jewish, visited synagogues in search of romantic adventures. The synagogues soon became so much the focus of all Jewish life that not only the "ten men of leisure," but many other members were to be found there at any hour of the day. To many diaspora Jews the synagogue enclosure must have appeared as the closest substitute for their lost patrimony in the Holy Land. They soon learned fully to appreciate R. Joḥanan's parabolic application of the Deuteronomist's blessing, "That your days may be multiplied . . . in the *land* which the Lord swore unto your fathers to give them . . ." to the regular attendants of synagogue services in the dispersion.[17]

The main functions of the synagogue were, of course, the closely related religious and educational activities. However diffuse and groping local rituals must still have been, they all centered in the reading and exposition of Scripture on holidays and Sabbaths (many a synagogue was known to outsiders only as a *sabbateion*). Rooted in a custom going back to Josiah and Ezra, this ritual gained ground with the growing veneration of Moses as mankind's foremost teacher and the belief that he was the real founder of the synagogue. Philo's description of what evidently was the practice in many Egyptian communities and the conclusions which may be drawn therefrom give an inkling of the character of the worship and of its appreciation by diaspora Jewry in general:

> In fact they [the Jews] do constantly assemble together, and they sit down one with another, the multitude in general in silence, except when it is customary to say any words of good omen, by way of assent to what is being read. And then some priest who is present, or some one of the elders, reads the sacred laws to them, and interprets each of them separately till eventide; and then when separate they depart, having gained some skill in the sacred laws, and having made great advances toward piety.[18]

It evidently was for the purpose of such public recitation that the Hebrew Bible was first transliterated and then translated into Greek, for the Hellenistic masses were rapidly losing their familiarity with the mother tongue. The Septuagint, work on which began within a century after the expansion of Hellenic culture, became the Bible of Hellenistic Jewry and, through it, of the Christian Churches.

Apart from the recitation of Scripture, there seem to have been no prayers and rites common to all the growing dispersion. Each congregation adopted its own ceremonies and liturgical forms. The richness and variety of diaspora services may perhaps best be illustrated by the beautiful prayers of Tobit and his associates, assuming of course, as is done generally, that the Book of Tobit was composed by an Egyptian Jew in the pre-Maccabean period. The ultimate decision concerning the content and form of divine services rested with the particular group, subject to all the influences of neighbors and of the numerous full-fledged or partial converts.

The variety found expression also in synagogue architecture. Members of each community, perhaps each individual builder and donor, could decide on style, on the religious or secular motifs to be used in their exterior and interior decoration, and on the inscriptions which would hand down to posterity the record of their deeds. Stylistic anarchy was due not so much to the absence of a definitely Jewish style, as to the fluidity of a new institution and the great social and intellectual variety among the different groups in Jewry.

Many groups evinced a desire to emulate the Temple. Rabbinic opinion, to be sure, here counseled caution, so as to preserve the superiority of the central sanctuary. The seven-branched candelabrum, it demanded, should be modified into one of five, six or eight branches. Many a diaspora community, however, brushed aside such scruples. In Rome, especially, the seven-branched candlestick became the standard symbol of Judaism to an extent unrivaled before or since. There also was a universal trend toward separating the sexes as in the Temple, but the women's compartments often were side by side with or behind those of the men. In the famous synagogue of Dura which, having served but a dozen years (245-56 C. E.), has been unearthed in an excellent state of preservation, the excavators found no trace of a partition between the two sections. Only gradually did there evolve the special women's gallery of which the Palestinian Talmud speaks. Even then, however, the distinction did not achieve the rank of a binding norm. Neither was there any recognized rule concerning the location of the building. While a talmudic regulation demanded, as a matter of prestige, that the synagogue should tower above all other houses in town, there is no evidence that the ancient communities attempted to meet the requirement, even where they were not hindered by contrary state legislation. Some congregations chose to place their synagogues on the banks of a river or at the seashore. Others, for instance in Antioch, disregarding the advantage of such facilities for ablutions, built their houses of worship in the heart of the city. Where local legislation required the concentration of cults outside the town limits, the Jews obeyed or sought a special exemption. Sometimes they could build in the neighborhood in which most of the members happened to live. Many synagogues had annexes to accommodate the manifold communal activities. The synagogue built in Jerusalem by the Roman Jew, Theodotos, son of Vettenos, "for the reading of the law and for the teaching of the commandments," contained in addition "the hospice and the chambers, and the water installation for lodging of needy strangers."[19]

Most synagogues were small, however. That of Dura, for instance, could seat comfortably only some 55 men and 35 women. A later Palestinian source describing the Temple services, but evidently having the contemporary synagogue in mind, emphasized that a hundred men could freely bow at the same time. Although no synagogue of a large community has thus far been excavated, it appears that even in such cases the Jews preferred small neighborhood houses in lieu of, or in addition to, a large central synagogue.[20]

Connected with the synagogue was the school. While we do not know whether the Palestinian system of obligatory communal education for children was adopted also in the Graeco-Roman diaspora, it appears that at least the larger communities tried to provide educational facilities for needy members, children and adults alike. Philo mentions, indeed, that his Jewish compatriots "had been taught ·in a manner from their very swaddling clothes by their parents and teachers and instructors" to believe in the unity of God. That they also tried to emulate the Greek *gymnasia* is the less astonishing the more such gymnastic training was regarded by their neighbors as not only the mark of a gentleman but also proof of superior civic status. Claudius' warning, sounded in his letter to Alexandria, that the Jews should not "strive in gymnasiarchic and cosmetic games," seems to have served as no more than a temporary deterrent. It appears that in Hypaepa, Asia Minor, there was, in the second or third century, a special sports-association of "young Jews."[21]

Synagogue annexes often housed communal archives and a library. For their frequent appeals to imperial authorities against the encroachments of native majorities, they required ready access to collections of privileges and records of precedents. Here, then, were kept the records of communal transactions, originals of the privileges granted local Jews, and copies of such grants to other communities of the Jewish people as a whole. Insofar as Jewish courts functioned, they, too, must have kept transcripts of proceedings. It is remarkable that, among the considerable number of known Egyptian papyri, very few seem to refer to transactions between two Jewish parties. Even the fourth volume of the Berlin papyri, largely deriving from the populous Alexandrian Jewish quarter, apparently contains but one such wholly Jewish contract. It mentions, moreover, a specific Jewish *archeion* as contrasted with the *politikon archeion* of the Alexandrians. An "archive of the Jews" is also clearly mentioned in at least one inscription in Hierapolis, Asia Minor. The deduction seems eminently justified that the Jews regularly repaired to their own courts of justice and deposited copies of their business deeds in their own archives. A lucky find may some day reveal material from such an archive, which would easily rival in significance the famous papyri of the Elephantine soldiers.[22]

Another highly important Jewish institution was the cemetery. The burning, in 489 C. E., of the Antioch synagogue with the bones of Jews interred in its vicinity, which elicited the characteristic remark of Emperor Zenon, "why did they not burn the living Jews along with the dead?" is not conclusive as to the location of cemeteries. The Alexandrian necropolis was, as we have seen, far from the

Jewish quarter where were, undoubtedly, most of the city's synagogues. Although by no means the first to have cemeteries in the ancient world, the Jews seem to have used them more consistently in the diaspora. Notwithstanding their burial customs, which must have appeared strange to the average Roman, and their growing exclusion of strangers, they seem to have greatly influenced the Roman change from cremation to burial. Placed under the general protection of Roman law with respect to tombs, communities and individuals defended their right to exclusive use by special provisions in wills or by announcing the founder's wish in an appropriate inscription. One such third-century inscription found in Smyrna is interesting for more than one reason: "The Jewess Rufina, archisynagogus, has erected this tomb for her freedmen and wards, so that no other person should have the power of burying anybody [there]. Should anyone dare to do so, he is to pay 1500 denars to the most holy fisc and 1000 to the people of the Jews. A copy of this deed is deposited in the archive."[23] It is, indeed, to the funerary inscriptions in Jewish cemeteries, especially the Roman catacombs, that we are indebted for much of our information concerning the ancient Jewish community organization.

Like the synagogues, the ancient cemeteries show great variations in style and arrangement. Had we sufficient records, we would undoubtedly see an equal diversity in funerary customs and rituals. It was here that ancient magic and folklore, coupled with religious syncretism, found a most receptive audience. The apparent absence of definitive regulation — the Pharisaic-rabbinic legislation on this point still was in its infancy — left ample scope to whim and fashion.

5. COMMUNAL ORGANS

Organizational forms likewise differed in accordance with the attitudes of members, the ambitions of founders and leaders and the accidents of historic origin. While there probably was some sort of basic pattern, determined by earlier historic evolution, interrelations between the diaspora communities, the influence of the common Palestinian center and, perhaps, by a certain similarity in external status, each diaspora community was "sovereign" in more than one respect. In formulating statutes the community could imitate the regulations of any of the local Hellenistic associations, which often differed from one another vastly, or follow previous experiences or the whimsical desires of its older and more recent members. Although no copy of such Jewish statutes, except perhaps for those of the Damascus sect, has come down to us, there is little doubt that many Jewish communities of that highly articulate and literary age committed their constitutional agreements to writing.

The main organ of the individual congregation was the plenary assembly of its members, readily available at weekly divine services. Rabbinic sources frequently imply the existence of such popular assemblies. Following a widespread Hellenistic custom, many probably met also in a gathering half religious and half social, the *synodos*, generally a common banquet or other form of conviviality. Our information, to be sure, is limited to ceremonial repasts among sectarian groups, such as the Essenes and the Therapeutai. The use of this term in connection with the Jews of Berenice, Sardes, Ravenna and, possibly, Nasli in Asia Minor, is inconclusive. Nevertheless, the Roman order to the people of Paros to allow the Jews "both to bring in their contributions and to make their common suppers" cannot be dismissed as a sheer misunderstanding on the part of a Roman official. With or without conviviality, the Jews doubtless gathered at stated periods for discussion, election and other common action. In an anti-Jewish homily long ascribed to St. Chrysostom but apparently written by Pontius Maximus before the time of Constantine, the Jews are accused of depravity or haughtiness for having changed the biblical New Year from March (Nisan) to September (Tishri), "in which month they also designate their own officials whom they call *archontes*." This evidently refers to some form of annual election, such as was a regular feature of many Hellenistic associations. If we may take a clue from a somewhat dubious reference to an edict of Emperor Alexander Severus, we learn that the Jews used to announce the names of candidates to office in advance of the actual election. They exhorted all who might know of a crime committed by any candidate to denounce it. An allegation which could not be proved was severely punished, however.[24]

All members seem to have enjoyed perfect legal equality. Women, of course, were generally excluded from the conduct of public business. The Palestinian rabbis agreed with Philo that women should abstain as far as possible from public appearances. The privilege publicly to recite the appointed scriptural lesson, originally granted women, was withdrawn by the Palestinian sages. The austere Alexandrian philosopher even demanded that, in visiting a sanctuary, they "should take pains to go, not when the market is full, but when most people have gone home." It is doubly remarkable, therefore, that contemporary records contain quite a few references to women holding offices, which may, however, have been purely honorary. The honorary charac-

ter of the various *matres* or *pateressae* of the synagogue is
the more likely as the male equivalents appear to have been
nothing more. The aforementioned woman archisynagogus
of Smyrna, if not merely the wife of an official, was very
likely a lady whom the congregation wished to honor, but
to whom it could hardly have entrusted the actual charge of
an office.[25]

Equality among male members remained unimpaired by
the distinctions between priests, levites and ordinary Israelites, carried over from the Temple. Found as early as the
diaspora congregation of Elephantine, this distinction was
maintained generally thereafter. The majority of rabbis
hesitatingly suggested, but never brought about the formation of a fourth category of proselytes.[26] In the light of the
great success of diaspora Jewry's missionary efforts in the
pre-Christian era, such segregation would have been but a
natural reaction. Only certain restrictions in the connubium
of proselytes and priests remained in effect. The exclusion
of semi-proselytes from full participation in communal affairs, on the other hand, although referred to chiefly in
relatively unfriendly rabbinic sources, undoubtedly became
the more imperative as the communities tried to stave off
the overwhelming forces of religious syncretism. But the
ritualistic distinctions among full-fledged Jews constantly
decreased in importance when diaspora Jewry refused to
apply to itself the strict laws of purity in the fashion then
elaborated by the Palestinian leaders. The priests and
levites retained some peculiar synagogue functions connected, for example, with the priestly blessing, which at
that time was prominent in the ritual. They may already
have enjoyed some precedence in the recitation of the Torah.
But they had long lost their position of leadership. The

few synagogue officials recorded in the inscriptions as
"priests" achieved their offices in the same manner as did
their lay colleagues, i. e., generally through election.[27]

The intriguing question of the extent to which differences
in economic status were reflected in communal rights unfortunately cannot be answered on the basis of available
sources. There is little doubt that, like political or intellectual eminence, wealth counted heavily in selecting leaders
and influencing communal action. In those fairly numerous
cases in which individual members endowed a synagogue
with all or a major part of the funds necessary for construction or maintenance, the donor's voice undoubtedly was
loudly heard in council. Since the communities collected
regular taxes from well-to-do members, it is conceivable that
the payment of a minimum tax or other property qualification was already a prerequisite for the exercise of electoral
rights or the holding of this or that office. The silence of
the sources does not in itself prove the absence of property
qualifications. Neither the literary nor the epigraphic material, the latter consisting mainly of funerary inscriptions
recounting the attainments of one or another individual,
would be likely to shed light on this subject. Only a fortunate discovery of a papyrus listing the statutes of a particular
congregation might determine the origin of the subsequently
numerous qualifications to the franchise. At present we may
only guess that in this respect, too, great regional and local
differences prevailed.

Much fuller is our information regarding communal offices.
While many important aspects of the origin, rise and characteristics of diaspora leadership and bureaucracy cannot
yet be clarified — indeed, many are likely to remain con-

troversial for many years to come — there is a solid background from which emerge the contours of the typical officeholder of the ancient community.

At the helm of each congregation there was, generally, a council of elders, individually frequently called by the traditional name, zekenim, or its Greek equivalent, presbyteroi. With the progressive decline of the family unit, these leaders were no longer literal elders. "An elder is he who has acquired wisdom," ran a contemporary talmudic adage. More concretely, anybody could be an elder in the diaspora — in Palestine the term was increasingly reserved for rabbinic sages — whom his fellow members elected to the council. Adopting a term common in Greek municipalities and associations, Hellenistic Jews called their council collectively gerousia. When there was a chairman, he was called the gerousiarches. The number of members varied widely in accordance with the size, the complexity of functions or the whimsies of each congregation. No regulations on these points are recorded, except for a talmudic precept that no council should consist of less than three members. This precept may or may not have been followed in the diaspora. The great council of Alexandria, in any case, consisted of seventy or seventy-one elders. Like the contemporary Palestinian Sanhedrin, it evidently adopted the traditional biblical figure. On one occasion thirty-eight of these venerable leaders were flogged by the Roman governor, Pomponius Flaccus, because of their resistance to the divine worship of Caligula. It is very likely that such large councils met in plenary session only for the deliberation on major legislative, judicial or administrative problems, while minor matters were the competence of smaller committees or executive organs. Such practice seems clearly implied in Philo's emphasis upon assembling "the entire council" to adjudicate certain difficult criminal cases.[28]

To the elders belonged also the so-called *archontes*. This term, which penetrated into the Hebrew-Aramaic of Palestine (not Babylonia), connoted chiefs or executives. In a larger *gerousia* it became necessary, of course, to delegate executive functions to a special committee, while in a smaller community all the councilors might serve in an executive capacity. The following resolution adopted in 13 B. C. E. by a public assembly during the Feast of Tabernacles in Berenice, North Africa, under the guidance of the nine archontes (here fully named) sheds interesting light on their position in a typical small community:

> Marcus Tittius, son of Sextus and Aemilia, a splendid and good man, having been called to the management of public affairs, has discharged his executive duties kindly and well and, while in this post, was found to have shown a peaceful disposition during the entire period of his administration. His behavior has been irreproachable not only in these matters, but also in those affecting the individual citizens. Discharging, moreover, in the best possible manner his executive duties for the Jews of our community [*politeuma*] in general as well as in individual matters, he did not fail to take the measures appropriate to their welfare. In consideration of all these circumstances the archontes and the community of the Jews in Berenice have resolved to honor him and, by naming him at every assembly and new moon, to decorate him with a wreath of olive branches and an honorary badge. The archontes are to inscribe this resolution [*psephisma*] upon a stele of Parian stone and place it at the most prominent spot of the amphitheatre. Unanimous consent.

These officers were generally elected for only one year but could be re-elected for a second. Subsequent re-election seems to have become less frequent as time went on. For the city of Rome, a single recently discovered tombstone inscription commemorates one Domnos as "thrice an archon," while nine other men are known to have been "twice archontes." On the other hand, Roman and other records speak of officers *dia biu*, which probably means men elected for life. Here, however, we may again be dealing with a merely honorary official who, like the *pater* or *mater* of a synagogue, participated in communal action only exceptionally.[29]

Some specific communal functions were entrusted to special officers, some of whom were probably simultaneously archontes and members of the general council. Some other officers seem to have been permanent, salaried civil servants, elected by the public assembly or appointed by the council or the archontes. Each community undoubtedly had its own organizational forms. "Even the smallest Greek ϑίασοι and Roman *collegia tenuiorum* paraded an imposing list of officers and dignitaries to satisfy the naive ambition of their members and protectors, and it is not surprising that the Jews yielded to the same temptation."[30] Multiplicity of titles was, moreover, the natural effect of local diversity and decentralization. Many different names encountered in sources may have connoted a single function, just as today comparable American associations are controlled by directors, trustees, governors, supervisors, superintendents or whatnot, having largely identical functions and prerogatives. To draw clear lines of demarcation between the numerous officers incidentally mentioned in one or another inscription or literary source, appears to be an altogether hopeless task. In the larger communities, on the other hand, the size and complexity of communal tasks required the services of many appointive or elective officials specializing in particular phases of communal service. Administrators of the communal treasury and other communal property, styled in Rome *archon pases times* and *phrontistes* respectively, were quite universal. Many communities must also have had special supervisors of charity, such as are frequently mentioned in the Talmud.

Three officers merit more than passing attention: the communal secretary or *grammateus*; the head of the synagogue or *archisynagogus*; and the latter's salaried assistant, or *hyperetes* or *hazzan*. Greek municipalities and associations, too, had secretaries, as did the Sanhedrin in Jerusalem. A *grammateus* or *sofer* could serve as secretary of an individual congregation or of a general community council. One might be primarily a clerk of a court or in charge of communal archives and membership lists. Another might be a mere expert in caligraphy or in the legalisms of contracts and wills; as such he would copy books, prepare rolls of Scripture and phylacteries and, in an altogether private capacity, write letters. On the whole, however, there was a trend to distinguish between the largely private *libellarius* and the official notary or *grammateus*. In another sense, at least in Palestine, the scribe, without altogether losing any official status, became primarily an expert in Scripture. Such an important official must have been found in many communities. In Rome are recorded no less than twenty-eight deceased *grammateis*. Only six are known to have been attached to a particular congregation. But whether the failure of the inscriptions to mention the connections of the others is due to chance or to a possible private or community-wide rather than congregational status, cannot be ascertained. The permanence of their function is, in any case, attested to by the complete absence of such limiting references as "twice grammateus."

The *archisynagogus* or *rosh ha-keneset*, the chief of the synagogue, may be called an ecclesiastical officer, just as is a church warden today. But to see in him the equivalent of a modern rabbi is to mistake the essence of the ancient synagogue. Services were still simple, ritual and liturgy formalized only to a minor degree. While a specially knowing member was always free to expound scriptural passages, it was still the average citizen who recited Scripture when called to the Torah. The archisynagogus maintained order, assigned seats, distributed honors, invited guest preachers and, when necessary, cared for the building. All our records, however, mention but a single officer of this kind in any congregation at any particular time. Of course, he must have exercised a spiritual influence as well. Frequently he led the Jewish opposition to Jesus and the apostles. Sometimes, apparently, he dabbled in the popular type of semi-magical healing, evoking the scorn of enlightened pagans and the opposition of Christian competitors. Among the Jews, however, he was held in high esteem. To belong to the family of an archisynagogus was a matter of great pride. He was, nevertheless, subject to the control of the entire congregation, to which he had to render an account of his activities and financial management. We possess a curious illustration in an inscription of Aegina, near Athens: "I Theodoros the ar[chisynagogus] who functioned for 4 years, built this s[ynagogue] from its foundations. Revenues amounted to 85 pieces of gold, and offerings unto God to 105 pieces of gold." The 20 gold denars difference may well have been taken from Theodoros' private resources.[31]

The archisynagogus was effectively supported by a permanent official, the *ḥazzan*. Like the *grammateus* this official had a variety of functions, and much of the confusion prevailing in scholarly discussions of the origin and meaning of this office is due to hopeless attempts to reduce it to a particular function. As a general assistant, he might rank second only to the archisynagogus, but he could also be a mere sexton with menial tasks. Sometimes he announced the approach of the Sabbath by three blasts on the trumpet from the roof of the synagogue. Often he led in prayers and recitations and directed congregational response, although as a rule the "public's messenger" in charge of services was still a mere layman. Sometimes he conducted the priestly benediction, delivered the Scripture roll to the reader and, after having publicly exhibited it, returned it to the ark. He often acted as bailiff, serving summonses, or as sheriff, executing sentences, such as floggings in the synagogue precincts. Frequently he was called upon to offer elementary instruction in Hebrew and Scripture. He was, in other words, a congregational factotum the number of whose functions was in inverse ratio to the size of the congregation. By a curious irony of history, it was the least frequent and least important of these functions, namely the conduct of services, which at a much later age came to be identified with the office of *ḥazzan* or reader.[32]

A curious phenomenon in diaspora communities was the conferring of communal offices or titles on women and children. Especially in Rome, leading citizens often sought the election of their minor children. One, Annianos, was called the "child archon" when he died at the age of eight years and two months. A certain Siculus Sabinus "served" as *mellarchon* (prospective archon) of the congregation of Volumnians at the age of two years and ten months. Another, Marcus Cuyntus Alexus, age 12, was both *mellarchon* and *grammateus* of the Augustians. In Venosa one, Kallistos, a child of three, was given the title of archisynagogus. Some sort of heredity is evidenced also by the aforementioned inscription of Theodotos, who gloried in the fact that both his father and grandfather had likewise been archisynagogi. None of these offices was, however, hereditary in the proper sense of that word. Even in Rome the successive officers of the various congregations do not seem to have belonged to the same families. Wealth, descent, political influence or personal merit doubtless created a certain tendency toward hereditary succession, but the ultimate decision among candidates remained with the plenary assembly.

A rather knotty question is the extent to which officers held community-wide competence. In communities having but one congregation, congregational officers were obviously also communal officers. But in larger cities such as Alexandria, Antioch and Rome, the co-existence of several synagogues is well attested. In Alexandria, indeed in all Egypt, the nearly totalitarian Ptolemaic economy and administration, although it left room for local and group autonomy, made a central agency desirable to both the state and the Jews. Whether or not many Jews were subjected to the *laographia*, the tax levied on the underprivileged mass of native Egyptians, they seem, in any case, to have paid a special tax. The Jewish community as such may have had no share in collecting imposts, since royal tax-farmers effectively managed this phase of government, but there must often have arisen questions of law and procedure requiring extended negotiations with the fiscal authorities by some formal Jewish representation. Such a central agency is, indeed, frequently mentioned in the sources. The only question is whether it was a council of elders, an ethnarch, or both. Apparently a single leader was deemed preferable under the more absolutist Ptolemies. He may have been assisted, however, by a council such as existed in each larger community. After the Roman conquest, and especially under Augustus and his successors, the *gerusia* seems to have found more favor with the new administration. In any case the *ethnarches* or *genarches* of the Jews disappears after the age of Augustus, even though Claudius is supposed to have renewed the Jewish privilege of having such a single leader. What, if any, influence was exercised on Jewish self-government by the *alabarches* remains highly controversial. But with or without an ethnarch, the great council of Alexandria undoubtedly had an important share in managing the general affairs of Egyptian Jewry.[33]

We hear little about such central leadership in other large communities in the same period. In Rome, it appears, some sort of city-wide management was required by cemetery problems arising from seven congregations apparently sharing a single burial ground. Political moves related to the renewal of privileges, the prevention of inimical actions, such as those of emperors Tiberius and Claudius, and the rather frequent embassies of Jews from Palestine or Egypt, likewise necessitated some sort of united leadership. Indeed, several scholars have seen in the title *exarchon* or *archon alti ordinis* mentioned in a few inscriptions, the chief of all Roman, perhaps of all Italian Jewry. Rabbinic sources mention a scholar, Theudas, who, apparently in the days of Hadrian, "led the Jewish inhabitants of Rome" and introduced ritualistic innovations which were clearly city-wide. More likely, however, is the existence of a general council of representatives of all congregations, which was more or less loosely organized and interfered but little with internal synagogue management. In any case, the hypothesis that here and elsewhere were single regional leaders, "little patriarchs," has created more difficulties than it has solved.[34]

6. Imperial Protection

The great organizational latitude was fostered by the absence of legal enforcement. The Hellenistic and Roman Empires, having decided to tolerate the Jewish religion as a *religio licita*, evinced little interest in the particular constitutional forms which their Jewish subjects adopted for their respective congregations.

The far-reaching Jewish claim of having obtained from the Empire and its predecessors full equality of civic rights (*isopoliteia*) was reiterated inferentially rather than directly, since it was difficult to persuade even such well-disposed Roman chiefs as Caesar and Augustus to embody this general principle in a sweeping proclamation. The Romans preferred, as a rule, to decide specific issues as they arose, leaving general principles, particularly with respect to the status of the Jews and later the Christians, to controversial, often partisan interpretation. As for self-government, the Jews were satisfied with a considerable number of negative privileges extending direct or indirect protection to religious and communal institutions.

Foremost among these privileges was that to form corporate groups. Like other dictatorships, that of Caesar became distrustful of the free associations of citizens. Following Caesar's example, Augustus dissolved all existing *collegia*, "except the ancient and legitimate ones," and decreed that thenceforth every new association would have to submit its charter to the government for approval. It was very important for the Jewish communities not to be classed among the new groups and thus be exposed to arbitrary decisions of the Roman bureaucracy. The danger was the more imminent as Caesar himself seems to have counted the Jewish congregations among the *thiasoi* and as public opinion then and later so designated the Jewish as well as the Christian communities. Although we possess no clear-cut legislative enactment — the decree addressed to the Parians is somewhat dubious — the Jews evidently succeeded in obtaining a general ruling classifying their *universitates* (communities) as among the "ancient and legitimate ones."[35] No application of a Jewish community is mentioned in any source. The only pagan Roman emperor who seriously interfered with Jewish self-governmental activities outside Italy was Hadrian, whose general prohibition of public gatherings went beyond the mere requirement of registration and approval. Although in line with the ever-tightening totalitarian control, this measure, like the corresponding prohibition of circumcision, was immediately relaxed by Hadrian's successor, Antoninus Pius. Here, too, we possess the text neither of a prohibitive decree nor of its revocation, but there is little doubt that the freedom of forming their own congregations "in conformity with the mores of their forefathers" was never thereafter denied Jews, insofar as they were tolerated at all in any ancient or medieval country. Being negative in character, this Roman privilege left the decision about the extent of such conformity largely to the Jews themselves.[36]

With the right of association went the freedom of instituting and electing the necessary organs, of owning property in the name of the community as a juridical person, and of erecting communal structures. For the main building, the synagogue, the Jews obtained from Augustus and his successors the protection implied in the classification of "sacred edifices." Theft or embezzlement of synagogue property was severely punished as a "sacrilege." Josephus reports the execution of a Roman soldier in Palestine by Cumanus, because he had torn to pieces and burned a roll of Scripture. Agrippa, Augustus' uncle, tried to reserve for the Jewish court the exclusive jurisdiction over such criminals, non-Jewish as well as Jewish. A desecration of a Jewish cemetery could be prosecuted by the *actio sepulchri violati*. Most far-reaching was the exemption of the Jews from imperial and local worship. Without ever saying it in so many words, emperor after emperor allowed Jews individually to abstain from all public ceremonies which they viewed as idolatrous, and collectively to exclude from their synagogues any form of worship objectionable to them. The emperors were satisfied with the Jews' regular prayers and sacrifices for their welfare and occasional dedications of particular synagogues. Flaccus' attempt in Egypt, followed by Caligula's general intention of abrogating this vital privilege of abstention, met with such stout resistance of the Jewish masses that no later emperor ever reverted to the attempt. Some emperors, individually friendly to Jews, aided them positively in the erection of synagogues and donated equipment. For such actions, Alexander Severus received the derisive nickname of archisynagogus. What is more, ecclesiastical officers of both the Temple and the synagogue enjoyed immunity from the ever increasing burden of taxation.[37]

Another implication of the right of association was the power to tax members. This authority was usually defined in the basic charter of each association. The Jews having but one generic charter, could make free use of this privilege within the boundaries set by their own laws and customs. Even the right of collecting funds, first for the Temple and then for the Palestinian patriarchs, was granted all Jewish communities, and the proceeds were under the protection of the laws governing sacred property.

The right of Jewish courts of justice to adjudicate all litigations arising among Jews was never contested in the pagan Roman Empire. The decree of Lucius Antonius to the magistrates, senate and the people of Sardes stated that, since the Jews had demonstrated to him "that they had an assembly of their own according to the laws of their forefathers, and this from the beginning, and also a place of their own, wherein they determined their suits and controversies with one another," he had given the order "that these their privileges be preserved." This decree is typical of a large number of such protective ordinances. Even in litigations of Jews against non-Jews, and in which state courts were to administer justice, the Jews enjoyed, since the days of Augustus, the privilege of not being cited as parties or witnesses on a Sabbath. At the same time, Roman public opinion often viewed the Sabbath as simply an expression of Jewish laziness.[38]

Even the Jewish "rebellions," culminating in the destruction of the Jerusalem Temple and the shutting of that of Onias, effected no general change in Roman legislation concerning Jewish autonomy. Some scholars assume that, having forfeited national status, the Jews were legally classified as a religious rather than an ethnic group and conclude therefrom that Jewish courts must have been transformed from the legitimate tribunals of an "alien" minority into mere optional organs such as all recognized associations possessed. Both assumption and conclusion have been effectively refuted, however. As before 70 C. E., Jewish judges continued to enforce the provisions of Jewish law not only with respect to religious life, but also in purely civil litigations. The main instrument of law enforcement, threat or decree of excommunication, was hardly affected by the change in political status which, incidentally, influenced Palestine much more than diaspora Jewry. The Roman authorities continued to support the Jewish communal organs in executing court sentences, collecting taxes and generally exercising an ever-tightening social control. Only in major crimes, especially those involving capital punishment, did the Roman administration reserve exclusive jurisdiction, since such crimes evidently threatened the general public order.

In short, the Jews, stubbornly insisting upon the full exercise of communal self-government, succeeded in winning at least the tacit approval of Roman legislation. For various reasons which cannot be enumerated here, this Roman support of Jewish autonomy went far beyond the Empire's general system of tolerating the mores and traditions of its heterogeneous population.

7. Christian Restrictions

This lackadaisical, often friendly, attitude of the Roman rulers came to an abrupt end when Constantine adopted Christianity as the main state religion. Basic indifference toward all purely internal Jewish affairs gave way to an intense interest in the religious as well as secular activities of Christendom's mother community. Although emperors as well as Church Fathers decided, for a variety of reasons, to tolerate Judaism as a *religio licita* and to continue recognition of the Jewish community as its organized expression, they drew an ever sharper line of demarcation between the Church, the new "Israel in spirit," and the Synagogue, the stubborn "Israel in flesh." In order both to impress the as yet unconverted masses of pagans and to fortify Christians, often still wavering, it became necessary publicly to degrade the synagogue and its sister institutions. The frequent complaints of such Church Fathers as St. Chrysostom that Christians were attending synagogue services on Sabbaths and Jewish holidays, listening to Jewish sermons, repairing to Jewish courts of justice and even taking oaths in synagogues because of their supposed superior sanctity, furnished a realistic background to harsh discriminatory legislation.

A series of laws was designed to place a mark of inferiority upon the synagogue as both congregation and structure. Insults were heaped upon insults even in the measured legal language of the *Theodosian Code* in regard to the "abominable superstition," the "Jewish perversity" and its "sacrilegious assemblies." Jewish law had demanded that the synagogue be placed in the highest elevation in town, and the new regulations emphasized that this place of honor be reserved for the Church. Attendance of Christians in the synagogue began to be punished as *lèse majesté*. According to a law of 423, evidently a re-enactment of older decrees,[39] no new synagogue could be erected without special permission, though records of such permits are extant only from the subsequent Ostrogothic period. This regulation, if carried into effect, would have completely checked the expansion of Jewish communities into new regions. Whether or not the legislator had such a check in mind — the Roman Empire, then on the defensive, was not much interested in expansion — it also interfered with possible attempts of Jews to make their services outwardly more attractive. The Jews were allowed, however, to keep existing synagogues in a proper state of repair.

The old severe sanctions on the desecration of Jewish houses of worship were long fully upheld. These laws, previously of slight practical significance, now became ever more vital. Christian mobs in various cities, unable to grasp the deeper social considerations which had influenced the leaders, repudiated all speculative niceties advanced in favor of toleration and began, often under the leadership of their bishops, to assail synagogues, burning them or appropriating them as Christian places of worship. Repeated decrees, especially in the turbulent years 393-423, sharply discountenanced such attacks. The Christian emperors no longer sent offenders to the mines, as had been, in the second century, the fate of the man who later became Pope Calixtus, but they still insisted that assailants be publicly flogged and forced to pay for rebuilding the synagogue. In 393 Theodosius I addressed to the *comes* of the Orient this order:

> It is sufficiently evident that the Jews' sect has not been prohibited by any law. Hence we are seriously aroused over the fact that their assemblies have been forbidden in various places. Your sublime Excellency will, therefore, upon receipt of this order, check with appropriate severity the overzealousness of those who, in the name of the Christian faith, arrogate to themselves illegal [powers] and attempt to destroy and despoil synagogues.

This ordinance is doubly remarkable since it followed a public demonstration of St. Ambrose in favor of offenders in Callinicum, Mesopotamia. Invoking Jer. 9.16, the Bishop of Milan had declared, in 388, that God authorized incendiary acts toward synagogues and that, had he known of this imperial law, he would have burned the synagogue of Milan in order to demonstrate the superiority of piety over police laws. He had finally threatened the emperor and his sons with eternal damnation. Although remaining firm in principle, Theodosius and his successors began compromising and finally modified the law to read that synagogues or synagogue objects appropriated by Christians must be paid for but need not be returned to the Jews if they had been consecrated. In cases of arson, the site was to be restored to the rightful owners. In this modified form, the law survived in Rome's barbaric successor-states in medieval Europe as well as in the Byzantine Empire. Another protective law for the synagogue, namely its exemption from the unpleasant and burdensome duty of billeting soldiers, was likewise frequently violated.[40]

The jurisdiction of Jewish courts continued to be respected and, whenever needed, supported by state organs until the days of Theodosius. This emperor, however, evidently impelled by the growing anarchy and the need for asserting the state's authority against the encroachments of the ecclesiastical courts — for which the above-mentioned threat of St. Ambrose may serve as a fairly typical example — decreed in 398 that

> in future they [the Jews] shall remain under our laws. However, if some of them should prefer in a transaction of civil law to submit their litigation by consent of the parties to the Jews or the patriarchs along the

lines of arbiters, the latter should not be prohibited by public law from issuing judgments. The provincial judges, moreover, should execute their sentences, as if approached on the basis of a sentence of a recognized arbiter.

With this decree (repeated also in the *Code of Justinian*)[41] Jewish jurisdiction in all religious matters was still upheld. Since, to Jews, all law was part and parcel of the Torah, the decision of a Roman jurist would have been required for each particular case to determine whether or not it fell under the provisions of this decree. It has also been pointed out that the intended parallel with courts of arbitration was not fully sustained. According to the rules of Roman law, a sentence issued by a court of arbitration did not possess the force of a court judgment and merely subjected the condemned party to the stipulated penalty in case of non-compliance. Here the decree itself ordered full execution by provincial authorities. Practically, it may be assumed, few Jews made use of the only important innovation arising from this parallel, namely an appeal to Roman courts against such judgments. Jewish solidarity in the face of common hostility and the still dominant control exercised by the Jewish community, whose power of excommunication was undiminished, effectively checked such unconventional moves.

The anti-Jewish legislation of the Christian emperors thus had no serious effect upon the self-governing Jewish community. On the contrary, the new emphasis upon religious life and conformity created an atmosphere decidedly favorable to the strengthening of communal bonds. If synagogues were destroyed or expropriated, this was primarily a financial problem affecting the life of the Jews less profoundly than had the oppressive yoke of taxation under the last pagan emperors. To combat the evils of extortionist taxation in a declining economy, the individual Jew was often assisted by his similarly placed coreligionists and his communal institutions. In case of dire need, he could appeal for aid from the increasingly effective communal charities. The community offered him also many social and cultural compensations for his declining status in state and society. Hence its cohesion and effectiveness was fortified rather than weakened by the wave of hostility.

8. INDIVIDUALISM AND SOCIAL CONTROL

Thus the Jewish diaspora community emerged from centuries-old obscurity and began to take definite shape under the aegis of the Hellenistic and Roman Empires. It continued to struggle for characteristic forms. Often modeling itself on the numerous Graeco-Roman associations, it shared their enormous structural and constitutional diversity. Stimulated by the long-prevalent individualistic trend, highly differentiated in origin, tradition, social status, intellectual outlook, degree of assimilation to the environment and extent of absorption of outsiders through full or partial conversion, each Jewish settlement in the Mediterranean world followed its own course. The influence of the Palestinian center, enormously significant in religion, culture and political status, was at first hardly noticeable in organizational matters, wherein the diaspora had its unique problems. To devise new structural forms to meet these problems was a task left wholly to the "creative élan of the masses."

Total disparity and extreme departures from the basic pattern developed in the Persian diaspora, however, were soon checked by the rising tide of social control in the increasingly feudalistic Roman Empire. This trend coincided with the rise of the new religion in the midst of Graeco-Roman Jewry. While the ever sharpening religious, social and political conflicts within the Jewish communities and the falling off of large numbers of Hellenistic Jews and proselytes undermined and finally eliminated many of the weaker organisms, it forced others to consolidate their position. Christian hostility, soon reinforced by the power of a vast Empire, made inner clarification and unity a prerequisite of survival. The task of reconstruction and unification in religion, law and community life was undertaken immediately after the fall of Jerusalem and Bethar by a vigorous and ambitious leadership in Palestine and a century later in Babylonia. The words of counsel and guidance emanating from the new centers of talmudic lore were soon heeded increasingly throughout the Jewish world; indeed, there developed a submissiveness greater than ever greeted the edicts of king and high priests who ruled in Zion.

CHAPTER V

TALMUDIC CONSOLIDATION

THUS far we have said little of the great Jewish communities of Palestine and Babylonia. Both countries were drawn early and decisively into the orbit of Hellenism. Even after the Maccabean revolt terminated what appeared to be the immediate threat to Jewish survival, the impact of Greek culture continued to be felt in all walks of Palestinian life. It was felt most strongly in the domain of community organization, where the vast constitutional experience of the dominant groups made emulation doubly desirable. Babylonia, too, for centuries under Seleucide and Parthian rule, could not escape the influence of Hellenistic political methods. When Hellenism's progressive decline in the Parthian Empire led to its nearly complete elimination in Sassanian Persia after 226 C. E., the Jews had behind them several centuries of autonomous community life. Although our information concerning these early developments is scanty, the rich source material in the Babylonian Talmud, whose beginnings precede the rise of Persia, pictures a community which was thoroughly organized and which functioned effectively.

The communal life of these two centers of ancient Judaism differed significantly from that of the countries hitherto reviewed. Since most Palestinian and many Babylonian communities embraced a majority of or all the inhabitants of a locality, ethnic-religious organization more or less coin-

cided with municipal government. On the other hand, the
Jews in many towns were confronted by a non-Jewish majority even less amicably disposed than those of the diaspora.
In the numerous autonomous Greek cities on Palestine's
Mediterranean coast and in Transjordan, the Jews had a
hard struggle for existence, notwithstanding frequent theoretical equality of rights. Contact with the wholly Jewish
municipalities and central organs, however, gave community
life even in such cities definite stimuli. Talmudic legislation
had to take cognizance of both types. This unusual combination led to no well-defined and comprehensive theory,
but it colored innumerable teachings, individual decisions
and incidental references of the talmudic sages, and left an
indelible imprint on the subsequent development of the
medieval and modern communities.

The presence of an influential class of scribes and rabbis
likewise accounts for certain peculiar aspects of the talmudic
community. Members of this class made ever more insistent
claims to exclusive leadership in public life, religious as well
as secular. The disappearance of the professional priesthood
and the downfall of Sadduceeism greatly facilitated the
realization of this program. We can still perceive, through
the haze of incidental controversies and homiletical allusions,
that the rabbis encountered strenuous opposition on the
part of classes whose major distinction lay in wealth, parentage or political connections. Talmudic theory was determined exclusively by the rabbinic party, however. The less
influential the individual teacher and the less his personal
responsibility for the practical implications of his theory,
the more could he indulge in doctrinaire postulates divorced
from the realities of contemporary life. With the growing
canonization of the Talmud as the compendium of divine

Oral Law, the original opposition and contradictory realities were forgotten, and all Jewry now tried to live up to the standards of communal life as formulated in the Talmud.[1]

1. REGULATED ACTIVITIES

In advising young scholars as to the choice of residence, the sages declared the following ten factors indispensable to a full and happy life: a court of justice with executive powers, a charity chest, a synagogue, a bathhouse, a public lavatory, a physician, a surgeon-masseur, a libellarius, a butcher and an elementary teacher. This succession was not intended to express relative values, since both synagogue and school undoubtedly ranked among the very first communal institutions, but to emphasize their equal indispensability. In any case, it was the business of the community to provide all these services. Only to the cost of a synagogue, however, and its most important equipment, the Pentateuch roll and the book of prophets, could a part of the population force all others to contribute.[2]

The rabbis soon set out to consolidate the ritual. The need for greater uniformity in worship was felt in Palestine's numerous synagogues (one had been erected in Jerusalem itself, on the Temple mountain) no less keenly than in the dispersion, whose great inner disparities could not fail to affect the center. There had long been in Jerusalem synagogues of foreign Jews, such as that of Theodotos, or those "of the Libertines [probably of Rome] and Cyrenians, and Alexandrians, and of them of Cilicia and of Asia," which disputed Stephen, the Christian apostle. Business, family bonds and pilgrimages constantly drew hosts of foreign Jews who, temporarily or permanently, joined the congregations of their respective origins. Others came to the Holy Land to be buried in sacred soil. All brought with them diverse rituals for both synagogue and cemetery. On Jewish tombstones in Jaffa, commemorating Alexandrian and Tarsian arrivals, we find Greek inscriptions with the single word *shalom* (peace) written in Hebrew characters.[3] Palestine itself, due to its checkered career, the numerous forcible or voluntary conversions, sectarian struggles and continued regionalism in social status and cultural outlook, seems to have developed diverse local traditions in and out of the synagogue.

Standardization of liturgy came about gradually. Daily prayer began concentrating on the *shema'* and the *'amidah.* The former, a public profession of monotheism with related passages culled from Deuteronomy, was preceded and followed by prescribed benedictions specially arranged for morning and evening use. The latter, also called *tefillah* (prayer) or *shemoneh 'esreh* (eighteen), consisted of a group of rather brief liturgical compositions evidently dating from hoary antiquity but re-edited under the direction of Gamaliel II soon after the fall of Jerusalem. In the lifetime of this patriarch was added a nineteenth section which, by invoking the wrath of Heaven on the Nazarenes and other heretics, was designed to bar all heterodox groups from communal worship. For the same reason the daily recitation of the Decalogue, theretofore practiced in many congregations, was now discontinued, thus impressing upon the worshiper the full equality of the Pentateuch's ceremonial and ethical sections. As a constant reminder of the Temple cult, the priestly blessing, uttered after the daily Temple sacrifice, was introduced into the synagogue, at first to be recited daily at all gatherings of ten or more worshipers. Only at a later date was this impressive ceremony restricted to a few festive occasions. The recitation of Scripture, too, became more regular. Originally, it seems, any number of men invited by the archisynagogus read verses selected at random from any section of the Pentateuch. Over a period of many generations there had gradually evolved a systematic division of the five books of Moses into weekly sections, to be read in toto on successive Sabbaths over a period of three years in Palestine, one year in Babylonia. As in many other phases of Jewish law, the Babylonian practice ultimately prevailed. In both countries, each weekly section was subdivided into seven parts for recitation by at least seven persons, although minor divergences with respect to the allocation of parts long persisted. The *haftarot*, selected sections of prophetic literature wherewith were concluded the recitations of Scripture, were now specifically assigned to particular Sabbaths and holidays. Here, too, minor differences prevailed and still do between the Sephardic and Ashkenazic groups.[4]

Growing standardization did not, however, altogether eliminate the pliability of the Jewish ritual. Sections from psalms were still freely recited. Individual prayers, often impromptu, might supplement official ritual. Most important were the regular homiletic explanations of recited verses which, of course, varied with each exegete or preacher. Following a widespread Hellenistic practice, Palestinian homilists wandered far and wide, often crossing the Roman frontier to Babylonia, in order to communicate their ideas on law and morality to synagogue audiences. Frequently itinerant preachers, including the celebrated R. Ḥiyya bar Abba, were appointed by the leaders of Palestinian Jewry. For the benefit of Jews unable to understand Hebrew — not altogether rare·even in Aramaic-speaking Palestine —

an interpreter translated the biblical verses into the vernacular in popular language. Obviously no such translator was needed in those diaspora communities where the Bible itself was publicly recited in the vernacular, but soon Palestinian hegemony made itself felt, and recitation in Hebrew was adopted universally. Neither the original liberalism of the rabbis toward vernacular recitation, nor such belated attempts as Justinian's severe order of 553 permitting minorities in congregations "to read the sacred Scriptures to the persons assembled in their synagogues in Greek or in their mother-tongue, i. e. Latin or any other language according to the locality, so that the recitation be understood by all those present," could stem the rising tide of conformity. Soon it became necessary both in Palestine and in the diaspora to employ official "readers."[5]

This reorganization clearly enhanced the role of scholars in synagogue services. The mere fact that certain prayers had to be recited in Hebrew in a peculiar sequence, gave to the learned a privileged position. The task of the interpreter (*meturgeman*), whether or not he was a permanent and salaried officer, was by no means as simple as it might appear. The ordinary meaning of Scripture being often at variance with accepted rabbinic exposition, the interpreter, who legally might be a male of any age, had to avoid both oversimplification and arbitrary elaboration. Rabbi Judah's irate remark that "he who translates a verse with exact literalness is a falsifier, and he who makes additions is a blasphemer" reveals the perplexities of this task. Public preaching, although likewise legally open to all, consisted of a skillful mixture of Bible exegesis and hermeneutics with ethical apothegms, moralistic anecdotes and legal maxims, and required the service of experts. Scholars without ora-

torical gifts or an aptitude for popularization were often
assisted by interpreters who tried to explain the sermon to a
heterogeneous crowd of men, women and children. Women,
we are told, would benefit by listening and celestial rewards
awaited those who brought children along. Little wonder
that scholars enjoyed preference for honorary appointments.
In their own estimation at least, they should follow priests
and levites in the assignment of scriptural chapters for
public recitation. As a matter of record, however, few rabbis
held the main synagogue offices, those of archisynagogus
and *ḥazzan*. In discussing preference in marital choice, the
rabbis advised prospective bridegrooms to choose in the
following succession:

> One should always sell everything one possesses in
> order to marry the daughter of a scholar; if he does
> not find a scholar's daughter, he should marry the
> daughter of the great men of the generation [the com-
> munal leaders]; if he does not find a daughter of great
> men, he should marry the daughter of archisynagogi;
> if he does not find a daughter of archisynagogi, he
> should marry the daughter of charity supervisors, he
> should marry the daughter of elementary teachers,
> but he should never marry the daughter of the [illit-
> erate] people of the land.[6]

If rabbinic ascendancy was thus guaranteed by the new
synagogue order, it was greatly fortified by the growing
emphasis on education. In the famous epigram of Simon
the Just, the "last of the Great Synagogue" ("the world is
built upon three foundations: Torah, worship and loving-
kindness"), study of the law took precedence. Indeed, the
synagogue itself paid equal attention to education and
edification. The services embodied lessons in Hebrew, Bible,
law and ethics, as well as opportunities for communion with

the Deity. Apart from the services, the synagogue's main hall or annexes frequently accommodated a school for both adults and children. In rabbinic theory the school was so superior that, while according to the general rule that "one may proceed from a lower to a higher degree of sanctity, but not from the higher to a lower degree," a synagogue could be converted into a school house, the reverse was not permitted.[7]

With this high estimate of education for both children and adults as guiding principle, the Pharisaic-rabbinic leaders embarked on their greatest and most successful venture: they made popular education obligatory for boys of six or seven on a scale unrivaled theretofore and long after. Ancient Jewish apologists already realized the enormous superiority of Judaism over the Graeco-Roman world in this respect. Josephus, perhaps unwittingly, echoed the Philonian exclamation concerning the universal familiarity of Jews with the entire structure of Jewish law. While the rabbis discouraged dismissal even of the most incapable pupils, they also could exaggerate in an opposite direction: "This is the way of the world: a thousand enter the Bible school, but only a hundred proceed to the study of the Mishnah; ten of those advance to the study of the Talmud, but only one achieves the rabbinic degree." Since the author of this statement was R. Simon b. Yoḥai, obviously Mishnah and Talmud do not refer to the works now known under these names but respectively to a general familiarity with traditional law and an ability to interpret and elaborate it independently.[8]

The ultimate responsibility for educating children remained with the parents. But the rabbis added an equal responsibility for the community. Innumerable utterances severely condemn communities which do not provide at least elementary instruction. The legal norm finally was that a community provide an elementary teacher for the first twenty-five boys over the age of six, an assistant teacher when their number should reach forty, and a second teacher when it should exceed fifty. The rabbis regulated curricula, insisting on progress from Scripture to Mishnah and then to "Talmud" (the ages of five, ten and fifteen were suggested for the respective courses, but were not considered obligatory), and generally gave preference to intensive over extensive study. The community was to supervise teachers, discharge moral and intellectual inferiors and prevent excessive chastisement of pupils. While the rabbis did not regulate salaries of elementary teachers, they exempted them from the general Jewish prohibition of charging for instruction in the law. This prohibition, intended to prevent the commercialization of learning, could not possibly be applied to the mass of professional elementary teachers whose manifold tasks often presupposed full-time employment. Unlike artisans or merchants, however, they were not protected against competition. "Rivalry between teachers will increase wisdom," was a popular adage. In small communities, several offices had to be combined in one man's hands. Levi b. Sissai, for instance, served in Simonias, without much success, as preacher, judge, ḥazzan, scribe, teacher of the Mishnah "and whatever else they might need."[9]

Another aspect of the term Torah was emphasized with equal vigor. Since Jewish law was viewed as divine, eternal and all-embracing, the Jews were to maintain their own administration of justice for all phases of ritual, civil and criminal law. They may have lost capital jurisdiction under the oppressive regulations of foreign conquerors, but Jewish law had long before made procedure in capital cases exceedingly cumbersome and practically eliminated executions. In all other respects Jewish jurisdiction remained intact, except during the brief Hadrianic persecution. Occasionally Jews repaired to Roman courts, which seem to have applied Jewish law to affairs affecting only Jewish parties. The Talmud has preserved the record of two Roman officials sent by their government to study Jewish law under Rabban Gamaliel. They are supposed to have expressed great admiration for the Torah, with the exception of two discriminatory provisions with respect to Gentiles. The rabbis, however, insisted that judges be Jews. Sometimes they conceded the operation of non-Jewish laws to litigations between Jews and Gentiles, but even then, at least in Palestine, they sought to reserve the judicial function itself to Jews. They were most insistent with respect to strictly Jewish lawsuits; such were to be submitted only to Jewish courts. They acknowledged, however, the validity of deeds registered at Roman archives, except for writs of divorce or manumission, which had to be countersigned by a Jewish archival office.[10]

Here, too, sages undertook to standardize procedure as they developed the minutiae of substantive law. The vestiges of the old people's courts did not speedily disappear. As in ancient Israel, an indigent old father, whose son refused support, could "summon an assembly" and publicly expose the ingratitude. Any three citizens could still sit in judgment in civil litigation, the parties usually selecting one judge each, and these two choosing a third. Such lawsuits as might lead to fines, however, must be submitted to three ordained judges. A tribunal "superior in wisdom and in number" (such as the "little" Sanhedrin of twenty-three members) could also annul the decision of a less distinguished court. With the growing complexity of the legal structure, moreover, it became more and more difficult for lay judges to find their way about, to relate cases to proper precedents, to decide between conflicting schools of opinion. No longer could they rely on common sense and a feeling for equity. When the rabbinic leaders finally introduced the principle of personal responsibility for judges' errors in fact and judgment, if not for those in the interpretation of clear-cut traditional law, they eliminated lay jurisdiction to all intents and purposes. Trained legal minds, of course, need not fear the pitfalls of increasingly complicated laws of evidence, and experts could escape legal responsibility for error by obtaining either the advance agreement of parties to abide by their decision or, preferably, a general "authorization" (*reshut*, akin to the Roman *potestas*) from the central Jewish authority in Palestine or Babylonia. Increasing numbers of permanent judges, qualified through rabbinic ordination, were protected by such authorizations. While rabbinic law still insisted that a judge, like the teacher of non-elementary subjects, must charge no fee, a loophole was easily found in the form of compensation for time taken off from gainful employment. From this to the evolution of a permanent, professional judiciary was but a step. Timidly made in Palestine, where, as mentioned before, Levi b. Sissai of the small community of Simonias combined his judicial office with several others, it led in Babylonia to the exilarch's authorization and later appointment of local judges. Courts began to hold public sessions for all litigants in a city and its environs on Mondays and Thursdays. As the law embraced with increasing exclusivity all walks of Jewish life and as the central authorities gained in power and influence, local judges gradually assumed functions going far beyond administration of justice. Soon they became the main leaders of communities, rivaling or exceeding elective officers in power, where they did not altogether replace such officials by their own appointees. A Babylonian teacher, Mar Zutra, finally denounced all scribes who were instructing laymen in the laws of communal administration.[11]

The influence of the court came to the fore also in communal regulation of economic life and social welfare. Increasing economic regimentation in the Roman Empire from the third century on, and the semi-feudal system of Sassanian Persia, forced Jewish leadership to assume ever more stringent control over Jewish economic activities, as the entire community now became responsible for the taxes levied on members. From the inception of Roman rule the Palestinian municipalities had been obliged to cooperate with government tax collectors and publicans in raising the exorbitant imperial revenue. Soon the Jewish minority community found itself in the same position. When, at the end of the second century, the Palestinian population complained before Pescennius Niger of the heavy yoke of taxation, he flippantly replied, "Verily, if I had my way, I would tax your air." The final step was made when, in 429, the Empire appropriated for its own treasury the *aurum coronarium*, theretofore voluntarily paid by all imperial communities to the Palestinian patriarch, and demanded that the communities continue to collect it. In Persia even earlier, the community had become the main tax collecting agency of the state.[12]

Partly under the dictate of an overpowering sense of social as well as individual justice inherited by the rabbinic leaders from their prophetic predecessors, and partly under the pinch of economic stress, the community began to control prices, supervise markets, check weights and measures, restrict speculation, assign streets to various crafts, regulate wages, hours of work and other employer-employee relations, prohibit interest, protect bona fide creditors, and generally to safeguard the interests of weaker members or of society against the encroachments of a powerful minority.

Even in the diaspora, many Jewish communities possessed markets of their own, as is evidenced by a papyrus found in Hermopolis Magna in the Egyptian district of Arsinoe (Fayyum). They appointed market-supervisors, usually called by their Greek title, *agoranomoi*. Philo, using this term in explanation of the laws of Lev. 19.35 f. and Deut. 25.13 ff., may already have had in mind an existing Jewish practice. These officials were to check measures and weights and, at least in Babylonia, control prices. When the revered teacher, Rab, apparently then still under the impression of his Palestinian experience, limited his supervision to the weights and refused to regulate prices, the exilarch threw him into prison. This economic self-determination of the Jewish community was, curiously enough, recognized by the absolutist Christian emperors. Theodosius I issued, in 396, a sweeping decree that "no one outside the Jewish faith should fix prices for Jews." This decree, repeated in the *Theodosian Code* and, with minor modifications, in those of Justinian and his successors, exercised great influence on Jewry's subsequent economic and communal destinies. From time immemorial there had existed the principle of *ona'ah*, whereby a sale exceeding or falling below the market price by more than one-sixth was, on demand of the injured

party, to be declared null and void. Now Samuel the Babylonian at least wished communal leaders to base all prices
on the allowance of a maximum merchant's profit of one-
sixth. While such sweeping postulates could never be fully
realized, there is little doubt that the communal authorities
had an increasing share in economic regimentation, which
deeply affected the life of all individuals.[13]

Hand in hand with this growing regimentation, went
provisions for the poor and needy. From the time of the
ancient Israelitic clans, charity had been deeply rooted in
Judaism. In the Bible the word *ṣedaḳah* is interchangeably
applied to charity and righteousness. This was recognized
by the Septuagint which, in fact, used the term, *eleemosyne*
in its new meaning of mercy and loving-kindness rather than
in its classical sense of simple compassion. Both elements
are equally emphasized again by such pre-Maccabean writers
as the Palestinian Sirach and the diaspora author of the
Book of Tobit. The inherent idea then and later was that
the poor had a right to support, and that failure to extend
it according to one's ability was a grievous sin. One need
recall only the immortal expostulations of Job:

> If I have withheld aught that the poor desired, or
> have caused the eyes of the widow to fail; or have
> eaten my morsel myself alone, and the fatherless
> hath not eaten thereof — Nay from my youth he
> grew up with me as with a father, and I have been her
> guide from my mother's womb. If I have seen any
> wanderer in want of clothing, or that the needy had
> no covering, if his loins have not blessed me, and if he
> were not warmed with the fleece of my sheep . . . .
> Then let my shoulder fall from the shoulder-blade,
> and mine arm be broken from the bone.

Less poetically but more concretely, Josephus summarized "the duty of sharing with others" which was "inculcated by our legislator" in the brief sentence: "We must furnish fire, water, food to all who ask for them, point out the road, not leave a corpse unburied, show consideration even to declared enemies."[14]

Although supported by the agricultural laws concerning gleanings, sheaves and corners, the triennial poor tithe, the Sabbatical year, and so forth, these forms of charity were primarily the obligations of individuals. Now communal charities, without in the least diminishing individual responsibility, were to organize social work systematically. A daily collection of foodstuffs for the so-called *tamḥui* enabled the community to establish a sort of public kitchen. Another larger collection for the *ḳuppah* supported the distribution of food for fourteen meals per capita to every needy family on every Friday. All persons claiming to be hungry were to be given food without further investigation. The community chest also provided clothing, after applications were scrutinized rather closely. Other funds financed burials, marriages of orphans (girls having precedence over boys), redemption of captives, and a variety of other needs. To discourage professional mendicancy, the rabbis not only coined many salty epigrams, but also declared ineligible for a share in the public distribution anyone who, begging from house to house, should receive as much as a dried fig. Penetrating more deeply to the roots of social maladjustments, they insisted on moderate living, the occupational training of children and the dignity of menial callings which made for economic self-support. They also urged every possible means of preserving private and communal resources, so essential in the economy of scarcity then prevalent.[15]

2. SCHOLARLY SUPERIORITY

The administration of charities was in the hands of a special committee. The rule was that there be two collectors of the charitable contributions, each of a character so un-impeachable that no check is necessary. Evidently this regulation, perhaps justified at the time of its enactment and helpful in preventing endless recriminations, subsequently led to many abuses. The distribution of charities, a more arduous and responsible task, was entrusted to a committee of three, a sort of tribunal adjusting conflicting claims. The ensuing controversies doubtless made many an officer echo R. Jose's exclamation, "Be it my destiny to serve among the collectors of charities rather than among the distributors." There were also special supervisors of certain communal institutions, such as schools, hospitals and cemeteries. To what extent these men belonged to the general communal council it is difficult to say. It seems that, unlike the Greek cities with their large councils of several hundred men, most Jewish cities and communities of the talmudic period were governed by small groups of seven to twelve members, the phrases "seven best men" (*tobim*) or "ten foremost men" (*dekaprotoi*) having become almost proverbial. Josephus, too, usually speaks of seven or ten councilors or judges. He himself "selected from the nation seventy persons of mature years and the greatest discretion and appointed them magistrates of the whole of Galilee, and seven individuals in each city to adjudicate upon petty disputes, with instructions to refer more important matters and capital cases to himself and the seventy." The rabbis, as a rule, speak of seven city elders, along with other special officers. Among these the "ten men of leisure" (*baṭlanim*) who, according to the Mishnah, characterized a large city, have given rise to endless discussions in modern scholarship. So has the generic name for the city council, the *ḥeber ha-'ir*, which, although rooted in a venerable tradition going back to ancient Ras Shamra, Israelitic proverbs and Maccabean coins, is referred to in the Talmud in such equivocal terms that many exegetes, from Maimonides to the present day, regarded it as the title of a single person. They, correspondingly, spelled it *ḥaber*.[16]

The paucity of our sources of information concerning the operation of these agencies is undoubtedly due in part to the frequent conflicts between the lay leaders and the scholarly authors of nearly all extant records. Except for a few hints, we learn nothing even about the division between the municipal and the more strictly religious agencies. To be sure, this modern distinction never carried much weight in antiquity, where religion was part and parcel of municipal life. Nevertheless, there undoubtedly existed an administrative division of functions, such as that illustrated by R. Joseph's decision between two contestants in a Babylonian community. To one of them, a rabbi, he assigned the "affairs relating to Heaven," to the other, who was distinguished neither by learning nor lineage (he was the descendant of a proselyte) the "affairs of the city."[17] In larger Palestinian cities, generally having a mixed Jewish and Gentile population, the city councils had perforce to abstain from regulating the inner affairs of each religious community.

Many of the city councilors, moreover, enjoyed little confidence on the part of the Jewish masses and their scholarly leaders. They were usually selected from among the wealthy classes. "A *boulé*, that is rich men," runs a talmudic definition. This was natural enough at a time when the Roman administration imposed severe financial responsibilities upon all municipal officers. Even before Diocletian's fiscal extremism, R. Joḥanan of Tiberias, for obvious reasons, somewhat cryptically advised his coreligionists: "if thou art elected to the *boulé*, make the Jordan thy neighbor," i. e. flee to the Jordan deserts. In contrast to other rabbis who preferred the municipal councilors to be men of leisure rather than hard-working scholars or busy physicians, R. Joḥanan also insisted that the heads of communities be scholars familiar with every law. Such scholars, particularly if they also were the authorized "judges," soon arrogated to themselves all authority in secular matters as well. The Talmud, indeed, speaks indiscriminately of a "city" acquiring or disposing of a street or a synagogue. No wonder that these extreme rabbinical demands were long and bitterly resisted by the ruling classes, as (through an analysis of the manifold hints preserved in the talmudic sources themselves) has been shown in the case of second-century Sepphoris, then the main center of Palestinian rabbinism.[18]

The lay heads were powerless, however, to stem the rising tide of rabbinic supremacy in Palestine and, still more so, in Babylonia. Although not democratic in the modern, electoral sense, rabbinic leadership cut across class and party lines and was, in some respects, more truly representative of the masses of the population than many an elective body. With their forceful insistence upon popular education, the talmudic sages opened wide to members of all social classes the gates to their own class, the aristocracy of learning. They themselves continued to ply all crafts, to live as nobles or as paupers as their differing private circumstances might require, and to devote, if at all possible, two-thirds of their time to study and worship and but one-third to earning a living. The separatism of the former Pharisaic fraternity and the sharp condemnation of the illiterate and insufficiently pious "people of the land," gradually gave way to a growing feeling of solidarity and brotherhood. The consolidating force of talmudic Judaism, buttressed by the progressive elimination of sectarian disparity and the increasing hostility of the outside world, greatly mitigated the conflict between the growing group of the learned and the mass of the uneducated. The sweeping, though somewhat equivocal principle, "all are equal before the Torah," had a decidedly "democratic" tinge. So had the provision adopted from Greek prototypes, that no close relatives be allowed to share an office or to serve as judges at the same court. This provision, consistently applied, served as a powerful check on the accumulation of power in the hands of a few families.[19]

Less obscure, although no less fragmentary, are the talmudic regulations of the basic requirements for communal membership. All Jews resident in a certain locality for twelve months automatically became members of the community. Transients had no membership rights, although they, too, must be supported by local charities which, incidentally, were open also to indigent Gentiles. On the other hand, short-term residents who possessed landed property within the confines of the community were obliged to pay their share of certain communal expenditures. All temporary settlers were obligated, after a sojourn of thirty days, to contribute to the communal kitchen; after two months, to the school budget; after three months, to the *kuppah* which distributed the weekly rations of food; after six months, to the expenses for clothing the needy; and after nine months, to the provisions for free burial.

In the general talmudic attitude toward taxation, it

may be noted, we find a streak of individualism not altogether congruous with the basic insistence upon social control and communal responsibility characteristic of rabbinic
law. It may not be too rash to assert that this peculiarity
was due to the influence of the more individualistic Greek
city constitutions, the emulation of which in this branch of
municipal administration may have been particularly stimulated by the apparent absence of regular municipal taxation
in pre-Hellenistic Palestine. True, precedence of a newly
formed municipality with respect to ownership of streets
was fully recognized. If a man tried to exchange a public
road for his private roadway, both became public property.
A four-ell strip along seashores or river banks was reserved
for the public despite the riparian rights of neighboring
landowners. None the less the general fiscal theory started
from the assumption that each member was to contribute
to specific communal expenditures only in proportion to the
benefits he might personally derive from such investment.
In the construction of a city wall, for example, one was to
consider its protective purpose. If the prospective assailants
were likely to be interested only in pillage, the contributions
were to be computed on the basis of property thus safeguarded. If, however, the enemy was bent upon the destruction of life, equal per capita payments appeared more justified. The nearer the outskirts of the city one lived, the
greater the danger, and hence also the larger was to be his
contribution. A bachelor was not bound to pay for the
defraying of the costs of education, but he was praised if
he offered voluntary donations.[20] Many of these discussions
undoubtedly are purely academic, but the existence of such
regulations opened many a loophole for tax evasion, particularly in the later medieval community.

By no means academic, however, was the desire of the rabbis to obtain general tax immunity for members of their own group. Such exemption was doubly important for them, as they desired to prevent the commercialization of teaching and of administering the law. Throughout the period of the Second Commonwealth the Temple priesthood had enjoyed such immunity, proclaimed as a matter of principle by its Achaemenide patrons. The rabbinic successors in the priestly ministrations to the religious needs of Israel felt that they should now enjoy the same privilege. With their usual vigor and insistence, the rabbis pursued this line of attack against the combined opposition of the lay communal organs and state tax collectors. Although it was rather difficult to draw such distinctions in the late Roman tax system, based as it was upon group contributions in so-called *jugera*, besides the drafting of citizens to forced labor and the billeting of dwellings for soldiers and officials, the rabbis persisted and won. Constantine tried in 321 to limit the immunity from municipal charges to two or three Jewish officers in each locality, but greatly liberalized his decree nine years later. In 331 he ordered, furthermore, that "the priests, archisynagogi and patres of the synagogues and others who officiate at synagogues be liberated from all corporal contributions."[21] In Persian Babylonia this postulate of rabbinic law, like many others, was carried out even more fully and, through the Babylonian Talmud, acquired authoritative validity in the medieval communities.

Tax exemptions alone could not, of course, solve the economic problem of the rabbis. In the first century after the fall of Jerusalem, they still lived largely as independent farmers, merchants or artisans. Even students were asked by R. Ishmael about their occupation before they were admitted to his school. With the increase in the number of rabbis and the simultaneous decline in the standard of life throughout the Empire, law and moral injunction had to step in and protect the interests of scholars. A series of homilies emphasized the great merit of taking a scholar into silent partnership, of working for him while he was studying the Torah, and so on. Workingmen in Babylonia exchanged their work for lessons in Jewish law. Regardless of their opposition to professional learning, the rabbis did not object to such an exchange of services. More, they extended to the scholarly merchant certain rights in competition with non-scholars which meant a great deal in that age of economic regimentation. When all these privileges did not suffice, active support had to be extended. We hear from St. Jerome, in 406, that

> according to a usage still persisting in Judea, not only among us, but also among the Hebrews, those who meditate day and night on the law of the Lord and have no portion in this earth except God alone, are maintained by the services of the synagogues and the rest of the world. This is done out of a sense of justice, lest some people live in well-being and others in care, but that the superfluity of the former alleviate the misery of the latter.

Women were especially active in aiding scholars financially.[22]

Whatever its economic status, the rabbinic calling was to be regarded as the most honorable of all positions attainable by Jews. Students were enjoined to honor their teachers even more than their fathers. To quarrel with one's master, to express a different legal opinion or merely critically to ponder over his deeds was compared with similar actions against the Deity. Not only a student, but every Jew was obliged to stand up before a scholar, however young in years. The scholars were to rank first in Jewish leadership, as when the sages enumerated, "the scholars, scribes, heads of the people and preachers" in this succession, or when they complained that "after the destruction of the Temple the scholars had become like scribes; the scribes like *hazzanim*; the *hazzanim* like the people of the land; and the people of the land had been getting poorer and poorer." The recurrent saying, "the rabbis are called kings," best epitomizes this type of wishful thinking which was destined to play a great role in shaping subsequent realities.[23]

3. THE PATRIARCHATE

Rabbinic hegemony became a definite reality with the establishment of the patriarchate which, originally derived from a primarily rabbinic office and constantly remaining in close contact with the rabbis, soon exercised supreme authority over the Jews of the Roman Empire. After the extinction of the Maccabean high priests and ethnarchs "of the Jews" (not of Judea), as Caesar called Hyrcanus II, central control over the religious life of Jewry gradually passed to the Pharisaic heads of the central academy in Palestine, which they often identified with the supreme court, the Sanhedrin. The family of Hillel, the Babylonian, holding this office in almost unbroken succession, was also distinguished by its reputed descent, in the female line, from the royal dynasty of Judah. Surviving its political superiors, the Herodian princes and the ever more disreputable high priests, members of this family, after 70 C. E., obtained from the Roman administration increasing grants of power. During the critical war years, to be sure, when Vespasian is supposed to have attempted to exterminate all alleged descendants of David, the leadership slipped into the hands of an outsider, Rabban Joḥanan b. Zakkai. But soon afterwards it was recaptured by Gamaliel II who seems to have obtained some Roman recognition. When Antoninus Pius, after the final suppression of the Bar Kocheba revolt, undertook to pacify the rebellious province and to appease all Jewry, he seems to have turned to Simon b. Gamaliel, who had apparently been less active during the conflict, and to have recognized him as the "ethnarch" of the Jews throughout the Empire. Simon assumed the high-sounding title, *nasi*, which, used already by Ezekiel and the authors of the Priestly Code for rulers second only to great and powerful kings, had been employed by the Maccabeans after their successful revolt and by the messianic Bar Kocheba. For some unknown reason, the Roman equivalent soon became the title "patriarch," which had apparently been introduced into the Greek language by the Septuagint translator of Chronicles.[24]

The patriarchate speedily grew in political and economic power. Judah I, the son of Simon, with his vast landed possessions, his luxurious court, his large retinue of slaves and a foreign bodyguard, resembled a hereditary vassal prince of Rome much more than the head of an academy of learning. The Jews, although paying heavily for the privilege, rejoiced in finding "learning and wordly greatness united" here in one person. In their endless controversies with Christians they could boast of the continued validity of Jacob's ancient blessing that "the sceptre shall not depart from Judah." Judah's great achievement in the compilation of the Mishnah likewise made them condone abuses which they never would have tolerated in other, freely selected, leaders. Because of the patriarchs' official position and their

necessary contacts with Gentile officials, they were specifically exempted from the prohibition of studying Greek wisdom and emulating Greek art and customs, a prohibition
otherwise more and more rigidly enforced as part of the
general policy of building "a fence around the Torah." The
patriarch, as the recognized chief of world Jewry, claimed
the right of appointing or deposing any communal officer
in Palestine and in the dispersion. To maintain direct contact with the individual communities, he often undertook
extended journeys. More regularly he sent out authorized
messengers, so-called *apostoloi* — a term apparently also
coined by the Jews — to supervise local administrators. In
364, Libanius, a Syrian pagan writer, asked the Roman
consularis in Palestine, Priscianus, in a characteristic letter,
to intervene with the patriarch in behalf of Antioch Jewry,
lest one of their communal officials, dismissed on the charge
of tyranny, be reinstated by him. By patriarchal authorization, Jewish judges in the Empire secured immunity from
personal responsibility for errors in judgment. We even
learn of patriarchal appointments of local teachers of Bible
and Talmud in Palestinian communities.[25]

The patriarch collected revenue not only for the state,
but also for his own chest. It is notable that, while we have
many complaints concerning the appointment of unworthy
officers and the authorization of unlearned judges by the
patriarchs for pecuniary reasons, there are relatively few
denunciations of their fiscal administration. The angry reply
of Judah II to such an attack by a Tiberian preacher, "Is
not everything that I ask for being taken away from me?"
evidently carried conviction, and at least the leaders of the
people placed the entire blame upon the Roman extortionist
system. Imperial Jewry was ready, moreover, to make

special contributions for the maintenance of its exalted chiefs. Renewing the ancient Temple tax of half a shekel or two drachmas for each adult male, each community gathered considerable sums which, soon known under the name of *aurum coronarium,* were paid to the patriarch's accredited apostles. Many of these messengers, such as R. Ḥiyya bar Abba, who visited Tyre (where he saw Diocletian), Emesa, Laodicaea, Gebalene and Rome, were distinguished rabbinic teachers in their own right.[26]

Perhaps the most significant patriarchal prerogative consisted in the exclusive right to regulate the Jewish calendar. It was extremely important for world Jewry to have a uniform calendar, to celebrate the new moon and the festivals all over the world on the same day, and to intercalate an additional month in the same leap year. Although the progress of astronomic science would have enabled the Jewish leaders at an early time to compute a permanent calendar (the scientifically trained Babylonian, Samuel, boasted that he could thus establish Babylonian independence and actually prepared a computation for the following sixty years), Jewry preferred to retain the accepted ceremony of witnesses appearing before the patriarchal court, testifying to their having seen the rising moon and the court, after appropriate judicial proceedings, proclaiming the new month to the world. Long after the patriarchs themselves possessed a perpetual astronomic calendar against which they checked the veracity of the testimony offered, they continued to go through the motions hallowed by an ancient tradition. When, after the Bar Kocheba revolt, Babylonian Jewry, led by Ḥananiah, the nephew of R. Joshua, made an attempt to end the rule of the weakened Palestinian center by proclaiming a leap year of its own, Judah I (or some of his predecessors) sent two messengers who, by using increasingly strong language, obtained the revocation of this measure.[27]

The progressive deterioration of the political and economic status of Roman Jewry, concomitant with the rise of Christianity to a dominant position in the Empire, entailed the gradual decline of the patriarchal office and its ultimate suppression by the Christian emperors. Christian leaders, beginning with Origen, had long resented the survival of this vestige of royal power among the Jews. The first Christian emperors, however, doubtless felt that continued maintenance of that office helped them better to control the inner life of the turbulent, still populous minority, whose rebellious record could be the less easily forgotten now, when it was under constant discussion. Down to Theodosius I, the emperors recognized the patriarchs as high officers of state, distinguished by the *praefectura honoraria*, addressed in honorific terms such as *viri clarissimi et illustres*, and legally protected against libel and assault. Jerome informs us of a Roman of high standing, by the name of Hesychius, who was executed by Theodosius because he had violated some papers of the patriarch Gamaliel. If Emperor Julian tried to persuade the patriarch to discontinue the collection of the contributions which he called the *apostolé*, he seems simply to have wished to relieve the Jewish masses from a burdensome surtax. Honorius I's more rigid decree of 399, prohibiting shipment of contributions from the Western Empire to the Palestinian "despoiler of the Jews," originated mainly from temporary rivalries with the Eastern Empire and, perhaps, from some difficulties in money transfer. The order was speedily rescinded in 404.[28]

The days of the patriarchate were numbered, however. Sensing approaching doom, they began relaxing their hold on world Jewry, and Hillel II promulgated, in 358–59 (or 344), a permanent calendar, thereby rendering the monthly proclamations altogether meaningless. That diaspora Jewry has ever since continued celebrating each festival for two days was due to deep-seated reverence for tradition rather than to any further validity of the original doubts concerning the exact date of the new moon. In his letter to the Alexandrines, R. Jose specifically enjoined them "not to change the custom of their forefathers" upon which incidentally, as the *patrios nomos*, had rested the entire fabric of their imperial privileges.[29]

In 415, finally, Gamaliel V was severely censured by the emperor because of his alleged violation of the imperial laws forbidding the erection of new synagogues, administration of justice in mixed litigations, circumcision of Christian proselytes and holding of Christian slaves. This censure was accompanied by the withdrawal of the honorary prefecture. With Gamaliel's death a few years later (about 425), the patriarchate was officially extinct and, in 429, the Empire appropriated the *aurum coronarium*.

4. The Exilarchate

Unlike the Palestinian patriarchate, the main office of Babylonian Jewry did not spring from scholarly circles. Individual exilarchs may have been learned men, but their claim to distinction did not rest on this personal feature. Theirs was a sort of hereditary monarchy, based upon their generally conceded claim to direct descent from the Davidic leaders of the Babylonian exiles. The genealogical list of fifteen generations from Zerubbabel to Nathan Ukban (the Mar Ukba I of the Talmud) in the third century C. E., apart from being poorly preserved and evidently emanating from official quarters, is too short to inspire any more confidence than other ancient genealogies. This account in *Seder 'olam zuṭṭa*, written shortly after 800 C. E., is obviously based upon the biblical chronicler's enumeration of the descendants of Jehoiachin combined with the usual erroneous telescoping of the two centuries of Persian history into a brief span of 34 years. To make the two accounts somewhat more congruous, Judah ibn Kuraish, a tenth-century Bible exegete, suggested that the genealogical list in Chronicles had been brought down to the end of the Second Temple. Nevertheless, the claim need not be altogether unhistorical. Our information concerning all the other phases of Babylonian Jewish history from 400 B. C. E. to about 200 C. E. is so sketchy and so much based upon casual references in outside sources, that the mere fact that we possess no reliable first-hand material is no proof that there had not been a succession of Jewish leaders in the same family throughout the period of Seleucide and Parthian rule. Were it not for a few incidental references in Palestinian and other outside sources, one might with equal justice deny the very existence, during that period, of Babylonian Jewry, which under Persia suddenly blossomed into the great achievement of the Babylonian Talmud.[30]

The exilarch's leadership was fully supported by the new Persian government. If we are to believe a somewhat confused talmudic statement, he ranked as the fourth highest officer of the Empire, immediately following its two military chiefs. This ranking may perhaps refer to the bureaucratic class alone which, as a whole, was placed behind the royal and the vassal princes. In any case the "prince of captivity" representing the numerous and affluent Jewish population, was a member of the chief council of state, advising the

Persian "king of kings" not only in matters directly relevant
to the Jewish community, but also in state-wide affairs.
Corresponding to this rank, the exilarchs wore princely
attire; held large courts, supporting not only their own slaves
and domestic or official attendants, but also numerous scholars and students; maintained extensive social contacts with
Gentiles; gave banquets and enjoyed musical and other en-
tertainments in the fashion of oriental dignitaries. Although
sometimes frowning on the laxity of law observance at the
exilarchic court and the overbearing attitude of the courtiers,
the rabbis acknowledged the exilarch's superior position and
called him by the distinguished title, *rabbana*. They even
allowed him to be honored in the synagogue in royal fashion.
When he was called upon to recite a weekly lesson, the
sacred roll was brought to his seat, an honor which, not
conferred upon the patriarchs, elicited the curiosity of the
Palestinians.[31]

Neither he nor the patriarch was legally recognized as a
true king, however, and the principle that "a king can neither
judge nor be judged" was never applied to them. Indeed,
both frequently exercised supreme jurisdiction over their
coreligionists. Only because of pressure of other business
or lack of legal training did many exilarchs delegate this
function to special officers, the *dayyane golah* (judges of the
dispersion). Apart from the members of this supreme court,
they also authorized or rather appointed the local judges
who controlled communal management in Babylonia even
more effectively than in Palestine. Being imperial Persian
officers, they often took cognizance also of Persian law.[32]

The peculiar fiscal structure of Persia and its semi-feudal
regimented economy gave the exilarchs a stronger hold over
the economic life of their people than was granted their

Palestinian compeers. More radically than in Rome, the theory was that all land belonged to the king and that a defaulting taxpayer could be deprived of his property by the agents of the Crown or replaced as tenant-owner by any person willing to pay the arrears. Since, according to the well-informed Arab historian, Ṭabari, the land tax ranged from one-sixth to one-third of the crop, such defaults must have been fairly common. In the case of poll tax defaults, the taxpayer could be put in bondage by a substitute payer. While the regional assessments and collections were principally in the hands of royal officials, their distribution seems to have been left largely to the local municipal or communal authorities. Little wonder that the Jewish communities and their official leader, the exilarch, had almost unlimited powers over the lives of their members. To a fuller extent than in Christian Rome, indeed, the state drafted the Jewish communal organs into its own fiscal services and for centuries to come the Jewish community was the main tax collecting agency for the state. While heavily encumbering communal management and sowing discord among the members, which at times reached the proportions of real class struggle, it immeasurably enhanced the prestige and power of the community in the eyes of both Jews and Gentiles.[33]

Only a few decades after the patriarchate, nevertheless, the exilarchate suffered a sudden eclipse and was not reinstated in power until after the conquest of Persia by the Arabs in 637 C. E. Under the reign of Firuz, foreign defeats combined with an inner famine to produce a severe depression. According to a talmudic source, land earlier worth 1000 denars found no buyers at one denar. It was in these stormy years of Zoroastrian fanaticism and the temporarily successful communist revolt under Mazdak, that anti-Jewish persecutions led, in 471, to the execution of the exilarch Huna Mari together with two leading rabbis. Soon afterwards Huna Mari's son, Mar Zutra II, led a Jewish rebellion against the weakened Persian regime. Successful for a time, he established a small independent kingdom which he ruled for seven years, until he was defeated and executed by the Persians (about 491). His son, Mar Zutra III, later left Persia altogether and, turning to the then leaderless Palestine, established himself as head of the academy in Tiberias. It appears that the Persian government, even after the restoration of more orderly conditions in the course of the sixth century, could the more readily dispense with a recognized exilarchic office as the effective fiscal reforms of Chosroes I Anushirvan (after 531 C. E.) greatly reduced the importance of the cooperation with the accredited chiefs of the religious minorities.[34]

In their relations with the patriarchs, the princes of captivity revealed conflicting attitudes which changed with changes in personal or social factors. As the older in line of succession and recognized descendants of King David in the male line, the exilarchs claimed decided superiority. For a time they demanded that their authorization of judges establish the latter's immunity even in Palestine, while no patriarchal authorization could have such effect in Babylonia. This demand was later repudiated by the more powerful Palestinian leaders. On the other hand, like all other Jews, the exilarchs had a sentimental attachment to Palestine. R. Huna, the first exilarch known to us from reliable sources, to whom, if he were to settle in Palestine, Judah I allegedly was ready to assign a seat of honor ahead of himself, was brought there to be buried in the sacred soil. The suggestion that the two officers divide their functions and the exilarch be invested, to use the medieval terms, with all the temporal power and the patriarch with the spiritual supremacy over all Jewry, could hardly appear satisfactory to either. It was doomed in advance by the inextricable blending of both elements in Jewish law and by the lack of an exclusively Jewish state power. Relations between these chief officers of Jewry were, on the whole, rather amicable. Separated by a boundary between two hostile empires and fostered by their home governments, so that they help maintain the independence of their respective communities from outside factors, they had few occasions to clash. The only serious menace of deep separation, the attempt of Ḥananiah to proclaim a leap year in Babylonia, was disposed of by the aforementioned energetic action of the Palestinians. If, in matters of law and ritual, divergent traditions, customs or interpretations threatened to lead to frequent misunderstandings and possibly grave conflicts, these were largely obviated through the growing cooperation and mutual toleration of the leading schools of learning in the two countries.[35]

5. The Academies

The power of the two leaders found its considerable limitations in the growing prestige of the scholars. Even discarding all obvious or likely exaggerations in the extant sources, the grandeur of the political as well as spiritual power wielded, without any state enforcement, by a handful of rabbis gathered around certain more or less permanent seats of learning, is really amazing.

The notable rise of the academies began in that memorable hour when Joḥanan b. Zakkai obtained from Vespasian the right to establish a school of higher learning in Jamnia (Yabneh). Modeled after the ancient Sanhedrin, these academies sometimes actually assumed the function of the "High Court" and operated simultaneously as schools, supreme judicial and administrative tribunals and, in a sense, legislatures issuing new ordinances. They often imitated the Sanhedrin's outward appearance. The latter consisted of seventy-one members (seventy-two, when the patriarch did not serve as permanent chairman), seated in three rows in a semi-circle about their chairman, who was assisted by a vice-chairman, the *ab bet din* (father of the court) and by a sort of rapporteur, called *ḥakam*.[36] They were surrounded by a gallery of regular students and more casual visitors.

In the first generations the leading members of the Palestinian academies lived in their respective localities, coming to the academy's public sessions only on certain major occasions. That is why certain important decisions were taken by sessions attended only by 24, 32 or 39 members. Attendance increased when many scholars, including the vice-chairmen, began to receive financial assistance which relieved them of the necessity of earning a living in their respective localities. No less a leader than R. Joḥanan seems to have received a regular stipend from the patriarchal chest. Although some members, trying to preserve their traditional independence, balked at such "gifts" from the patriarchal treasury, there were increasing collections of funds "for the maintenance of the rabbis." These contributions were sent to Palestine by local chiefs, such as Theudas in Rome, or were collected by the patriarchal apostles.[37]

Later, especially in Babylonia, it became customary for the academy to maintain a permanent body of scholars and students. It was really in Babylonia, in the academies of Sura, founded by Abba Arika (Rab) in 219 C. E. and re-established, after an intervening decline, by R. Ashi (about

375) and of Pumbedita, which merely continued the old native academy of Nehardea destroyed by the Palmyrene invaders in 259, that the institution reached its highest degree of development. When the Palestinian academies, anticipating the formal suppression of the patriarchate, had gradually withered away in the severe clime of the Christian Roman Empire, the two schools in Babylonia shone ever more brightly as the main beacons of Jewish culture.

The academies undertook to organize, unify and compile a growing mass of tradition. To overcome serious divergences among them, as well as differences of opinion among individual scholars or rival schools of learning, the principle of majority rule was adopted. Even such powerful chairmen as Gamaliel II and Judah I were overruled by majorities.[38] Recalcitrants, such as the sturdy conservative R. Eliezer b. Hyrcanus, were excommunicated, until an academy decision, out of fear of abuse by the concentrated patriarchal power, eliminated this disciplinary measure.

Another method of obtaining uniformity was to follow the lead of certain recognized authorities in some or all fields, with a number of specified exceptions. Thus it was agreed that the opinion of the school of Hillel was generally to prevail over that of the school of Shammai, that of R. Joshua over that of R. Eliezer, that of Raba over that of Abbaye, and so forth. Rab's decision was considered authoritative in ritualistic law, while that of his opponent, Samuel (perhaps because the latter's Nehardean teachings better reflected Babylonian economic realities), was accepted in civil law. Many majority resolutions, moreover, were given universal validity by being anonymously rendered in the numerous compilations prepared by the chiefs of the various academies in collaboration with other members.

Such a compilation of "testimonies" was undertaken by the academy of Yabneh about 100 C. E. Other partial compilations by R. Akiba, R. Meir and others led to the authoritative edition of the Mishnah under the direction of Judah I (about 200). Other collections of tannaitic traditions followed, to be climaxed by the great, though really unfinished, compilation of the Palestinian Talmud, accomplished by the academy of Tiberias in the course of a century and a half, beginning with the work of R. Joḥanan (died 279). Even this great work was largely superseded for world Jewry by the still more imposing structure of the Babylonian Talmud, compiled by the academy of Sura under the direction of R. Ashi and his successors during the fifth century.

The patriarch, being from the beginning the head of the main Palestinian academy and soon also in charge of the appointment of new members, never came into conflict with the academy as such, although in quite a few instances he was severely criticized by individual members. Once, due to such a quarrel, Rabban Gamaliel II was deposed by his colleagues until he made amends, but this event took place before the patriarchate was fully established by Gamaliel's son, Simon. Simon himself, threatened by a conspiracy of R. Meir and R. Nathan the Babylonian, who as a member of the exilarchic family had superior genealogical standing, barred both distinguished members from many sessions. Nevertheless, the opposition of the rabbis became quite articulate after the death of Judah I, and the academies, less and less frequently presided over by the patriarchs, arrogated to themselves ever more functions. At first mere patriarchal messengers who communicated calendar proclamations to distant localities, and at most assistants to the chairman as members of a committee of seven, the rabbis ultimately transferred the main handling of the testimony to the academy. Ordination, originally a power of individual teachers, had become an exclusive patriarchal prerogative, especially under Judah I, who used it sparingly. Later, however, the academies began sharing this right and ordained Palestinian as well as Babylonian students some of whom subsequently assumed leading positions in their respective alma maters.[39] Although living a shadowy sort of existence, the academy of Tiberias survived the extinction of the patriarchate and received a new lease on life under the Babylonian *archipherekitai*. It was to blossom again in the more friendly atmosphere of the Muslim domination.

The Babylonian academies made an increasingly successful attempt to become independent of both Palestinian and exilarchic control. Rab and Samuel had already called parts of Babylonia "the land of Israel," and minimized the importance of the Palestinian ordination. Their disciple, R. Judah, although bowing to R. Joḥanan's learning, enjoined his pupils not to study in Palestine. The academies at first recognized the superior authority of the exilarch. Their heads congregated in the princely residence on various festive occasions, prepared the exilarch's addresses and behaved like his critical, but generally obedient, subjects. It was also his sole prerogative to communicate to the public the recurrent patriarchal proclamations concerning the calendar.

With the second generation of Babylonian Amoraim, however, headed by R. Naḥman, who was related through marriage to the exilarchic family, the rabbis began to assume a position of equality. The calendar proclamations were now issued by the chiefs of the academies. The festive gatherings, and even the regular sessions of the semi-annual *kallah,* that remarkable month-long assembly open to both scholars and laymen, were transferred to the seats of the academies. In the days of R. Ashi, who assumed the exilarchic title, *rabbana,* the exilarchs themselves attended such sessions in Sura. The ordination of rabbis, for which the Babylonians had long turned to Palestine, was now less solemnly performed at the Babylonian academies and soon exceeded in importance the exilarchic authorization. Only the ordained scholar could venture to adjudicate civil litigations single-handed, in the place of the usual three judges. The authorization itself could be granted to none but an ordained scholar. In short, just as the local scholar-judge dominated the individual community, so the central academies of scholars rivaled the exilarchic authority in managing country-wide Jewish affairs. Indeed, more than one member of such an academy may have reiterated the homily formulated by the sons of R. Ḥiyya in the presence of Judah I: "The Messiah will not come until the two families in Israel, that of the exilarch in Babylon and the patriarch in Jerusalem, shall have ceased."[40]

6. Communal Survival

The enormous discrepancies in Jewish life were welded by the talmudic sages with remarkable finality into a common basic pattern, which was to last until the break-up of the Ghetto during the three centuries of the modern period. Centered in the hardly tangible synagogue of any ten adult males and the even less tangible *bet ha-midrash* (school) of students gathered around a recognized teacher, the Jewish community was eminently equipped for its subsequent struggle for survival under varying conditions and in changing environments. Having successfully faced semi-capitalist and, later, semi-feudal Rome, as well as nearly feudal Persia, having met and compromised with polytheistic Hellenism, dualistic Zoroastrianism and monotheistic Catholicism in their most decisive stages, the reconstructed communal organism acquired a vitality and adaptability which stood it in good stead among all civilizations which it was to encounter in its historic career until the Industrial Revolution and the rise of modern science. Not until then was the Pharisaic-rabbinic doctrine and way of life discarded or even modified in any essentials. The Jewish communities of seventeenth-century Frankfort and Cracow, of Constantinople and Cairo bore an uncanny resemblance to those of Tiberias and Nehardea at the beginning of the third century.

It was, nevertheless, unavoidable that the dynamic forces of Islam and of the youthful civilizations of medieval Europe should bring about considerable modification and elaboration in detail, and that the uniform pattern should receive new and variegated hues from the rich fabric of the outside world. This remarkable combination of basic uniformity with richness of individual variation characterizes the fascinating story of Jewish communal evolution in the millenium following the rise of Islam.

CHAPTER VI

PROTECTED COMMUNITY

THE rise and expansion of Islam injected a powerful new element into Jewish communal history. The dualism of Rome and Persia was now replaced, and on a much wider scale, by that of Christendom and Islam. For centuries Muslim countries harbored the overwhelming majority of world Jewry. Even after the Mongolian invasions of the East and the Christian reconquest of the Iberian Peninsula, they included a substantial minority. The expansion of the Ottoman Empire, extending to Budapest and to the frontiers of India and Morocco, soon opened new economic and cultural opportunities for the harassed western as well as eastern Jewries.

After Caliph Omar's memorable conquests, Muslim lands thus served as a reservoir of biological, economic and cultural strength for the entire people, or as places of refuge and shelter for its stranded fragments. Islam, always including Babylonia and, except for the brief interlude of the early Crusades, Palestine, also long embraced the chief intellectual and communal leadership of world Jewry. Even when its decline, concomitant with Christendom's rise to heights of economic and cultural power never before achieved by man, entailed the loss of such unified leadership, Palestine remained the cynosure of all eyes. It still attracted settlers, pilgrims and donors from all the Jewish world, strengthening, in return, the moral backbone of the people and fortifying

157

its unswerving messianic hope. More realistically, the permanent division of the world, as far as the Jews were concerned, between Edom and Ishmael (Christianity and Islam) helped them weather the severest storms in subsequent centuries. As far back as the ninth century a farsighted observer explained that God had so divided the world "in order to preserve Israel."[1]

1. Muslim "Protection"

The Great Caliphate of the first three centuries after the Hijra (622 C. E.) combined in more than one respect the main political and administrative features of its immediate predecessors, the Persian and the Byzantine Empires. Soon reverting economically and culturally to the more capitalistic, liberal and scientifically-minded age of Hellenism and the early Roman Empire, it nevertheless persisted in adhering primarily to governmental methods developed by Sassanian Persia. In its relations to religious minorities, however, it followed in the footsteps of the Christian Roman emperors, with such important modifications as sprang from the special historic origins and world outlook of the dominant Arabic group.

The Jews shared with Christians and Zoroastrians, long the substantial majority of the imperial population, the status of "protected peoples." Although exposed to constant infiltration of new ideas and modes of life and faced by disruptive forces of sectarianism, they found a bulwark of strength in the integrity of their communal structure and resisted conversion more effectively than any other group. The new type of protection extended to them enhanced their ethnic and religious self-determination, reinforced their communal ties and paved the way for a marvelous economic and cultural regeneration.

The "tribute" paid by the Jews in return for toleration was speedily converted into a major concern of the Jewish community. Although primarily consisting of a poll and land tax to be paid per capita or as part of a crop, its collection was more often entrusted to established Jewish communal agencies than to government officers. This arrangement accrued to the advantage of both parties. From time to time the government regulated the amount due from individual citizens. For example, in the days of Harun al-Rashid, farmers and workers were to pay 12 silver dirhem annually, the middle class 24 dirhem each and the more well-to-do (bankers, textile merchants, shopkeepers, landowners and physicians) 48 dirhem each; women, children, unemployed, aged or infirm persons were exempted. But the application of such mechanical rules would obviously have encountered staggering practical difficulties without the assistance of the better informed leaders of each religious group. A famous provincial governor, Ziyad ibn Abihi, undoubtedly reflected both widespread practice and personal experience when he counseled that "the functionaries of the Treasury should be taken from among the chiefs of the conquered peoples who well understand this matter." Since there was no effective apparatus for a thoroughgoing census of population and taxable land, such as had long existed under the Ptolemies and the Romans, the state had to rely on the inefficient and rapacious bureaucracy which ultimately turned out to be a major source of weakness. Bureaucratic greed, on the other hand, was often ruinous to the entire population and fostered solidarity and communal bonds among taxpayers. The Jews did not object to the taxes as such. Much as they individually disliked to pay the poll tax and to part with anywhere between one-fifth and one-third of their crop, they felt that this was their main *raison d'être* from the standpoint of the Muslim administration. There is probably more than a grain of truth in the story of Neṭira, a Jewish banker at the end of the ninth century, who allegedly dissuaded the humane caliph, Al-Mutadhid, from relieving the Jews of special taxes. Arguing "that through the tax the Jew insures himself, and that, by eliminating the tax, the Caliph would give free rein to the Arabs to shed Jewish blood," this spokesman of the Jewish community is supposed to have sought and obtained only a reduction of the tax to its original low level.[2]

Neṭira's intervention was not necessarily altogether disinterested, however. As the wealthy leader of the community, he must have suffered from more than one extralegal extortion by a high official seeking to enrich himself during his short tenure of office. With the community's fiscal authority left intact, Neṭira and others in a similar position were reimbursed by their coreligionists, for which practice they found ready support in the Jewish tax laws. That law's persistent exemption of scholars, generally respected by Muslim legislation as well, likewise fostered communal control. The community alone could effectively discriminate among such claimants and, in view of the proportionate increase in the burden of its other members, would also try to reduce their number to a minimum. Nevertheless, it was in Muslim Lucena, the central section of which resembled an autonomous all-Jewish municipality, that Joseph ibn Megas applied this exemption in its extreme form, when he decided "in favor of a man in a certain locality who owned gardens and orchards for which he would have had to pay thousands of denarii, but whom he [R. Joseph] declared free of all imposts — because he was a scholar, even though that tax had to be paid by the poorest in Jewry." This sweeping provision echoed by his student, Maimonides, was soon accepted as authoritative law, and it was the more readily invoked as its main exponents and administrators were also its main beneficiaries.[3]

Other discriminatory provisions of Muslim law likewise intensified Jewish communal solidarity. The obligation to wear cloth of distinctive color or other distinguishing marks which, beginning with the so-called Covenant of Omar, led to a variety of local observances, although perfectly in keeping with the oriental predilection for colorful professional and class attire, exposed the Jews and other "unbelievers" to contempt and, perhaps, attack. Other forms of discrimination, such as that which forbade riding horseback, together with their generally inferior status, undoubtedly increased the cohesion of these dissident groups. Positive laws enabled the Jewish communities to possess an inalienable *waqf* (sacred property) and to inherit the estates of members dying without heirs. These legal provisions were greatly reinforced by age-old customs of segregation. A ghetto was as natural a phenomenon in a medieval oriental city as are numerous separate foreign quarters today. The absence of compulsion prevented the oriental Jewish districts from becoming so exclusive, overcrowded and marked out for disdain as some of the later European ghettos. On the other hand, their existence greatly facilitated the exercise of social control by the community. The prevailing personal principle in Muslim law, whereby every person was judged in accordance with his or her own law, rendered

Jewish courts of justice the usual, if not exclusive, forum for Jewish litigants. The following statement of an eleventh-century Muslim writer typifies the prevalent usage:

> If there be quarrels among the infidels with respect to their religion, or if their opinions be divided in regard to their religious principles, one must not interfere in their affairs and exercise any pressure upon them. If there be litigation among them and they submit it to their own judge, one shall not prevent them from so doing. If they should come, however, to our judge, he shall judge them according to the laws of Islam and impose upon them, if they should prove guilty, such penalties as are prescribed in our law books.[4]

In one major respect, on the other hand, Muslim legislation proved to be inimical to the self-governing Jewish institutions, and the ensuing hardships were aggravated by the lack of a universally accepted rule. The Caliphate had inherited from the Byzantine Empire the desire to elevate the houses of worship of the state religion above all others. Timidly and rather inconsistently it prohibited the construction of new synagogues and churches and forbade that their construction be at an elevation exceeding that of the local mosques; and, more radically, it prevented the building of private houses taller than those of one's Muslim neighbors.

Since it was a fairly late foreign importation rarely adhered to in practice, this prohibition did not fail to produce a variety of interpretations in the leading schools of Muslim jurisprudence. The Ḥanafite school contended that new synagogues and churches might be built only in such villages or hamlets where there was no token of Islam. Elsewhere they could be only in private houses, which, however, could be handed down as *waqfs*. In this respect, too, the Shafi'ites. frequently drew the line of demarcation between territories conquered at the point of the sword and those which had been acquired by treaty. In the latter case new structures. were to be allowed if this right had been stipulated in the original treaties; in the former even the right of repairing old buildings appeared dubious to some members of the school, while others denied it categorically. These views are,, on the whole, shared by the Malikite school, while Ibn Hanbal simply declared that all repairs of synagogues and churches in a Muslim city or its vicinity were to be outlawed. These controversies were accompanied by the usual endless. casuistry in detail, such as whether the walls might be repaired inside, if not outside. When a synagogue had already been converted into a mosque, there arose special difficulties, analogous to those which had vexed many a. Christian Roman emperor. The Jews of Tripolis, in such a case, asked merely for permission to erect a new synagogue on another site (about 1020). The authorities, as a rule,, however, severely punished illegal appropriations of syna-. gogues by an aroused populace. In 1473–75, such a con-troversy in Jerusalem ended with the removal of two Muslim judges and the flight of a guilty sheikh to Mecca. After the Covenant of Omar, conflicting opinions concerning the right of private houses led a Mameluke sultan in 1301 to issue an order to the governors of his newly conquered provinces to. bring down all dwellings of Jews and Christians to the level of neighboring Muslim houses and also to lower the floors. of Jews' and Christians' shops below those of their Muslim neighbors. As late as 1858, the so-called *Ḥatti-humayum*,, the new liberal constitution of the Ottoman Empire, in-sisted that repairs on churches and synagogues be made only in accord with their original plans, permitting no increase in size.[5]

The Jews fought back with legal and extralegal means. Forced to show pre-Muslim origin for particular houses of worship, they often fabricated evidence. A synagogue inscription in Fustat announced to the world its supposed erection in 336 Seleucide era, i. e. 23–24 C. E. A tradition in Damwah had it that the local synagogue had been constructed 40 years after the destruction of the first Temple. As late as 1854, J. L. Porter, a British visitor in Busrah, Transjordan, was shown a dwelling called "the house of the Jew," a name, it was explained, which went back to the Arab conquest. A Jewish owner, forced to give up his house to make room for a mosque, appealed to Omar I in Medinah. The latter allegedly sent an order written on the jawbone of an ass: "Pull down the mosque and rebuild the Jew's house." These legal difficulties, incidentally, doubtless added stimulus to the growing worship of ancient shrines and the spinning of legends concerning their alleged foundation by Ezekiel, Ezra and other celebrated biblical heroes. Benjamin of Tudela, the renowned twelfth-century traveller, found a considerable number of such "ancient" synagogues in the Muslim Orient. As late as 1855–59, appeals were sent to European communities soliciting funds for the upkeep of these holy shrines. Where such evidence of antiquity did not help, bribes frequently proved effective. Occasionally a liberal monarch or governor deliberately shut his eyes to rampant breaches of the prohibition. The orthodox philosopher, Al-Ghazali, was not altogether wrong in his complaint that the vast number of existing churches and synagogues testified to the relaxation of religious observance under the non-conforming rulers of the preceding two centuries. On the other hand, there were intolerant monarchs who, like Ḥarun, Mutawakkil or Al-Ḥakim, ordered the destruction of all obnoxious new structures.[6] In view of the Jewish community's relative independence of the house of worship, however, these chicaneries caused property losses rather than serious interruption in religious or communal life.

2. Centrifugal and Centripetal Forces

Legal uncertainties, fostered by the absence of clearly defined and detailed privileges; the recognized power of local custom and chance precedent; the varying authority of individual Muslim jurists; and the sweeping principle of the *ijma*, the catholic consent, strengthened centrifugal forces within the Jewish community. Much depended on the whim of rulers, their advisers or such Jews as had their ear. The tenacity of Jewish community life was undermined by individualist rationalism and sectarianism combined with the overwhelming power of big business in the period of the "Renaissance of Islam." In the intermittent periods of persecution, the need for defence and mutual support often reinforced the shaky communal structure, but in the frequent protracted periods of genuine toleration and good will, inner class struggle, heterodox deviation and repudiation of the existing leadership generated widespread unrest.

In an inquiry addressed to a Babylonian academy we read the characteristic complaint, "There is among us a place of Jewish heretics who deride Israel, separate themselves from Israel's way of living, observe neither the commandments nor the Sabbath, slaughter their animals differently, consume [forbidden] fat, blood and the eighteen types of *ṭerefah*, live in sexual licentiousness and write neither marriage contracts nor writs of divorce." From another complaint we learn of "strong men who disobey the courts and commit hateful acts. The times are bad, the government fierce and hard, and we cannot enforce the law against them." The masses, on their part, often had equally just causes for complaint against the leaders. It was unavoidable that some Jewish officials should be affected by the prevalent standard of morals of Muslim bureaucracy, and natural that they, too, should try to promote their own or their friends', rather than the common, good. The great gaon, Hai, uttered a curse against those "judges of Sodom, robbers and racketeers" who conspired with wealthy moneylenders to deprive insolvent debtors of household articles not legally subject to seizure. He urged his interpellators to give wide publicity to such wrongdoings, to expose perpetrators to public contumely and to deprive them of a further share in administering justice. His father, Sherira Gaon, had with equal sharpness attacked those students of the law who, applying literally one of the talmudic sages' venomous denunciations of the "people of the land," allowed themselves liberties with the property of analphabets. Sherira ingeniously declared that, were certain related talmudic utterances taken literally, these students themselves would have to be classified as "people of the land," and it would be permissible to butcher them on a Day of Atonement falling on a Sabbath. Little wonder that propagandists, especially Karaites, stirred mass discontent against the recognized leaders. Sahl b. Maṣliaḥ, an eleventh-century Karaite, was particularly eloquent in denouncing the exploitation of the poor by the rabbis:

> They rule them with an iron hand and "whoso putteth not into their mouths, they even prepare war against

him" (Micah 3.5). They elevate themselves and suppress the people through bans, anathemas and the assistance of Gentile officials. They punish their poor, force them to borrow money on usury in order that they give it to the officials so that their rule may be perpetuated.

The rabbis replied in kind and placed all such agitators in a class with the biblical rebels, Dathan and Abiram, for sowing discord between the communal leaders and the people.[7]

Another source of weakness was the ever growing dispersion and the plurality of custom and outlook. In the talmudic period, there had already arisen considerable legal and ritualistic differences between the Jews of Palestine and Babylonia. Even in the centuries of Babylonian supremacy Palestinian Jewry persisted in adhering to its cherished customs. The attempt of Pirkoi b. Baboi, in the eighth century, to influence at least African Jewry to follow Babylonia, rather than Palestine, met with only partial success. Under Islam these divergences became more pronounced, as subjection to one Empire put an end to the artificial isolation of the two countries and as expanding business, migrations and travel brought Jews of both communities into ever closer contact. Soon there arose in various Syrian and Egyptian cities (Fustat, Damascus, Ramleh, etc.) congregations of Babylonian ritual existing side by side with those adhering to the Palestinian rites. The dissolution of the Caliphate did not abolish the essential legal, economic and cultural unity of Islamic civilization. But it entailed the creation of increasingly autonomous regional groups, each developing a set of new customs and rituals, which further aggravated internal Jewish clashes. Single families or business firms often had connections in several Mediterranean countries. When, from the fourteenth century on, increasing masses of Spanish Jews settled in northern Africa, western Asia and the Balkan Peninsula, the pulverization of the communities into small ritualistic units, largely based upon the age-old *Landsmannschaft* congregation, reached a degree unheard of since the days of the early Roman Empire. Constantinople in the sixteenth century had no less than forty-four Jewish congregations divided by origin and ritualistic disparity.[8]

To prevent complete break-up, communal leaders under the Great Caliphate adopted harsh disciplinary measures against the slightest non-conformity. Going far beyond the stringent rules of the Talmud, they flogged people who dared shave on a half-holiday or wear shoes during the days of mourning. Naṭronai Gaon declared that a man who, in reciting the Passover *Haggadah*, omitted the rabbinic passages, was to be treated as a heretic. "All communities ought to banish him and to exclude him from the community of Israel." Similar punishment was to be meted out to all who, by refraining from warm dishes on the Sabbath, betrayed Karaite sympathies. At times the communal organs sent out special investigators to ascertain whether any member had concealed leaven on Passover eve. The geonim admitted that, according to talmudic law, flagellation was limited to transgressions of biblical negative commandments, not exceeding 207 in number according to the enumeration of the Maimonidean Code. But by distinguishing between regular *makkot* or *malḳot* and the rabbinic *makkat mardut* (flagellation for disobedience), the Talmud enabled the medieval judges to impose flogging for any breach of dis-

cipline, however trifling. Such flogging was even more severe
than the official type, inasmuch as it was not dependent
upon medical sanction or restricted to a maximum of 39
lashes. The talmudic type of excommunication was now
likewise developed in great detail and made a common
instrument of law enforcement and general communal control. Refusal to appear before a judge was punishable first
by a temporary *niddui*, followed after thirty days by anath-
ema, the *ḥerem*. A formula for notifying other communities
of the imposition of *ḥerem* gives an inkling of its ruthless
severity:

> ... As soon as this decree of banishment will reach
> you, you will likewise excommunicate him, and make
> a public announcement that his bread is like the bread
> of Gentiles, his wine wine of oblation, his fruit un-
> tithed and his books books of sorcerers. And you
> shall cut off his show-fringes, remove his *mezuzah*, not
> call up his children in the synagogue, nor include him
> in the prescribed quorum for services, nor circumcise
> his infant, nor bury his deceased relative, nor let him
> join any of the prescribed or free associations, angrily
> exclude him from your midst, not do any business (?)
> with him, pour a cup [of water] after him [as a sign of
> contempt], shut him out of the community of the
> dispersion and treat him like a Gentile. Any commu-
> nity which will see this decree of banishment and not
> excommunicate him, [the Lord's] wrath shall rest
> upon it.

The most dangerous offenders, informers, were subject to
the extreme penalty, wherever the community could exercise
capital jurisdiction.[9]

Community control was further enhanced through its
economic and fiscal administration. As in ancient times,

many medieval communities possessed their own markets or bazaars. Several are recorded to have had special "inspectors of the merchants," who evidently were in charge of markets and other forms of economic activity. The leading jurists restated and amplified the talmudic regulations affecting civil transactions with a view toward application. Through interpretation or new enactment, a so-called *takkanah*, they modified laws as required by new economic realities. The Jews soon found that the elastic system of Jewish legislation promoted their new pursuits. Notwithstanding occasional grumbling, they also realized that their interests were better safeguarded by Jewish rather than by Muslim courts. Apart from the possible anti-Jewish bias or contempt of Muslim *cadis*, they had to fear, in the often disreputable and corrupt state and city courts, miscarriages of justice. It is remarkable how few complaints against bribery of Jewish judges have come down to us. This cannot be wholly explained by the one-sided nature of the rabbinic sources, but must in large measure reflect reality. On the other hand, the rabbis, perhaps not quite disinterestedly, suspected most Muslim lawyers and scribes and rather recognized their signatures on deeds as valid proof only by exception. While Hai Gaon was ready to acknowledge testimony accepted by Bagdad tribunals, he and others were quite outspoken in their condemnation of the proceedings of many other courts. The Muslim judiciary of Spain and Kairowan was held in bad repute among all rabbis writing in those countries.[10]

The fiscal authority of the community over its members was invariably recognized by the Muslim states. The ceremony accompanying the payment of the poll tax by each Jew and Christian, as described by a fourteenth-century author, is by no means typical. At that time, we are told, the Emir sitting on an elevation, received the money with his hand above that of the "infidel," knocked him down with his fist and had him speedily ejected by an attendant. This description seems to be the outgrowth of the overheated fantasy of an author who expressed the hope that such personal payment would make the infidels "feel the humiliation, and they will perhaps believe in God and his prophet; whereupon their shame shall cease." The rule was for the community to pay a stipulated sum based on a general estimate of the taxpaying population and its relative wealth. It was, of course, in the interest of the Jewish community to obtain as low an estimate as possible. The absence of a reliable census greatly facilitated the manipulation of figures, but the government had drastic legal and extralegal means to obtain its due and more. In some communities, especially in Turkey, it demanded that, when paying, the communal chiefs bring along a sacred scroll and take an oath to the correctness of their computation. In certain recorded cases suspect officials were thrown into prison and, without any process of law, despoiled of all their property. An accusation of tax fraud brought about the imprisonment of twenty-three elders of the Fustat community in 1011 C. E. So excited was Muslim fanaticism, that Fustat Jewry, indeed that of all Egypt, feared a general massacre. Only the intervention of Caliph Al-Ḥakim, then in a rather tolerant mood, prevented large-scale bloodshed.[11]

In collecting taxes, the community did not follow the mechanical division of the official imposts. It disregarded the official scale of the 12, 24, and 48 dirhem, recorded by Abu-Yussuf, and the early Turkish scale of 10, 20 and 40 dirhem (roughly 1 to 5 ounces of silver). It imposed greater burdens on the rich, while relieving some struggling members of all contributions. Neither did it necessarily adhere to the governmental classification for land and special taxes, nor altogether separate the revenue due the community from that owing the state. It often simply assessed its members lump sums destined to cover all communal expenditures, including state taxes. In an interesting responsum, a rabbinic authority expressed the opinion

> that the community ought to appoint three men, expert in tax matters, to assess each member according to his wealth. He who has land, this should be taken into account; so also the fact that one has neither vineyards nor fields, but possesses ready cash wherewith he trades and derives income from Gentiles. Everyone should be assessed, but they must not deviate from the local custom observed by the forefathers before this day to impose a tax upon everyone who owns land valued at 100 denarii or has 100 guilders in business.

Only with respect to charitable funds did some communities, following a talmudic injunction, demand that even public charges make a contribution, however small. Taught by experience, some communties (e. g. fifteenth-century Brussa) assessed a higher total than that required by the budgetary deficit, placing the excess in a sort of reserve for tax deficiencies resulting from deaths or emigration. At times taxation became so oppressive that Jews as well as Gentiles fled, leaving a proportionately heavier burden upon those who remained behind. To prevent the utilization of the religious ban by extortionist state organs, Sheshna Gaon (before 689) proclaimed a principle, often reiterated in the middle ages, that "if an official or tax-collector order a community to issue bans for his purposes and needs . . . and it is impossible to resist the compulsion, such bans are null and void, and may be disregarded."[12]

We should not be misled, however, by statements in the juristic and moralistic literature, communal statutes and minute books, into believing that the communities, as a rule, pursued a policy of "soaking the rich." Those in power, usually members of the wealthy classes, prevented discrimination against themselves. The numerous regulations were intended rather to stem abuses in the opposite direction and to maintain some sort of balance. The power of law and ethics and the influence of their accredited expounders make it likely, however, that equilibrium was widely achieved.

3. EXILARCHS AND GEONIM

Upon the conquest of Persia by the Arabs (637), the exilarchate was re-established in its ancient glory. After Mar Zutra II's execution and his son's emigration to Palestine, other members of the exilarchic family apparently carried on as the heads of their people, although perhaps no longer recognized as such by Persian law. Two holders of the office, Kafnai and Haninai, seem to have lost their lives in quick succession in the political disorders preceding the final disintegration of the Empire (581, 589 C. E.). When the Muslim conquerors, however, proceeded to reorganize their new and vaster Empire on the basis of denominational self-government, they were easily persuaded to entrust to one outstanding leader the main responsibility for each religious community. The Nestorian *catholicos*, as chief of the most populous and influential Christian sect, represented all Christians in the caliph's inner council, the imperial Diwan. The exilarch, too, alone of all Jews regardless of sectarian divisions, took his seat among the highest dignitaries of the Caliphate. Both these officers naturally received their appointments from the head of the state, but the caliphs usually respected the wishes of their *dhimmi* subjects.

It soon became customary for each new investiture to be accompanied by expensive tokens of gratitude which, varying with the individual appointee, very likely increased in proportion to the opposition elicited by his appointment. Hence comes the accusation, so frequently voiced in later generations, that the exilarchs "purchased" their office. But the caliph's choice was clearly restricted to the immediate relatives of the deceased or deposed exilarch, and, except for periods of inner dissension, it followed the usual hereditary succession. For the most part, the candidate had previously been designated by a Jewish public assembly headed by the chairmen of the two academies. In his subsequent audience with the caliph, the exilarch-elect, after the usual introductory words of praise and blessing, reminded his sovereign of "the customs of his fathers and his fathers' fathers" (reminiscent of the *patrios nomos* of the Graeco-Roman rulers), and obtained from him a written confirmation of his authority. We possess but a brief reference to such royal appointment of an exilarch, but it may be taken for granted that it did not differ in any essentials from similar formal decrees installing the Nestorian chiefs.[13]

The exilarchs' prerogatives resembled, and perhaps even exceeded, those which they had enjoyed in Sassanian Persia. They appointed, and at times deposed, the heads of the academies and the increasingly powerful local judges. They exercised supreme jurisdiction through their own "judges of the gate," they corresponded with the Jewish communities in and outside the Caliphate, and generally acted as hereditary rulers of the Jewish nation. They gloried in their unbroken line of succession over some two thousand years. A Muslim writer reports the boast of one of them that "seventy generations have elapsed between King David and myself, and yet the Jews greatly honor me, recognize the prerogatives derived from my royal descent and feel it their duty to protect me. Between you and your prophet there was but a single generation and you have already slain his son [grandson], Hussein." While our information concerning their fiscal rights and responsibilities is rather limited and equivocal, it appears that, for a time, they had general supervision over local tax collections. Al-Kasim b. Ibrahim, an Arab jurist of the ninth century, lists, with evident exaggeration, the following items in their regular revenue: a tax of one-fifth on all Jewish property, fees from the redemption of all first-born children and animals, $1\frac{1}{3}$ dirhems per head of ritually slaughtered cattle, 4 dirhems for each Jewish marriage, divorce and newly constructed house. Besides, they were supposed to raise illegitimate Jewish children and those born to unknown fathers, all of whom they could sell as slaves. From the more reliable, though picturesque account of Nathan the Babylonian, we learn that they annually derived some 700 gold denarii (over $2,800 by the present American gold standard, but at least three times that much in purchasing power) from three provinces, mainly from imposts upon ritually slaughtered meat. Two centuries later, Benjamin of Tudela found the exilarch, Daniel b. Hisdai, not only possessing vast estates, but also enjoying the right to impose annual taxes on Jewish markets and merchants. According to one version of the *Itinerary*, the exilarch's weekly income from this source amounted to 200,000 denarii.[14]

Little wonder that some Christians resented what they regarded as the preferential treatment of the Jewish (as well as the Zoroastrian) chiefs. The Jews and Parsees, complained Michael Syrus, "call their heads 'kings' enjoying hereditary dignity. They pay their taxes to their respective chiefs; such never was the case with the Christians." The Jews themselves, whatever their personal attitude to individual exilarchs, basked in the glory of the office to which they sought to attach the glamor of royalty. The ceremonies accompanying an exilarch's election and installation had all the earmarks of a coronation. In far-off France, an eleventh-century author echoed the talmudic identification of the exilarchate with Judah's rod of the blessing of Jacob, explaining it to mean

> that even today, when on account of our sins monarchy and power are lost, we the children of Exile are commanded to appoint unto us a prince of the progeny of David to serve as exilarch. We are to obey him and to lend him authority over us to the extent of our ability under the yoke of kings and masters and with the impoverishment of the masses, so that on our part he may still possess greatness and government, and no one should rebel against his words.[15]

At the time when these words were written, the exilarchate was but a shadow of its former self, however. Even within the Great Caliphate, tremendous inner and outer forces operated to weaken the hold of this central agency. Sooner or later it was bound to reveal the usual weaknesses of hereditary power, with all the accidents of age, training and personal character. Jerome's malevolent comment on the Palestinian patriarchs whom he considered to be "youngsters or boys, effeminate and indulging in luxuries,"[16] must have held true in much higher degree of some exilarchs living in the glamorous Bagdad of the "Arabian Nights."

From its re-establishment under the caliphs, moreover, the main exilarchic line lived under a cloud. Centuries afterwards the story of Bustanai, the first prince of captivity under Islam, was being retold with many a semi-legendary embellishment and contradictory bias. Caliph Omar I, ran its main line, wishing to show his regard for the Jewish chief, gave him a captive Persian princess-royal whose sister he had taken himself. For some reason Bustanai, before cohabiting with her, either did not liberate her ("out of inertia or pride," says one version), or at least failed to make sure that a writ of manumission was duly recorded. While such failure would have made no difference in the ruling dynasty — many caliphs were sons of slave-girls — the sons of Bustanai's other wives, after the father's death, treated the children of the princess as slaves in accordance with Jewish law. It so happened that a century later (before 771) the princess's descendants, legitimized in the meantime through the intervention of both the caliph and the Jewish academy, succeeded to the exilarchic position. Friends of the ruling line fell back upon the talmudic principle that "a man does not cohabit illicitly [if he can help it], and still less so a prince in Israel," and contended that Bustanai could not possibly have failed to manumit the Persian girl. Others harped on the illegitimacy of the reigning dynasty, pointed out the greater purity of descent of some other living families claiming Davidic ancestry, or, at least, expressed the hope that the Messiah, allegedly predestined even before the fall of Jerusalem, would be of unblemished lineage. Everyone familiar with the importance of dynastic legitimacy in the entire history of medieval Islam, beginning with the conflicts

over the succession of Ali, will realize how deeply these
controversies must have lowered the prestige of the exilarchate.[17]

Another source of weakness lay in the frequent struggles
over succession, which doubtless were greatly stimulated by
the unceasing dynastic quarrels in the ruling houses under
Islam. "In the absence of a principle of hereditary succession," says Prof. Levy, "or of primogeniture, and in the face
of legal disapproval of such a principle, it was generally the
most powerful member of the royal family who secured the
throne for himself." Since, moreover, both the Jewish people
and the caliphs claimed the right of selecting a new exilarch, controversies at least between two brothers became
rather frequent. The first, between 'Anan and Ḥananiah
(about 767), ended with the removal of the older brother,
suspected by the rabbis of heretical leanings. Thereupon
'Anan, supposedly acting on the advice of Abu Ḥanifa, the
distinguished Muslim jurist, declared himself the head of a
sect within Jewry. He thus escaped the severe penalty which
otherwise would have awaited him for rebelling against his
brother's authority, in the meantime confirmed by the
caliph. This declaration is said to have marked the beginning of the great Karaite schism. No less eventful in the
history of the exilarchate was the conflict between David b.
Yehudah and Daniel, the latter allegedly a professed Karaite. The matter was finally submitted to the caliph in 825.
Combining Muslim heterodoxy and rationalist tolerance
toward sects with pronounced anti-Jewish feelings, Caliph
Al-Mamun settled the controversy by issuing a far-reaching
decree that thenceforth "if ten men of whatever creed, be
they Jews, Christians or Magi, should get together and wish
to constitute an authority over themselves, no one should

prevent them from so doing." This decree, which opened
new opportunities for separatist trends, would have spelled
the end of Jewish communal unity, were it not for the deeply
entrenched communal control and the continued support
of the recognized chiefs by Al-Mamun's successors. Apparently without revoking the decree and despite the fact that
on occasion they allowed organized Jewish sects to withdraw
from exilarchic supervision, the later caliphs persisted in
confirming elections, receiving gifts and recognizing the
exilarchs as the main spokesmen of Jewry in the imperial
council. Opponents of individual exilarchs could, nevertheless, cast aspersion on the entire institution. Samuel b. 'Ali,
the energetic head of the Bagdad academy in the second
half of the twelfth century, climaxed his vitriolic attack upon
the exilarch by stating that "in the days of Exilarch David
b. Yehudah they were removed from royal service. They
joined the scholars and the academies, but were not admitted
until they accepted in writing the conditions of the academy
which had ordained them." Samuel derived therefrom the
radical conclusion that Israel in the dispersion have "neither
a king nor war, nor anything that would necessitate a king."
They only require a spiritual leader who would teach them
and administer justice to them.[18]

In the heads of the academies of Sura and Pumbedita,
now called geonim (an abbreviation of "head of the academy,
the pride [gaon] of Jacob," cf. Ps. 47.5), the exilarchs always
faced a rival, though not always an inimical authority.
Exceptionally, as in the days of Hezekiah b. David, the
exilarchic and geonic office were combined in the hands of
a single leader for as long as twenty years. Usually, too,
the princes of captivity maintained scholars of their own,
issued judgments through their own "judges of the gate,"

and even answered occasional legal inquiries addressed to them. These functions, however, were gradually concentrated in the academies, which, emerging again into the full light of history about the middle of the eighth century, were now better organized, had greater stability, remained in more direct contact with world Jewry and, for a time, commanded even more universal respect than their ancient predecessors. Sharing in the glory of the exilarchic house, geonim were likewise installed with quasi-royal pomp. In the ninth century a prayer for the welfare of the exilarchs and the officers of the academies was incorporated in the liturgy; it is still recited today by most orthodox Jews at Saturday morning services. Several other benedictions, recited at the academies in honor of individual exilarchs and geonim, have likewise come down. During an exilarchic interregnum, the gaon of Sura served as acting exilarch, and both geonim in a joint session of the two academies proceeded to "elect" a new chief. Through an arrangement of unknown date, each took direct supervision over certain districts, appointing local judges, as did the exilarchs (perhaps in cooperation with them) in other provinces. Thence they derived considerable revenue through meat and other imposts. The gaon of Sura received at one time as much as 1,500 gold denarii (some $6,000) a year from this source. Apart from their private fortunes, the geonim seem to have controlled also considerable accumulations of property belonging to the academy, from all of which they maintained a considerable staff of permanent officials and pupils, as well as the more prominent non-resident students attending the semi-annual *kallah* gatherings.[19]

Another substantial source of income was donations from all over the world. Following both talmudic precedents and a Muslim custom, become imperative in the vast expanse of the Caliphate, Jews of all countries addressed legal inquiries to either academy. Such inquiries were usually accompanied by gifts for the maintenance of the academy, its members and students. These "gifts" soon became so regular that they began to be regarded as dues rather than voluntary donations. Many geonim, including Nehemiah, Sherira, Hai and Samuel b. Ḥofni, solicited communities abroad, often breaching the dignity of high office. Local unpaid representatives gathered contributions and shipped them to the academy. For example, the distinguished eleventh-century scholars, Ḥananel b. Ḥushiel and Nissim b. Jacob, filled the post in Kairowan, each receiving in turn the high-sounding title of chief rabbi (*rosh ha-rabbanim*). Renewing also the ancient patriarchal "apostolate," some geonim began sending out regular collectors. An interesting specimen of a messenger's authorization is the diploma issued in 1191 by Samuel b. 'Ali to Zechariah b. Berekel, his son-in-law and vice-chairman of the Bagdad academy.[20]

Such proceedings, of course, elicited occasional protests. Maimonides undoubtedly was not alone in antagonizing contemporary scholars and running counter to ancient precedents, when he attacked the commercial exploitation of learning. He turned sharply against those who, by erroneously interpreting older sources, "imposed regular dues upon individuals and communities and induced them to believe in their simplicity that it was their duty to support scholars, students, and all those who professionally pursued the career of learning." Somewhat unhistorically, he contended that in talmudic times collections had never been made on behalf "of the honorable and precious academies, nor of the exilarchs and their judges" nor of any scholar or leader.

Such sporadic voices proved entirely ineffective, however, against the combined forces of tradition, reverence for learning, vested interests and the legitimate requirements of an organized community.[21]

Contact with the people was further maintained by the geonim through the renewal of the ancient *kallah* gatherings. While honoring the exilarch by assembling at his residence at the now stated occasion, the third Sabbath after the Feast, of Tabernacles, they developed the semi-annual congregations at the seat of the academies into major events in national life. If we accept Nathan's idealized description, learned Jews in various localities spent five of every six months studying an assigned section of the Talmud, and then appeared at the academy for a month (Adar and Elul) to be examined and to exchange ideas with confreres under the gaon's personal guidance. There they could also observe the judicial and interpretive machinery in full swing, since it was the custom for geonim to submit inquiries received in the intervening months to public discussion during the sixth month and then to announce the replies. It was, therefore, more than sheer formality when, having adopted the flowery letter style of the Muslims, the geonim addressed their inquirers more or less as follows:

> Amram b. Sheshna, the head of the academy of Mata Meḥasia (Sura), to all the rabbis and their disciples and the rest of our brethren, the house of Israel, living in the city of Barcelona, who are dear, honored and beloved before us, may their well-being grow and increase forever. Receive greetings from us and from R. Zemaḥ, the judge of the gate, the heads of the *Kallahs* and from all the ordained scholars who are in the place of the Great Sanhedrin, and from the candidates who are in the place of the Little Sanhedrin, and

from the other scholars, teachers and students of the entire academy. We always inquire about your welfare and implore the Lord's great compassion to be with you. We have commanded that the inquiries which you have sent us be read before us in the presence of the head of the court, the *allufim* [masters], the scholars and all the students. We have had them under advisement and considered all that is written therein. And we were enlightened from Heaven as follows . . .[22]

This idyllic situation could not last indefinitely. The exilarchs, having the right of appointment, also arrogated to themselves the right of deposing unwelcome teachers. During the conflict between David b. Zakkai and Saadia, the greatest of the geonim, which arose when the gaon found fault with some deeds issued by the exilarchic court, the gaon tried to replace David by his brother Josiah, and the exilarch deposed the recalcitrant master. In the ensuing controversy, which resembled some of the struggles between the papacy and the empire, both parties resorted to undignified language and personal vilification.[23] David's predecessor, Uḳba, on the other hand, fell victim to a conspiracy between Kohen Zedek, the gaon of Pumbedita, and a few leading Bagdad bankers, and was banished by the caliph.

The dissensions between the two academies and the personal rivalries in each were no less suicidal. Sometimes a special prayer was recited, soliciting God's help for peace in the academies. At first, relations seem to have been well regulated, with the academy of Sura recognized as the superior in rank and in bounty. While the head of Pumbedita always had to address his colleague by the distinguished title, gaon, the latter omitted this designation in his letters to Pumbedita. Even when younger in years, the gaon of

Sura sat to the right of the exilarch, was called to the Torah first and had precedence in all communal honors. Donations received by the academies, without designation of the particular recipient, were divided in the ratio of 2:1 in favor of Sura. Pumbedita often objected. Under the powerful leadership of Kohen Zedek, it asserted its equality with the Suranic school. Although the latter received a new lease on life under Saadia (928–42), the rise of Pumbedita could not be checked after its removal to Bagdad in 890. Having overcome a general crisis which affected the entire population of the capital and which reduced it to next to nothing under Sherira (967–1006) who, in 987, complained of having but one student at the *kallah*, it obtained full equality with Sura in 1006. The academy shone brightly once again in the days of Hai, Sherira's son (1004–38), the last of the great and universally recognized geonim.[24]

Hai's successor, Hezekiah, combined for twenty years the offices of exilarch and gaon of Pumbedita. The influence of both offices was, however, rapidly sinking. Western scholars, viewing the history of the Jews from the standpoint of western countries, ever since Abraham ibn Daud, dated the extinction of both these world-wide Jewish agencies at about 1040. We now know that this dating is erroneous insofar as a continuous line of exilarchs and geonim ruled the Bagdad community for more than two centuries thereafter. The conditions of the twelfth century, partly known before from the brief reports of the travelers, Benjamin and Petahiah, and a few references in the correspondence of Maimonides, have been greatly illumined by the letters of Samuel b. 'Ali which came to light a few years ago. They, as well as other sources, show both the gaon and his first exilarchic opponent, Daniel b. Hezekiah, to have been vigorous leaders, comparable in stature to most of their predecessors. Daniel's influence was felt strongly in Egypt, where in 1161 he confirmed in office the head of a local academy and where a writ of divorce of 1164 seems to have been issued in his name. Daniel's nephew and successor, Samuel of Mosul, was held in such high regard by Maimonides and his associates that the audience stood while his letter was recited in the philosopher's home.[25]

These two princes of captivity and their gaonic adversary were, nevertheless, essentially provincial dignitaries. Their influence outside Babylonia, Persia and the adjoining countries was completely overshadowed by Maimonides and others. The decline in status was due much less to personal deficiencies or administrative faults than to international developments. The disintegration of the Caliphate into a number of independent countries, often at war with one another, put an end to unified Jewish leadership. Distinguished individuals, such as the great geonim Saadia, Sherira, Hai, and the latter's colleague of Sura, Samuel b. Ḥofni, could for a time maintain a semblance of unity because their voices happened to carry considerable weight in religious, legal and even organizational affairs. Their personal authority would have been widely recognized had they held no office whatsoever. But the rival caliphates of Cairo and Cordova were bound to foster separatist tendencies which, conspicuously supported by the local governments, led to the establishment of new, independent provincial centers both of learning and administration.

The Bagdad chiefs were thenceforth obeyed only in those eastern lands over which the religious, if not political, pre-eminence of the Bagdad Caliphate still was generally recognized. The suppression of that caliphate by the Mongol conqueror, Hulaju, in 1258, followed by the frightful decline of all western Asia as a result of the subsequent Mongol invasions, spelled final ruin for the age-old Jewish leadership as well. To be sure, the first Mongol conquerors, retaining their pagan creed, left the bulk of the Muslim, Christian and Jewish population in the undisturbed exercise of their respective religious and communal rights. Not only was the general status of the Jews considerably improved, but Jacob b. Elijah of Valencia, in his *Polemical Letter* against Fra Pablo, boasted, after 1258, of "our master the exilarch, Rabbana Samuel, who is of the House of David, a foremost leader and one of the royal councilors and dignitaries of state." The Mongol government, however, seems to have withdrawn effective state support of the denominational chiefs. Allowed to shift for themselves, both the exilarchs and the geonim seem to have sunk further to a position of purely local leaders. Although as late as 1288 we still find a gaon, Samuel ha-Kohen, in Bagdad, and in 1341 and 1376, respectively, Azariah b. Yehallelel and David b. Hodayah signed themselves princes (*nasi* rather than *rosh*) of captivity, this was mere pretentiousness. David, in fact, claimed descent from the patriarchal, not the exilarchic branch of the Davidic house, a claim otherwise encountered only in the case of the Ben-Meir family and of a private citizen found in Tiberias by Petaḥiah of Ratisbon. Thus vanished from the stage of history — as quietly as it had entered upon it at least eleven centuries before — the longest-lived dynasty and one of the most enduring communal institutions in the history of mankind.[26]

4. PROVINCIAL LEADERSHIP

The autonomous central government of the Jewish people now gave way to regional powers. Whether adopting the same titles of princes of captivity (or, more proudly, of all Israel) and geonim, or resuscitating the ancient designations of *nasi* and *nagid*, the provincial chiefs claimed supreme authority in their respective domains. Even when an Egyptian *nagid* declared that he held sway over the people of the Lord "by permission of our master the exilarch under whose royal sceptre we and all of Israel come, and all of us gain our strength through the true God and the authority of his princely office, may it be elevated,"[27] it was but a literary flourish and may not even have referred to the Babylonian prince of captivity.

There had always existed in the imperial and provincial capitals of Islam a sort of collateral Jewish government which often was more powerful than the accredited authorities. Like other absolutist regimes, those of Islam fostered the rise of individuals or small court camarillas who became the real powers behind the throne. Among these influential advisers were often Jewish bankers, tax farmers, physicians or courtiers who had the ear of the monarch, the chief wazir or the more or less independent provincial governor. Many caliphs, defying the reiterated prohibitions often reissued under their own names, employed the *dhimmis* in high positions of state. Since a large part of the state revenue came from the non-Muslim taxpayers, treasury departments were particularly crowded with Jewish, Christian or Parsee officials. Due to their ubiquity, familiarity with foreign languages and foreign conditions, Jews were also useful diplomatic agents. Throughout the middle ages and early modern times we find a host of Jewish ministers, consuls and interpreters serving African and Turkish princes. Such officials, court bankers and physicians often used their connections to affect Jewish communal matters. Sometimes official communal leaders had to appeal to such influential coreligionists to obtain favorable government action or to forestall unfriendly measures.

No wonder that at times these well-connected bankers and government officials proved to be dangerous rivals of the established leadership. They often appeared as the main spokesmen of their people, sided with one or another party within the community, caused the appointment or deposition of certain communal officers and generally interfered with the management of communal affairs. Being independent of both electorate and communal treasury, they had only as much responsibility as was dictated to them by their consciences or by the degree of their reluctance to antagonize Jewish opinion. Reference has already been made to Neṭira's intercession with the caliph concerning the Jewish poll tax and to the successful intervention of a coterie of Jewish bankers in Bagdad (including Neṭira) in the controversy between Kohen Zedek and Uḳba. Another interesting sidelight is offered by a letter of Saadia, who tried with these words to win the good will of the leaders of an Egyptian community:

> And thus whenever you have transactions with the Government, I admonish you to let us know about them, that we may consult with the prominent members of the Bagdad community in the midst of which we dwell, namely the sons of R. Neṭira and the sons of R. 'Amram . . . and then the Government will so deal

with you as the Lord may lend success to our helper.
Thus do ye and not otherwise.[28]

Similarly in the Caliphate of Cordoba, Ḥisdai ibn Shaprut,
diplomat and court physician, exercised a memorable influence over the communal affairs of Spanish Jewry.

Not all prominent Jewish bankers and diplomats were
satisfied with such an unofficial position, however. International developments, combined with the inner dissensions
inside the exilarchic dynasty, greatly favored their ambitions. It was soon after the establishment of the Fatimid
caliphate in North Africa, in 909, that Mar Uḳba, the
exilarch deposed by the Gaon Kohen Zedek and subsequently exiled from the entire Abbasid Caliphate, settled
in the young and prosperous community of Kairowan. We
have the testimony of Abraham Yarḥi stating that the new
arrival was accorded princely dignity by the Kairowan
leaders, that "a seat of honor was assigned to him near the
ark in the synagogue and, after the recitation of the weekly
portions allocated to a priest and a levite, the scroll of Law
was brought to his seat" for the reading of the next section.
This clearly was the exclusive prerogative of an officiating
exilarch. Thus the foundations were laid for an independent
North African leadership. When, after the conquest of
Egypt in 969, the Fatimid caliphs sought to wrest the hegemony over their large and populous Jewish communities
from the exilarchic appointees of their rivals in Bagdad,
they allegedly turned to a man who had faithfully served
them for many years and to whose organizing ability were
due, in no mean measure, their rapid conquests. Palṭiel, of
a distinguished, though non-Davidic, South-Italian family,
is said to have assumed the leadership "of the communities
of the people of God living in Egypt, Palestine, Palermo

[Sicily], Ifrikiyya [north-central Africa] and all the Arab kingdom [of the Fatimids]." To what extent this tradition, undoubtedly colored by both the appointment of 'Ali ibn Ḥayyun, a Moroccan participant in the Fatimid conquests, as supreme judge of the Egyptian Muslims and the narrator's family pride, represents the truth is still controversial. But there is no doubt that about that time some such powerful leader of Egyptian Jewry assumed the high-sounding title *nagid* or *negid 'am el* (prince of the people of God), which had been used a millennium before by Simon the Maccabean. Whether or not he realized that the Egyptian Greek translators of the Bible usually rendered this royal attribute by *ethnarches*, he thus resuscitated the long discontinued line of Jewish ethnarchs of Ptolemaic Egypt. The office was ultimately entrusted to the family of Maimonides (it is still doubtful whether the codifier himself assumed the title), in whose tenure it remained until the end of the fourteenth or the beginning of the fifteenth century.[29]

The conquest of Egypt by the Turks in 1517 augured badly for the continuation of an office which, with its hereditary and non-rabbinic features, sharply contrasted with the prevalent type of organization in other Turkish communities. When, after one of the recurrent rows, the *nagid*, Jacob ibn Ḥayyim Talmid, was excommunicated by the distinguished rabbi, Bezaleel Ashkenazi, the government abolished his office and replaced it by the more typically Turkish chief rabbinate (1556). The new officer, combining much temporal with spiritual power, was called in Turkish, *tchelebi*, and was usually sent to Cairo from Constantinople. Throughout the six centuries of its existence, however, the Egyptian *negidut* enjoyed, within its more limited geographic boundaries, the high governmental prerogatives of the exilarchate.

The *nagid's* functions, in the words of their careful modern investigator,

> were to represent all the Jews, to serve them as legal authority and as judge in conformity with their laws, to watch over the contracting of marriages, the pronouncing of the ban, and the turning in prayer to the proper *Kiblah* [the direction of Jerusalem]. The Muhammedans looked to him for protection against Jews. The custom has been that the *Rais* [*al-Yahud*, the Arabic equivalent of *nagid*] should be of the Rabbanite community to the exclusion of the other communities, though he sat in judgment over all the three sections, Rabbanite, Karaite and Samaritan. In short, the *Rais* of the Jews took the place of the Patriarch of the Christians.

In the period of the suppression of the office, the renowned Cairo rabbi, David ibn Abi Zimra, described the emoluments paid by the Egyptian Jewry for the maintenance of the *nagid*, so "that he may devote his entire time to administering justice among them and representing them before the king and the authorities. Like the exilarch he was entitled, by virtue of a royal grant, to flog and to imprison them." From Egypt, office and title were taken over by Jewish leaders in Kairowan, the Yemen and Granada.[30]

The contrast between exilarchs and *negidim* was duplicated, in the domain of Law, by that between the Babylonian and the Palestinian geonim. The academy of Tiberias seems to have continued to function in some form or other under the descendants of Mar Zutra III even in the dark ages of Byzantine persecution. Justinian's prohibition of the Jewish study of Oral Law (this seems to be the meaning of the much-debated term, *deuterosis*) may have put further obstacles in the way of creative legal investigation which, even before the sixth century, had largely been abandoned to the Babylonians. Together with another Byzantine prohibition of unknown date which forbade the recitation of the *shema'* and the *'amidah,* because of their anti-Trinitarian or anti-Christian slant, it stimulated the Jewish leaders to new creativity in the realm of legend and liturgy. To convey to the audience some of the outlawed talmudic lore, they hid it behind the mask of poetry and introduced it into the synagogue in the form of free liturgical additions, the *piyyutim.* The school of Tiberias concentrated also upon the final redaction of the Old Testament and related grammatical and lexicographic studies. The Palestinians did not cease, however, to cultivate their ancestral customs which often greatly differed from those in vogue in Babylonia, and they staunchly resisted occasional attempts of Babylonian chiefs to establish greater uniformity. The impact of these differences was felt also in neighboring lands of Africa and Europe.[31]

What is more, even after the calendar proclamation of Hillel II, the Palestinians retained the ritual of announcing the new moon. Unimportant as this function was in fixing the generally accepted leap year, it retained some significance with respect to the months following the New Year, which could still be made to count either 29 or 30 days. As late as 835, the Babylonians ungrudgingly acknowledged Palestinian supremacy in this field, the exilarch himself writing "And I, the heads of the schools, the scholars and all Israel rely on the calendar dispatched by the scholars [of Palestine]." Soon afterwards, however, the Babylonian academies declared their independence of Palestine in this respect, too. With Saadia's arrival in Babylonia, moreover, a new fighting spirit was injected into the Babylonian leader-

ship. Since the Palestinian academy was at that time headed
by Aaron Ben-Meir, a no less vigorous personality, the
clash was unavoidable. After a prolonged personal controversy, with many invectives hurled by each side (e. g. the
allegedly Davidian Ben-Meir denounced the plebeian Saadia
as a descendant of proselytes) and many pamphlets making
the rounds of the Jewish communities, Saadia seemed vic-
torious (921). But his was a truly Pyrrhic victory. Within
half a century, Palestine was incorporated into the Fatimid
Caliphate and, utilizing fully its political independence of
the Babylonian exilarchs, claimed exclusive leadership in the
new Empire.[32]

Once again political boundaries prevented complete rupture. Under Hai even the Palestinians dispatched inquiries
to Bagdad, and the Palestinian gaon, Solomon b. Yehudah,
sent his son there for advanced study. But in all important
aspects the Palestinian geonim who, incidentally, now
adopted the same title, were independent. In externals
they emulated Sura and Pumbedita. Their academies, too,
consisted of 70 members sitting in seven rows before the
chairmen. Supported by regular contributions from communities under their jurisdiction, they, too, sent out collectors and wrote pathetic, none-too-dignified letters of
solicitation. They even went beyond the formal election of
the exilarchs by their colleagues in Babylonia and "authorized" several *negidim* in succession. In that period of progressive decentralization of Jewish communal life, however,
they could attract only local attention. Few communities
outside their immediate jurisdiction sent inquiries to Jerusalem or Tiberias. Even the renowned eleventh-century
scholars of Kairowan preferred to correspond with the leaders in Bagdad.[33] The little prestige that the Palestinian

schools began to achieve was destroyed in the catastrophic years of the Crusaders' invasion which all but wiped out the Jewish communities in the Holy Land.

In addition to the Egyptian *nagid* and the Palestinian *gaon*, the Fatimid Caliphate included also one or another *nasi*. Although thus renewing the exalted title of the ancient patriarchs, its holders were little more than dignified mendicants. Many, though not all, claimed Davidic ancestry. They settled in Fustat, Jerusalem, Damascus, and so forth, and were maintained by charitable contributions. Some, however, achieved more than passing prominence. Benjamin and Petaḥiah found two cousins serving as local exilarchs in Mosul, and two brothers holding such a hereditary position in the Yemen.

Genealogy being less important in the selection of a head of an academy,[34] the decentralization of scholarship made much more rapid and definitive progress. The story of the four Babylonian captives who, sold by their pirate captors to Egypt, Kairowan and Spain, founded there new centers of learning, was long cherished by the protagonists of the biographic-anecdotal type of historiography. While perhaps containing a kernel of historic truth, it need not be credited any more than is the story of the rise of the *negidut* out of a query of a Fatimid princess. It reflects reality insofar as the intellectual emancipation of western Jewry had made it increasingly independent of both Palestinian and Babylonian tutelage. Maimonides, the greatest teacher of oriental Jewry, in his pathetic letter to the rabbis of Lunel, was looking forward to European leadership in the evolution of Jewish learning. Only partly justified in his own day, this expectation was to be realized in the future far more than the sage of Fustat imagined.

5. TURKISH *Hakam-Bashis*

Legend spun its yarn also about the origin of the office of
Chief Rabbi of Turkish Jewry, which, for a time, seemed
destined to resuscitate the vanished glories of both exilarchate and gaonate. Transmitted by the hero's nephew,
Elijah Capsali, the story undoubtedly contains more than
a grain of historical truth, although it hardly gives us an
inkling of the real forces behind the rise of the new institution. Sultan Meḥmed II, we are told, after the conquest
of Constantinople in 1453, visited the populous Jewish
quarter and wondered who might be in charge of such a
large community. Told that it was an old and saintly rabbi
living an extremely ascetic life, he was duly impressed. To
test the saint's impeccability the sultan, in disguise, attended
a trial and witnessed how an overbearing rich litigant was
humiliated by the rabbi. After a final test, an inquiry concerning the rabbi's and general Jewish views of Ishmael,
Islam's purported ancestor, which was answered, with several friendly quotations from the Talmud, to the sultan's
complete satisfaction, Meḥmed appointed Moses Capsali to
serve as the head of all his Jewish subjects and as their
representative in the imperial council.[35]

These incidents which, in view of oriental methods of
government need not be altogether fictitious, reveal the
true historic sequence, viz. that the sultan took the initiative. This he did for a variety of reasons. Having inherited
from the successor states of the Caliphate most of its governmental machinery, the Turkish administration, long before
the conquest of Constantinople, was used to entrusting the
management of non-Muslim affairs to the heads of the
respective communities. It was also in the imperial interest

to have single men responsible for the substantial taxes
paid by the various groups of "infidels." Since the Greek
patriarch of Constantinople was speedily recognized as the
supreme officer of the millions of Greek-Orthodox Christians living under the Sublime Porte, similar arrangements
had to be made also for the Jewish subjects whose number
was rapidly increasing through waves of immigration from
Christian countries. During the subsequent rapid expansion
and gradual disintegration of the Ottoman Empire, the Jews
proved to be the most reliable among the "infidels." We
may readily believe therefore, that their *ḥakam-bashi* (a
combination of the Sephardic title *ḥakam* for rabbi and of the
Turkish designation *pashah* for a high dignitary of state)
ranked in the councils of state even higher than the respective Christian patriarchs. None of them, however, was a
regular member of the Supreme Council, the Diwan, in
which the *sheikh al-Islam*, next to the sultan-caliph the
highest officer of the Mosque, had the sole permanent religious seat.

The Jews, mainly Greek and oriental, at first submitted
meekly to the rule of Capsali. For forty-three years he
judged the Jews of the Empire, imposing bans, prison terms
and flagellations. He appointed many local rabbis, even
over the renowned community of Adrianople. He issued
ordinances modifying existing law, declaring null and void,
for example, every Jewish marriage performed in the presence of less than ten adult males. This measure, become
necessary in order to secure wider publicity among the
immigrants hailing from many lands, cut deeply into Jewish
law, even disrupting existing marriages.[36]

Under Capsali's successor, however, it became apparent

that unified Jewish communal control along the lines of the Great Caliphate was a matter of the past. The mass influx of western, especially Spanish Jews, who ultimately succeeded in imposing their Ladino speech and their Sephardic ritual upon most Balkan and western Asian communities, brought forth a growing opposition to such centralized and state-imposed leadership. The rise to power of individual court bankers, physicians and diplomats — from Moses Hamon, through the cousins Joseph Nasi and Solomon ibn Yaish (Alvaro Mendes), the dukes of Naxos and Mytilene, respectively, to Count Abraham Camondo in the nineteenth century — established in Constantinople the same sort of irresponsible parallel rule as had proved detrimental to official leadership in Bagdad. Even women, such as Esther Kyra (16th century), gaining access to influential members of the sultan's harem, often exerted more effective pressure in behalf of their coreligionists than did the accredited chiefs. The numerical and cultural strength of other communities, such as Salonica, Safed, Jerusalem or Cairo, and the preeminence of some of their rabbinic authorities, often reduced the preponderance of the capital to a mere shadow. Last, but not least, the progressive disorganization of the administrative machinery of the vast Empire undermined the effectiveness of all central agencies of both the state and the churches.

Even in the days of Elijah Mizraḥi, the government found it necessary to entrust the general supervision over Jewish taxes to a new officer, the *kehaya*. The Jews at first disliked this arrangement and, in 1519, the communal leaders of Constantinople called upon Shealtiel, the first to hold this office, instantly to resign. He and his descendants were ordered not to accept the appointment even if threatened with execution by the sultan. Shealtiel obeyed, but the Jews soon reconsidered and, apparently under government pressure, allowed him to resume his post. They stipulated, however, that he first "promise, under sanction of excommunication, to enter no negotiations with the Crown, judges, cadi or other official in any matter, major or minor affecting the community at large without consultation with and authorization by representatives elected by the community."[37] Subsequently we find such central as well as local fiscal agents in charge not only of taxation but also of the registry of births and deaths and of transfers of real estate. *Kehayas*, who performed such intermediate governmental and communal functions, existed in Constantinople as late as the nineteenth century.

Even in purely spiritual matters, the authority of the *ḥakam-bashi* rarely went beyond the confines of the capital. He still served as Jewry's main spokesman in imperial deliberations. To him were still addressed most imperial communications for forwarding to individual communities. From the official standpoint he still had general control over all provincial and local rabbis. In the sultan's decree (*bérat*) of July 10, 1909, confirming the election of the last *ḥakam-bashi* of the Ottoman Empire, Ḥayyim Nahum (here for the first time styled *effendi*), we still read such passages as this:

> The appointment of rabbis through our imperial decree in other cities will not be valid without the chief rabbi's approbation . . . . When, at the chief rabbi's written request signed by him, a rabbi is appointed for a particular city, his rights will be specified, on our

part, in the decree to be addressed to him. No one is entitled to demand the appointment of a rabbi for a particular city nor to solicit from the chief rabbi the assignment of a particular synagogue to a particular rabbi.... [The chief rabbi] is free to perform his tasks and administer his office according to his own judgment, and in no case and under no excuse whatsoever may anybody prevent him from so doing or [otherwise] interfere with his administration.

In practice, nevertheless, the influence of the *ḥakam-bashi's* office on the local management of the individual communities throughout the Empire was constantly waning, and in 1836 an attempt had to be made to renew its glory by obtaining for it, as well as for the provincial chief rabbinates, regular imperial confirmations and by installing the then newly-elected chief, Abraham Levi, with unusual pomp. For the sake of both prestige and increased security, the Jews did not mind paying anywhere from 12,000 to 30,000 aspers for the privilege of such an imperial *bérat*, which was publicly proclaimed at the Porte or at the seats of the provincial governors and was accompanied by special vestments to be worn by the newly-elected officers. This payment seems to have been officially abolished by the *Ḥatti-humayum* of 1856, but unofficially all persons so honored continued to express their recognition in tangible fashion. The Porte's interference made itself disagreeably felt, however, when Abraham Levi's successor, Samuel Ḥayyim, was deposed after one year of tenure, allegedly because he was a foreigner. While such rigor is fully understandable under the system of capitulations which exempted resident aliens from local jurisdiction, it demonstrated to the Jews the disadvantages of state control of religion.[38]

6. Local Organs

It would be entirely beyond the scope of the present treatment to describe the great variety of local officers, functions and electoral methods found in literally thousands of communities which, during thirteen centuries, existed in Muslim lands. Many aspects of local self-government were common to the Jews under both Islam and Christendom and will often be referred to in the forthcoming chapters. We shall, therefore, limit ourselves here to a few general remarks concerning certain peculiarities of the near-eastern communities and some basic trends in their millennial evolution.

From Morocco and Muslim Spain to India and Turkestan innumerable smaller or larger groups of Jews, often subdivided into many congregations, were ruled by officers of their own, bearing various names and exercising a variety of functions. Names did not always correspond to functions. Jewish predilection for titles derived from the Talmud, coupled with the growing Muslim fashion of heaping honorific designations on men in power, often obscure the meaning of the simplest terms. For example, Benjamin of Tudela was astounded, upon arrival in Bagdad, to find the heads of the ten academies — or rather the ten leading members of the main academy under Samuel b. 'Ali — going under the archaic name of the "men of leisure." Maimonides, too, seems to reflect contemporary practice when he gives equivocal explanations for this term. The talmudic *hazzan* increasingly became the reader of the congregation, as is evidenced by several geonic and post-geonic sources. Nevertheless some communities persisted in attaching to this title the entirely different function of preacher. About 1400,

Al-Kalkashandi still drew the distinction between the ser-
monizing *hazzan* and the *sheliah sibbur*, the Jewish equivalent
of the Muslim *imam*, or leader in prayers. The *hazzan* now
often served also as author and composer of liturgical songs,
and *hazzanut* appears as a frequent synonym of *payyetanut*,
or the art of liturgical composition. On the other hand, it
is not surprising to find men addressed in glowing terms,
such as "the pride of *hazzanim*" or "the crown of *hazzanim*."
Ordinary officials sometimes were styled "fathers of wisdom"
or "crowns of wisdom." Benefactors and well-wishers of the
academies, with no official connection whatsoever, were
designated in letters as the "beloved of the school" its
strength, glory, crown, pride, banner or even foundation.
A Karaite officer, not the head of his community, was called
"the banner of the Jews and the joy of their glory." Both
Maimonides and his son sharply derided this plethora of
titles. "It is known among men of discretion," writes
Abraham Maimuni, "that most of these designations given
to men are nonsense and meaningless flourish. Wise men
use them sparingly and hate them, but ambitious and
domineering persons like them in great profusion, because
in them alone lies their greatness and distinction." Nevertheless, the conferring of such flattering titles was a substantial source of income for the geonic academies and
became increasingly significant in the period of the Caliphate's decline. Under these circumstances, to define exactly
the nature of each high-sounding office often appears
altogether hopeless.[39]

Of fundamental importance was the appointment of the
local judge, under the Caliphate the most important official
leader. At first all appointments came from the exilarch

and the geonim. A geonic responsum, probably addressed by Hai to the sages in Kairowan in 1011, informs us that

> it is a custom in Babylonia for the High Court [the designation of either of the two academies] to appoint judges in every district and to hand to each judge a letter of authorization, called in Aramean, the *pitka de-dayyanuta*. They clearly write therein: "We appoint X, the son of Y . . . to serve in such and such place, and give him the authorization to adjudicate litigations and supervise all affairs relative to the commandments, the prohibited and the permitted, and the fear of Heaven. With those who refuse to accept his decision he is entitled to do what appears to him to be the duty imposed upon him by Heaven . . ."

These letters of authorization, or rather decrees of appointment did not fully specify the extent of the judge's authority, but let local custom provide the details. According to Nathan's description, the judge, upon his arrival at his destination, would appoint two local notables to sit in judgment with him so that the talmudic requirement of three judges would be fulfilled. The same, or two other local assistants, helped supervise the fiscal administration. The judge's revenue consisted, in Nathan's days, of a capitation tax of two dirhems annually from every man over twenty, of a dirhem weekly from each butcher and of fees for various services. For every marriage contract, writ of divorce and deed of gift or sale, the judge was to receive 4⅓ dirhem, unless he voluntarily reduced the amount for the needy. The regular secretary, or notary who wrote deeds, did not share in the fees, but received an annual salary. "He who orders a deed to be written secretly (out of court) may be banished, fined in the amount of the fee and flogged by the judge." Only if the latter grossly abused his powers could the community impeach him before the exilarch (or gaon) and obtain his dismissal. The government, too, enjoined the local organs, to quote the caliph's decree of 1209 appointing Daniel b. Eleazar ibn Ḥibat as head of the Bagdad academy, that "it is the duty of the Jewish community and its judges in Bagdad and the districts of Iraq to submit to that which he orders, to demean themselves according to his word in the disposition of their affairs and to act according to the degree required thereby."[40]

The powers of the judge were at first little affected by the decline of the Babylonian center. In Egypt and Palestine, under both the Fatimids and the Mamelukes, his authority stemmed from that of the *nagid* or Palestinian gaon. Obadiah Bertinoro, traveling through Egypt in 1487–88, observed that the *nagid* "has authority from the king to imprison and flog, at his discretion, the recalcitrant Jews in all the neighboring communities. He also appoints the judges for each community." Occasionally the government appointed the local leaders directly. In North African communities, for example, the Spanish arrivals of the fourteenth century found a local elder, a sort of sheikh, in the enjoyment of almost absolute powers which, according to them, he wielded with little wisdom and discretion.[41]

The self-determination of the individual community was nevertheless on the increase. Even in the most authoritarian periods, many officials must have been elected by the local communities to assist their appointive chiefs in fiscal and other affairs. In small communities the local elders exercised even judicial functions, without eliciting the protest of the geonic leaders. One of them, Ḥananiah Gaon (938–43), proclaimed a general principle: "From these [biblical] verses and traditions we clearly learn that the city elders have the right to issue ordinances for the inhabitants of their city and to force the latter to adhere to these regulations." With the weakening control of central or provincial leadership, the elected officials, often men of great learning or wealth who sometimes also enjoyed the confidence of the government, began displacing appointed chiefs. In the western countries, especially in Spain under Islam, the "democratic" traditions of the ancient Graeco-Roman community persisted with such vigor as to make elections the predominant, if not the exclusive, method of choosing officers. Although building entirely on geonic foundations and imitating similar works by Saadia and Hai, Judah b. Barzilai of eleventh-century Barcelona has in his *Book of Deeds* only formulas for decrees of appointment and deposition by the community at large. In electing a "head, elder, judge or *nasi*," the author opines, the community is to specify their rights and duties, while in deposing "a reader, slaughterer, scribe . . . or even judge, God forbid," it ought to describe his previous functions and the reasons for his dismissal. Al-Barceloni betrays, however, his personal bent when, in suggesting a long formula for a decree of appointment, he describes the appointee as a "local scholar, wise, understanding, pious, wealthy and incorruptible."[42]

Self-government not only of the local community, but also of any of its subdivisions reached its peak during the extensive migrations of Sephardic Jewry throughout the Mediterranean basin. Arriving in increasing masses, imbued with a feeling of cultural and, one might almost style it, racial superiority, and often astoundingly successful in their economic and political ventures, these immigrants into Moorish or Turkish possessions looked down upon the community life of the native Jews. Disunited in themselves, each regarding the ritual, the customs and the communal management of their particular city of origin in the Iberian Peninsula as infinitely superior to all others, the newly established congregations were in constant conflict both with the indigenous communities and with one another. The Marrano antecedents of many members introduced another discordant element into the communal structure.

This ferment is reflected in the perennial controversies between the outstanding rabbis which fill the annals of that period. Written chiefly by the new arrivals, the extant records give a one-sided picture in which lights and shadows are inequitably distributed. But they clearly reveal the intolerant mood of the immigrants which, in turn, provoked a widespread reaction, sometimes even attempts to close the gates to further immigration. For example, Simon Duran, answering an inquiry from Bugia and urging the enactment of certain new communal regulations, paid his inquirers, without further provocation, the left-handed compliment, "Unlike many other localities in these parts, you happen to possess elders who are familiar with public administration and know the requirements of the Law." A city like Constantinople, at the same time harboring ten Sephardic congregations in addition to Romani (Byzantine), Italian and Ashkenazic groups, would have generated endless friction, if the communities had not developed some sort of *modus vivendi* by respecting one another's autonomy. It was at that time that David ha-Kohen of Corfù, amplifying a talmudic discussion, proclaimed the general principle that "no congregation can enforce its will upon another congregation, however small, since each is to be treated as a city apart." This principle, widely adopted and often quoted, did not altogether eliminate the talmudic prohibition of fostering local separatism. These two essentially contradictory principles, calling for varying, often casuistic, attempts at harmonization, formed a broad and elastic basis for the adjustment of many communal conflicts.[43]

7. PROGRESSIVE SELF-DETERMINATION

The evolution of the Jewish community under Islam reveals trends which are in direct contrast to those prevailing during the preceding millennium of Hellenistic, Roman and Persian rule. In antiquity the trend was from enormous local diversity to talmudic uniformity. In the Muslim countries uniformity was at first greatly reinforced through the interpretation and amplification of talmudic law in the Babylonian academies, but soon gave way to a new outcrop of local customs, constitutional forms and administrative methods. The ancient evolution toward centralized control by the patriarchate and exilarchate likewise reached its peak, about 800 C. E., in the accumulated powers of the exilarchs in Bagdad. From 825 on, however, the oriental communities underwent a process of steady decentralization resulting from the rise of mighty rivaling forces led by the geonim, the Egyptian-Palestinian *negidim* and academies, and the other regional authorities. Toward the end of the middle ages local autonomy was so deeply entrenched that the attempt to revive a central agency for the great Ottoman Empire was doomed to failure. Even the local community had to make increasing allowances to many smaller units, particularly those founded upon the "city of origin" principle.

Hand in hand with decentralization — in fact, often as its cause or effect — went the progressive decline of state control. The Christian Roman Empire and Sassanian

Persia had succeeded in making the Jewish community increasingly subservient to imperial needs. Under the first caliphs the state was in still fuller control. The caliphs appointed the exilarchs who, in turn, chose the heads of the academies and, directly or through the latter, determined who should govern the individual community. This hierarchic system, become a branch of government rather than the free expression of the community, was accepted by the Jews only because the government respected the hereditary succession of the exilarchs, because such succession flattered Jewish political ambitions, and because all Jews recognized the cultural supremacy of the academies. Unsupported by the vast resources of the Empire, however, after the disintegration of the Caliphate, this system gradually broke down in favor of the free, more or less "democratic" community, as it was simultaneously developing in Christian Europe.

CHAPTER VII

EUROPEAN CORPORATION

IN MEDIEVAL and early modern Europe, the Jewish community reached its apogee. In many countries and periods it came close to justifying complaints that it constituted a "state within the state." In fact, such complaints became vocal only during the eighteenth century when complete non-religious assimilation began to be viewed in many quarters as both feasible and desirable. Before that time, extensive Jewish self-government was universally accepted as the necessary and welcome complement to recognized religious disparity. Over professing Jews the community often exercised more authority than the most powerful secular regimes. Buttressed by the legal recognition of State and Church; imbued with the spirit of a nomistic and ethical, i. e. activist religion; bound together by strong economic ties, outside animosity and a communal responsibility both theoretical and practical; permeated with a profound reverence for tradition, it was a sort of little state, interterritorial and non-political, but none the less quasi-totalitarian. What it lacked in police or military facilities for law enforcement, it more than compensated for by super-natural sanctions of religion, which made of every deviation from the norm, however slight and however secular in character, a serious offense against religion. Even the offender who felt he was sure to escape earthly justice, was likely to be troubled by conscience, haunted by fears of supernatural damnation.

This memorable state of affairs was made possible by a concatenation of many external and internal forces. Feudalism's dissolution of European society into a hierarchy of corporate bodies, each with a separate economic function and political status, the Church's adherence to tradition and its need of external testimony, the State's perennial fiscal difficulties, met half way an irrepressible inner urge of the Jews to survive in no matter how hostile an environment until the messianic end of days. Out of this extraordinary combination arose the European ghetto. Often territorially delimited, it furnished the people in exile, by means of its remarkable interplay of social and religious forces, an effective substitute for the lost state and territory. A brief review of these manifold internal and external factors may help us better to understand the complexity of the political evolution of the Jewish communities in the various Christian states and cities.

1. Jewish Perseverance

The majority of European Jews had come at one time or another from Muslim lands. While the traditions of Roman rule were not altogether forgotten, few communities could pride themselves on unbroken continuity since the days of the Christian Empire. The severe persecutions and expulsions of the seventh to the tenth centuries in the Byzantine Empire and the intolerant outbursts of the seventh century in Visigothic Spain, the Frankish Kingdom and in Langobard Italy, annihilated many ancient settlements and reduced many others to a state of utter cultural dependence on more prosperous brethren in the East. The conquest of Spain by the Muslims, followed by a briefer Saracen domination over Sicily, brought the most populous and hardiest communities of the western Empire into direct contact with the civilization of the Caliphate. Even the city of Rome, where alone the Jews were allowed to pursue their historic career without violent interruption, still turned to Palestine for guidance in all communal and religious matters. No better illustration need be found than the speedy adoption of Palestinian titles by the communal leaders of the papal capital. Jacob b. Yekutiel, visiting Rome in 1007, found there three rabbis, distinguished by the titles *nasi, gaon* and *resh kallah,* two of which Palestine herself had not so long before borrowed from Babylonia.[1] As in Palestine, the position of gaon, or head of the academy, was held for several generations by members of one family. Spain, on the other hand, gravitated toward Babylonia. Having taken over some of Babylonia's observances, administrative methods and religious doctrines, it perpetuated the influence of the Babylonian academies long after the elimination of the gaonate and exilarchate as political factors in the West.

Coming from economically and culturally far superior regions, the new Jewish arrivals in the West, especially north of the Alps, must have looked down upon their "barbarian" neighbors. Their own business methods, educational facilities and cultural amenities were so much more "advanced" that they would have resisted assimilation even if the local corporate system had not encouraged them to persevere in their own folkways. Their law, in particular proved extremely useful to them in their new situation. From the days of the Carlovingian Empire they had increasingly been called upon to perform special tasks in international and local trade and banking. They found in their law — originally developed under the semi-capitalistic civilization of the Hellenistic and early Roman empires, then modified under the semi-feudal regimes of Christian Rome and Persia, and once more reinterpreted to suit the needs of the expanding economy of the Caliphate — a much more pliable instrument than the varying local primitive regulations and procedures. Confronted by an often hostile world, they had to be on constant guard as individuals and as a community. In 1130 the community of London was fined the enormous sum of £2,000 for the misdeeds of one man. Informers denouncing fellow Jews or the community at large before the mighty became a grave menace and had to be severely dealt with by Jewish judges. The common fiscal responsibility for governmental taxes, enhanced by the realization that "taxes are our saviors," as Asher b. Yeḥiel unwittingly paraphrased Neṭira's argument, likewise necessitated the exercise of effective communal control.[2] These and other weighty considerations intensified the Jewish urge for religious, judicial, educational and economic self-government even beyond the extent hallowed by a tradition already a millennium in antiquity.

Solomon ibn Adret of Barcelona (died 1310) proclaimed it as a general principle that "no man is entitled to withdraw and free himself from a communal ordinance by saying 'I shall not participate in the issuance of the ordinances' and the like, because the individuals are subjected to [the will of] the majority. Just as all communities are subjected to the High Court or the *nasi*, so is every individual subjected to the congregation of his locality." This principle, underlying all discussions on Jewish communal law, was elaborated by many old and new regulations designed to fortify the community against outside interference. In this respect the early medieval Franco-German communities went further than even their Babylonian predecessors under Persia or Islam. A synod at Troyes about 1150, attended by some of the greatest luminaries of northern Jewry (the brothers Jacob Tam and Samuel b. Meir, Eliezer b. Nathan, and so forth) adopted the following sweeping resolutions:

1. We have voted, decreed, ordained and declared under the ban, that no man or woman, related or unrelated, may bring a fellow Jew before Gentile courts or exert compulsion on him through Gentiles, be they prince or common man, superior or lower official, except by mutual agreement made in the presence of proper witnesses.

2. If the matter is accidentally brought to the attention of the government or other Gentiles, and pressure is exerted on a fellow Jew, the man [so assisted] shall save his fellow from their hands and shall secure him against the Gentiles . . . and he shall make amends to him in such manner as the seven best men of the city will ordain . . . .

3. We have also declared under a ban that no one may intimidate the seven best men of the city through the power of Gentiles. And because the masters of wicked tongue and informers perform their deeds in obscurity, we have also decreed excommunication for indirect action unless he makes amends imposed upon him by the seven best men . . . .

5. We have also declared under ban that no man shall feel entitled to gain control over his fellow Jew through a king, prince or judge, in order to punish or fine or coerce him, either in secular or religious matters . . . .

The synod allowed, however, to cite before non-Jewish courts litigants who demonstrably refused to appear before a Jewish court. By a curious inconsistency, it also invoked the aid of Jews influential with the government "to coerce, through the power of Gentiles, all those who shall transgress any one of our commandments."[3]

As a matter of fact, equipped with the power of imposing fines, flogging, excommunicating and, exceptionally, executing recalcitrant members, the Jewish communal authorities rarely required direct governmental assistance. Many communities disregarded the synodal exception in favor of mutual agreements to repair to Gentile courts, and required that in each case the special permission of the communal leaders be obtained. In the face of often contradictory state legislation, the rabbis insisted upon the exclusivity of Jewish law on both practical and theoretical grounds. In the arguments advanced, emphasis on the educational advantages of the practical administration of Jewish law is particularly characteristic of the workings of the medieval Jewish mind. Maimonides pointed out that in Christian countries (he had primarily Byzantium in mind), where the Jews did not possess civil jurisdiction, even experts were unfamiliar with the intricacies of civil law. Ibn Adret sharply attacked submission to Gentile jurisdiction and bitterly exclaimed, "Of what use will then be the sacred and holy writings which Rabbi Judah and after him Rabina and R. Ashi have composed for us [the Mishnah and Talmud]? God forbid that they teach their children the laws of the Gentiles and build for themselves altars in Gentile academies! Nothing of the kind shall happen in Israel." Deeply convinced of the superiority of the Jewish judiciary, he branded as "foolish" the attempts of some litigants to escape non-Jewish judges by ribbing their opponents. In his opinion the Jewish court could easily reverse any sentence disagreeing with the provisions of Jewish law.[4]

Reality and government power, of course, forced compromise on some of these exalted claims, a trend which could readily be justified by the old talmudic recognition of "the law of the kingdom." This principle, without which life in Exile would have been well-nigh impossible, could be interpreted with the latitude dictated by each teacher's personal temper or circumstances, or by the changing needs of each generation or locality. In its root essential, however, rather than proclaiming the supremacy of the non-Jewish state and its laws, it merely reaffirmed the eternity and inviolability of the divinely instituted Jewish law and, hence, the sovereignty of the Jewish community. The law of the kingdom was law, because, and insofar as, Jewish law acknowledged its validity.

Authoritative teachers of Judaism must pass judgment on each state regulation and decide whether or not it fell under the provisions of this voluntarily announced rule. Vast domains of law referring to strictly religious matters, which included all questions arising from marriage and divorce, were from the outset reserved for exclusively Jewish administration. Rashi, who otherwise belongs to the more liberal interpreters of the principle, argued that the original "Noahidic" commandments included a provision for universal courts of justice, but none regulating marriage or divorce, and that hence Judaism must in these matters pursue a wholly independent course. Even in purely governmental affairs, such as taxation, the rabbis often arrogated to themselves the power of acknowledging or repudiating the validity of a particular enactment. Sharing with their non-Jewish contemporaries an extreme reverence for custom, they often denounced innovations unfriendly to Jews as an illegitimate royal usurpation of power which need not be recognized. They also generally repudiated royal enactments which they considered discriminatory between groups of royal subjects. One may easily gauge the opening thus given to divergent interpretation under the medieval system of special corporate rights and duties. Two great Spanish rabbis taught that "if a king enacts a new law, even though he issue it for all [subjects], insofar as it is not part of the legislation of the early kings it is not valid law in the Jewish sense." Two other authorities, on the other hand, although likewise influenced by Spanish Jewish teachings, recognized the validity of such an enactment. But whether recognizing or rejecting a state or city ordinance, it was the rabbi who, by weighing its merits in strictly Jewish legal terms and invoking strictly Jewish precedents, made the ultimate decision.[5]

2. The Church

Christendom, of course, refused to acknowledge this ultimate supremacy of Jewish law and the sovereignty of the Jewish community. The status of the Jewish people was viewed as that of a subjected group of "serfs" belonging to either the Church or the Christian princes, whose very right of sojourn in a country depended upon the will of their masters. Some rabbis, too, recognized this dependence to the extent of drawing a distinction between the strictly delimited constitutional rights of the Jewish kings and the legislative freedom of the Gentile kings in all matters concerning their Jewish subjects. Neither Christians nor Jews ever contested the legality of the various decrees of expulsion, whatever else they may have done to have them rescinded. In Christian eyes, consequently, the validity of Jewish law was contingent upon its recognition by the legislation of each particular state. Pope and emperor, king, duke and baron were entitled to delimit, as they saw fit, the functions of the Jewish community, the operation of its laws and the activities of its officers. That there existed, nevertheless, a certain basic homogeneity in the entire fabric of medieval and early modern legislation concerning Jewish self-government is due not only to the force of tradition and the stubborn insistence of the Jews, but also to the uniform standards laid down by the Church.[6]

The Jewish question was often and hotly debated in ecclesiastical circles. To be sure, not all the innumerable utterances of popes, Church Fathers and teachers concerning Jews and Judaism have a bearing upon the Jewish problem in their day. From its inception, Christianity had to justify its departure from the mother religion. The arguments advanced in the difficult early stages of Christian propaganda were reiterated endlessly even after the victory had been won. By attacking the "Jewish perdition" or "perversion" and the "Synagogue of Satan," Popes Gregory I and VII, for example, had in mind Christian audiences more than they did serious measures against the Jews. As a matter of fact, through the endless variety of legal enactment, theological debate and extralegal episodes, there runs a thread of Church preachment of limited toleration of Jews in Christian society. Naturally, there were many shades of opinion among the popes (acting in their double capacity of spiritual heads of western Christendom and temporal rulers of the Pontifical State), ecumenical and provincial councils, bishops and Church philosophers. But with few exceptions, all agreed that professing Jews, living in a state of physical subjection and legal inequality so as outwardly to demonstrate the superiority of the new dispensation over the old, should be allowed to exist until the end of days. This compromise, subject to a multiplicity of practical solutions, had considerable effects upon Jewish self-government.

Every newly elected pope was greeted by the heads of the Roman Jewish community — in 1165 at the entry of Alexander III they are described as *stratores, scrinarii, judices cum advocatis* — with the scrolls of their Law. From Innocent II (1130) and Eugenius III (1145) to Gregory XIV (1590), it was customary for the pope to accept the scroll and to answer: "We praise and revere the Sacred Law . . . but we condemn your religious practices and your futile interpretation thereof . . ." Some popes (e. g., Leo X) emphasized this condemnation by dropping the scroll to the ground. The Jewish community, expecting from the tone of the answer a clue to the personal attitude of its new sovereign, sometimes prepared itself for the ordeal by public fasting and prayers. Shortly after installation, popes from Calixtus II (1119–24) on, with ever fewer exceptions, confirmed the privileges of Roman Jewry. Their bull, called by its beginning, *Sicut Judaeis* (a phrase dating back to Gregory I's epistle of 598), increasingly standardized in substance but subject to modifications in detail, was addressed primarily to Christians in Rome. Indirectly it served as an appeal for toleration to all Christendom. The following passages from Innocent III's bull of 1199 may be cited here:

Although Jewish perfidy is in many ways worthy of reprobation, nevertheless, because through them our own Faith is truthfully confirmed, they are not to be severely oppressed by the faithful . . . . Therefore, just as the Jews [*sicut ergo judaeis*] in their synagogues must not have the license to undertake anything beyond what the law permits them, so ought they not to suffer any prejudice in those rights which have been conceded to them . . . . We decree that no Christian shall use violence to force them to be baptized as long as they are unwilling and refuse . . . . Moreover, without the judgment of the authority of the land, no Christian shall presume to wound or kill them or rob them of their money, or change the good customs which they have thus far enjoyed in the place wherè they live. Furthermore, while they celebrate their festivals, no one shall disturb them in any way, by means of clubs and stones, nor exact from them enforced services except such as they have been accustomed to perform in the past. To counteract the wickedness and avarice of evil men in this respect we decree that no one shall dare to desecrate or reduce a Jewish cemetery, or for the sake of gain to exhume human bodies . . . . We wish, however, to place under the protection of this decree only those [Jews] who have not in any way ventured to plot the subversion of the Christian Faith.

Innocent IV added in 1247 the provision, likewise reiterated by his successors, that no one shall accuse the Jews "of using human blood in their religious rites."[7]

From the communal point of view this decree guaranteed freedom of worship, extended special safeguards to the synagogue and the cemetery and offered a measure of protection against forced conversions. The term "forced," to be sure, had many shades of meaning, and the baptism of minors without parental approval was especially often to envenom Jewish-Christian relations. The Jewish community itself soon had to assist in conversion. In 1278 Nicholas III introduced regular missionary sermons by Christian preachers before Jewish audiences, and before long Jewish communal leadership was made responsible for the attendance of a specified number of adult Jews and Jewesses. To add insult to injury, the fiscal exploitation of the community was climaxed by new imposts for the maintenance of houses of catechumens or prospective converts. The result was that, with each new conversion, the community "lost a taxpayer and acquired a pensioner."

The perennial question of new, tall, enlarged or ornate synagogues troubled the Church no less than it did its imitators under Islam. True, Gregory I, soon revered as the Great and the Saint, sharply reiterated the protective laws of the Theodosian Code against the destruction of synagogues and twice (591, 598) rebuked overzealous priests for such acts of lawlessness — an interesting contrast, indeed, to the theories expounded by St. Ambrose. But in view of the growing Christianization of Europe and the spread of Jewish settlements throughout the Continent, the disability to erect houses of worship in the new communities became of paramount importance. As a rule the Church, like Islam, was ready to condone a practice whose inevitability, once toleration had been granted, was obvious. Under the very eyes of the popes and the Roman inquisition, several new synagogues were built in the spiritual capital of Christendom. The famous Jewish lexicographer, Nathan b. Yeḥiel, erected there about 1100 both a new synagogue and a bath-house.[8]

The tenure of such structures, which were in defiance of established law, was extremely precarious, however. Honorius III, upon learning that the Jews of Bourges "have dared to build new synagogues," ordered the archbishop "to cause these synagogues to be destroyed." Local authorities who should try to shield them were threatened with severe ecclesiastical censure not subject to appeal (1221). In 1250 Innocent IV unqualifiedly condemned the "presumption" of the Cordovan Jews in building "a new synagogue of unnecessary height, thereby causing a scandal among faithful Christians and much harm to the Church of Cordova." In 1415, when anti-Jewish feeling, fostered by the preceding "holy war" and the disputation of Tortosa, ran high in Spain, Anti-Pope Benedict XIII issued a bull demanding, among other disabilities, that there be no more than one synagogue in each locality and that it should be neither vast nor sumptuous. This bull, subsequently restated in a royal decree of Ferdinand I of Aragon, paved the way for the conversion of many Spanish synagogues into churches. In Maqueda, near Toledo, the larger of two synagogues with its vineyeards, fields and olive-groves was munificently granted to its former rabbi who, upon embracing Christianity, had found himself without a job. The synod of Polish clergy, meeting at Piotrków in 1542, decided to ask the king for "an order to destroy the new synagogues, including those built in Cracow. While the Church tolerates the Jews in commemoration of the Savior's passion, their number ought not to increase." Sometimes, as in the case of Łuck in 1627–28, the local clergy obstructed the erection of a new Jewish house of worship, in contravention of a royal permit whose sole qualification was that "the height of the building shall not exceed that of the local churches." Two decades before the French revolutionary armies occupied Carpentras an attempt to enlarge the synagogue, then four centuries old, caused a general outcry. After a litigation extending over several years, during which the local bishop went so far as to complain that the interior decoration was unduly attractive, the Sacred Congregation in Rome ordered in 1784 that the synagogue be restored to its former size. On the whole, however, these chicaneries, although a source of constant friction and an additional strain on financial resources, hindered but slightly the free development of the autonomous Jewish community.[9]

Otherwise popes, councils and local clergy rarely interfered with the inner workings of the communal organs. It is a rather dubious source which tells us that Eugenius IV, in extending in 1442 the provisions of his Spanish bull to Italy, not only suppressed the Jewish administration of justice, but also forbade Jews to study their law, except insofar as it is incorporated in the Pentateuch. He would thus have gone beyond Justinian in meddling with matters of innermost Jewish religious concern. But these outbursts of intolerance were as sporadic and ineffectual as were the more dramatic decrees of expulsion from parts of the papal possessions in 1322, 1569 and 1593. Theoretically the popes claimed full jurisdiction over those Jewish religious practices which might in any way affect the orthodoxy of Christians. From this point of view, the spread of heresies within the Jewish community could have undesirable repercussions among its Christian neighbors. Eymeric who, in his handbook for inquisitors, greatly elaborated the principle of papal intervention, admitted, none the less, that the popes usually found it inopportune to exercise their right.[10]

As a matter of record, ecclesiastical courts rarely claimed jurisdiction over professing Jews. The flagellation and expulsion of a heretical Jew by the Roman inquisition in 1736 was quite exceptional. Where local clergy, interpreting freely the elastic regulations of Canon law, attempted to cite Jews before their courts for civil offenses, the secular authorities, acting in the self-interest of the state, immediately intervened. Only transgressions against the Christian faith as such, blasphemies against Jesus and the Virgin and missionary efforts among professing Christians, were the recognized subjects for the jurisdiction of the inquisitorial and other ecclesiastical judges. Suspicion of having aided a backsliding Jewish convert became a source of endless tribulation for individual Jews as well as for communal leaders, especially in periods of mass conversion and frenzied heresy hunting. The prosecution, in 1489–90, of many leading members of the community of Huesca for a series of such offenses revealed the precarious status of communal organs trying to steer a middle course between the duty of preserving their community and the fear of opposing the missionary interests of the Church. There were innumerable dubious cases of child conversion by such outsiders as nurses and servants without parental consent. Here the inner insecurity of the Church organs, confronted by many contradictory ordinances and teachings of canonists, made more arbitrary the persecution of Jewish abettors of alleged relapses. Among numerous incidents of this kind one, in 1784, attracted most widespread attention. Because an applicant for conversion informed the papal authorities in Rome that two of his kinsmen, boys aged ten and thirteen respectively, lived with their closer relatives in the ghetto, the demand was made that they instantly be delivered to the baptismal font. Not being able to locate them, papal officials imprisoned sixty other Jewish boys as hostages and subjected the communal chiefs to torture. Finally the two boys were forcibly baptized and the community of Rome severely fined for attempted resistance.[11]

These prosecutions, however severe, were overshadowed in Jewish communal life by Christian censorship of Jewish books for the avowed purpose of eliminating passages prejudicial to Christianity. Beginning with the burning of Maimonides' *Guide* by the ecclesiastical court of Montpellier in 1232 and the public auto da fé of the Talmud in Paris in 1244, Church organs arrogated to themselves ever increasing powers over Jewish letters. With the spread of printing, moreover, and the gradual development of the papal Index, the procedure of expurgating or entirely suppressing undesirable Jewish books became highly refined. Even then, however, the papal administration did not wish to assume full responsibility for the work of often unreliable "revisers." These censors, mostly recruited from among converts with a smattering of Hebrew knowledge, were frequently baffled by the complicated dialectics of rabbinic texts. They worked under pressure or with excessive speed — Domenico Hierosolymitano, the most prolific among them, claimed to have expurgated over 29,000 Hebrew printed books and manuscripts. Sometimes they pursued personal profit rather than the interest of the Church. Suspicion was rampant, and reiterated expurgation of a single book, as well as the imposition of penalties for possession of books which once had been passed, made ownership of Hebrew works of any kind precarious, often dangerous.

Little wonder that this type of censorship involved many Jewish communities, especially in Italy, in unpleasant and costly negotiations. It also induced them to institute a rabbinical pre-censorship of Hebrew books by the Jewish courts. The papal bulls of 1553–54, ordering all princes, bishops and cities to burn both the Palestinian and Babylonian Talmuds and to investigate carefully all other Hebrew books, were speedily followed by the memorable rabbinical assembly in Ferrara, which introduced a permanent Jewish book licensing system. Nevertheless, in the years 1731–53 there were no less than four large-scale confiscations of all Hebrew books in Rome. A papal bull of 1775 regulated, in great detail and under truly Draconian sanctions, the entire process of publication and distribution of Hebrew books, as well as their importation from abroad. More than once the Roman community had to turn to other Jewries for financial assistance. In one appeal, addressed in 1590 to the communities in northern and central Italy, the Roman elders urged, "if you have done so much to prevent a threatened expulsion, how much more ought you to do for the preservation of the sacred writings which are 'thy life, and the length of thy days.' "[12]

These vexatious policies of the Church, although a source of endless irritation, strengthened rather than undermined the communal control. The suppression of all heterodox deviation in practice or in literature was as urgently desired by the Jewish communal chiefs as by the Christian authorities above them. Communal responsibility for individual attacks on the dominant creed and for individual missionary ambitions enhanced the power of the leaders charged with prevention. More, the Church's insistent teachings and enactments, designed to segregate Christians from Jews and Jewish influences, presupposed the existence of a self-sufficient Jewish community, whose contacts with the outside world were limited to but a few, unavoidable business transactions. Even before its seizure of political power in the days of Constantine, the Church, through the Spanish council of Elvira (about 300), sharply condemned not only intermarriage and free sexual relations between Jews and Christians, but also simple conviviality. Subsequent provincial and universal councils, as well as popes, elaborated this principle in great detail, increasingly postulating actual physical segregation of the two groups. After the provincial councils of Narbonne and Oviedo (both meeting in 1050) had demanded that the Jews should not be allowed to live together with Christians, the universal Third Lateran Council in 1179 enacted for all western Christendom a general canon that Christians "who will presume to live with them be excommunicated." The provincial council of Breslau adopted a more specific resolution at least for the archdiocese of Gnesen (Gniezno):

> Since the Polish country still is a young plant in the body of Christendom, the Christian people might the more easily be infected by the superstitions and the depraved mores of the Jews living with them. In order that the Christian faith be more easily and quickly implanted in the hearts of the faithful in these regions, we strictly prescribe that the Jews inhabiting this province of Gnesen must not dwell indiscriminately among the Christians, but should possess contiguous or adjoining houses in a segregated location of each city or village. This should be so arranged that the Jewish quarter be separated from the common habitation of the Christians by a fence, a wall or a ditch.

Elevated by Paul IV in 1555 to an integral part of the papal program and elaborated in various minute ghetto ordinances such as those issued in 1602 in Padua, in 1603 by Cardinal

Borghese in Rome and in 1624 by Cardinal Aldobrandini in Ferrara, the separate, tightly shut and closely supervised Jewish quarters became the most effective substratum for the little Jewish "state within the state."[13]

The Church also insisted upon the superiority of the testimony offered in court by Christian witnesses over that of Jews. Its demands thereby were, if anything, more moderate than the complementary provisions of both the Jewish and the Muslim laws. Confronted by a paradoxical practice in many countries, which, for fiscal reasons, actually favored Jewish witnesses, the Third Lateran Council merely declared that "the testimony of Christians against Jews shall be accepted in all law-suits, since the latter make use of their own witnesses against Christians." The Council felt obliged to threaten with excommunication those judges who would give preference to Jewish testimony. Other ecclesiastical resolutions and enactments went much further and, in some cases, repudiated Jewish witnesses altogether. The more radical this repudiation, however, the stronger must have grown the conviction that litigations among Jews should be left entirely in the hands of Jewish judges acting in accordance with the provisions of Jewish law. In short, in order more effectively to keep Christians out of Jewish reach, the Church did everything in its power to develop an increasingly self-sufficient Jewish communal organism.

3. MEDITERRANEAN COUNTRIES

Unlike Islam, the western Church was not identical with the Christian state, and although Canon law greatly influenced the various legal systems, it did not enjoy automatic validity. Individual states were free to adopt as much of it as suited their own purposes and to reject the rest. They could also modify such acceptance or rejection under changed circumstances, varying pressures of interested groups or whims of individual rulers. There was, nevertheless, a certain basic pattern moulded by the fundamental views of the Church, particularly in the state's relations with the Jewish community. This is the less astonishing, since the entire fabric of medieval culture received its coloring from the uniform *Weltanschauung* of the Church and the sense of belonging to one universal body of Christ. When the acids of Protestantism, early capitalism and modern science dissolved that unity of Christian culture, state legislation concerning Jews underwent a sharp change. Before the Emancipation period, however, any Spanish or French Jewish community was much like one in England or Poland.

Within the general framework of medieval society the Mediterranean countries reveal some marked peculiarities in Jewish communal evolution, as they do in all other aspects of social and cultural history. Not only was the Byzantine Empire permanently outside the range of western Christendom, but also Italy, particularly its southern sector, southern France and the Iberian Peninsula differed in many ways from the northern lands in the opportunities they offered for the economic, political and cultural development of the Jewish community. The antiquity of the southern Jewish settlements which, in most regions, preceded and paved the way for the spread of Christianity; the continued traditions of Roman law and Roman institutions; the prolonged domination of vast areas by Muslims and Islam's permanent proximity to all the Christian lands in the South; the lesser development of feudalism — these and other factors had far-reaching effects upon the status of the Jew and his autonomous life. As late as 1402 the popes themselves treated the Jews of Rome as *cives Romani*, as citizens differing in some of their rights and duties from other citizenry, but an essential element of the political structure of the pontifical city.[14]

The Byzantine Empire, too, for all its frequent outbursts of extreme intolerance and its recurrent decrees of expulsion and enforced conversion, treated those Jews whom it allowed to live in its provinces essentially on the basis of the laws codified under the Christian Roman Empire. Concentrating in their office supreme religious and secular authority like the caliphs, the emperors in Constantinople were more ruthless in extirpating heresies and infidelity. But they also exercised greater liberty in adhering to the ancient traditions of limited toleration and, with certain serious restrictions, of fundamental civic equality. Despite the appropriation of the Jewish fiscal tax and later the *aurum coronarium* by the Roman Empire, Byzantium may not even have singled out the Jews as objects of special taxation. The sources are so few and equivocal that some investigators have denied the existence of any special Jewish tax such as was common under both Islam and western Christendom. This does not necessarily imply that the community had ceased playing a role as a tax-collecting agency for the state. It still could be, and apparently was, drafted for the task of gathering the general imposts from the Jewish citizens. It had long performed such services in Sassanian Persia, whose administrative machinery so greatly influenced the Byzantine system of government.[15]

The old crucial laws governing Jewish judicial autonomy, evidence in mixed Jewish-Christian litigations and the construction of new or enlarged synagogues, were generally upheld. True, in his recodification of Roman law, Justinian eliminated more than one-half of the nearly three-score provisions which are found in the Theodosian Code concerning Jews and Judaism. Thereby he abolished many ancient Jewish privileges respected even by his Christian predecessors. He omitted especially Theodosius the Great's sweeping assertion of 393 that "no law prohibits the Jewish faith." He repeated, none the less, the law of 398 allowing the Jews to repair to their courts as specially privileged tribunals of arbitration, further accentuating this privilege by basically altering the character of other courts of arbitration. In specific *Novellae* he also modified his original sweeping disqualification of Jewish witnesses in cases involving Christians (affirmed also, evidently with imperial approval, in the *Canons* of the African Church), by allowing them to testify for a Christian or for the state against a Christian. These discriminatory provisions, moreover, could not fail to strengthen the authority of the Jewish courts among Jewish parties who based their claims upon the testimony of Jewish witnesses or deeds.[16]

As a matter of principle, on the other hand, the Jews remained subjected to the jurisdiction of the general courts. After the establishment of the separate Jewish quarter in Constantinople under Theodosius II, the *strategos* of that quarter served as their supreme judicial officer. Under Manuel Comnenus (1143–80) they began to be "judged before every court in accordance with the laws." This change, curiously, seems to have been regarded by them as the bestowal of a favor, a sentiment understandable only in the light of the increasing neglect of Jewish civil law in Byzantine Jewry. Similarly, new synagogues were not legally tolerated in the Empire, but old ones were usually protected against popular violence. Such protection, particularly in the early period, may not always have been effective. John of Ephesus publicly boasted that during his mission in Asia he had converted seven synagogues into churches. The eastern Church, too, possessed in its Gelasian Sacramentary a special liturgical composition for the dedication of a church building which had previously served as a synagogue. Justinian's sweeping "concession" to the African church in 535 "that no synagogues be allowed to stand, but we wish that they be rebuilt in the fashion of churches," was neither extended to the other provinces nor emulated by his successors, however. Nor did his prohibition of a public celebration of Passover before the Christian Easter or his outlawry of the *deuterosis* permanently impair the autonomous life of Byzantine Jewry. In any case, a Babylonian gaon once approvingly cited a "distinguished court" in the land of Byzantium, and Benjamin of Tudela, traveling through the Balkans in the 1160's, found well-established communities in the capital as well as in many provincial cities. In southern Italy, then under Byzantine domination, Jews are recorded as exercising some sort of capital jurisdiction, whether or not recognized by state law. Christian complaints of this latitude, which sometimes affected them personally, shed a remarkable light on the life of the much-harrassed Byzantine communities. The antecedents of Moses Capsali's elevation to the post of *hakam-bashi* of Constantinople likewise give the impression that he held a somewhat similar post under Byzantine rule.[17]

When southern Italy, after a brief but significant Muslim interlude, reverted to western Christendom, it included many populous and affluent Jewish communities. Until the expulsions of 1492, 1510 and 1541 the Jews played a notable role in the economic and cultural life of these regions. In the crucial period of Norman domination, to be sure, the conquerors, needing assistance from local powers and especially the Church, often divested themselves of their fiscal and other rights in favor of bishops, feudal lords or cities. But these transfers did not necessarily imply the complete renunciation of royal overlordship. Even if specifically granted "for all time," they could be revoked. The Church of Palermo, after having obtained in 1210–11 such an "eternal" grant, gladly accepted, in 1215, its renewal for six years only. Nevertheless the eleventh and twelfth centuries marked a period of general decentralization of control over Jews throughout the kingdom. It was partially interrupted, but not checked under the strong rule of Emperor Frederick II. Only from the end of the fourteenth century on do we find the state making serious efforts to recover full jurisdiction over the Jewish communities through the appointment of a royal *baiulo generale* or *iudice universale* to protect and judge all Jews in the realm.[18]

The jurisdictional division which prevailed during preceding centuries, although introducing elements of instability and insecurity into Jewish life, also prevented uniformly excessive fiscal exploitation and outbursts of radical intolerance such as characterized the periods of unified control. The expulsions of 1492–1541 were, in many ways, the outgrowth of the same forces which had operated before in the direction of administrative centralization, as well as of the reaction thereto among burghers, clerics and nobles. To the end of the fifteenth century, occasional persecutions and regular fiscal exploitation were largely offset by many extensive privileges safeguarding Jewish rights as citizens (*cives*) and often placing them on an equal footing with the Christian burghers. As late as 1470 the community of Trapani obtained governmental approval of its statute and the order to the royal authorities that "the Jews ought to be treated... as are treated the Christians of that city." The same principle was proclaimed by the Viceroy in 1471 with respect to the Jews of Palermo. The Aragonese dynasty long protected also the autonomous functions of the community. Ferdinand I, in granting to the Jews permission to repair to state courts, specifically mentioned that this be done without prejudice to their own Jewish courts. By disqualifying converts from testifying in litigations involving Jews and Christians, and by rejecting, in 1463, the demand of the burghers of Bari for exclusion of Jewish testimony from general courts, he further upheld the principle of fair play in the administration of justice. The Aragonese rulers also allowed the Jews to construct "synagogues in every locality and to do everything else required by the observance of their law." In 1484 the king frustrated an attempt of the populace of Aversa to "reduce the *moscheta* [synagogue] of the Jews erected by Raphaele Perosino," probably without special ecclesiastical license. Privileges secured protection for and government non-interference in the free celebrations of the Sabbath and the Jewish festivals.[19]

Under the Aragonese dynasty, Naples and Sicily had thus come into the orbit of Spanish influence. Spain, as well as Portugal, with their even more pronounced Muslim antecedents, harbored the largest, economically most powerful and progressive and intellectually most alert agglomeration of Jews in medieval Europe. Here, too, Jewish autonomy at times achieved heights rivaled only by a few Muslim

lands or early modern Poland. The Spanish Jews, proudly
claiming for some communities an antiquity going back to
the first or second Jewish Commonwealth and thus incidentally repudiating all ancestral responsibility for the cruci-
fixion of Jesus, increasingly asserted independence of outside
leadership. The Christian rulers, on the other hand, often
justified favors extended to Jewish self-governing agencies
by the Jews' usefulness in the struggle against Islam. In
1342 Alfonso XI of Castile asked Pope Clement VI to
legalize a newly erected synagogue in Seville because "the
Jews are highly necessary, since they contribute to the
needs of the state and sometimes participate in the Christian expeditions against the Saracens, not fearing to expose
themselves to death."[20] Such arguments must have carried
weight with the popes who themselves sometimes preached
the toleration of Jews on the ground that the Jews should
be treated in Christian countries in the same way as one
wishes to see the Christians treated in heathen lands.

Alfonso XI's admission of the self-interest of the state in
the protection of Jewish communities strikes the keynote
for all medieval state legislation concerning Jews. Everywhere, in the northern countries even more than in the
southern, the Jews found themselves sooner or later inti-
mately attached to the royal power. Somewhat mislead-
ingly termed "serfs" of the king or of the royal treasury,
they were objects of special fiscal exploitation and a source
of substantial revenue much beyond their relative numbers. The kings, as a rule, zealously guarded what Pedro IV
of Aragon, in 1367, called "our property and our treasure."
To maintain and enhance this source of revenue, the kings
long encouraged Jewish immigration and discouraged emigration, sometimes to the extent of threatening would-be

emigrés with slavery or execution (Affonso IV of Portugal, John II of Castile, and others). The resolution adopted by the Jewish deputies of Aragon in 1354:

> to make every effort to obtain a privilege from our lord, the King, may His Majesty be elevated, to permit all the Jews living under his sceptre to trans-fer their residence from places in the realm and to localities belonging to the nobles or any other place they might choose — which right they have enjoyed from ancient times — and to revoke every [contrary] law hitherto promulgated,

failed to stem the growing restrictions upon the Jews' free-dom of movement largely motivated by fiscal exigencies. In 1291 Sancho IV of Castile concluded a treaty with James II of Aragon in which he pledged himself that "if a Jew or a Moor should arrive from your country to ours, we shall be bound to send him back to you with all his possessions as soon as you will let us know." The kings favored Jewish economic pursuits even at the expense of vested interests of Christian burghers or clerics, and long paid little heed to the Church's demand that Jews acquiring land from Christians continue to pay the customary eccle-siastical tithe. Able to threaten recalcitrant Jewish land-owners only with a rather ineffective boycott by Christians, the Church sometimes preached complete elimination of Jewish landholdings. In 1205 Innocent III severely, but futilely, rebuked Alfonso VIII of Castile for his failure, several apostolic letters notwithstanding, to compel the Jews to pay the tithe, and for his "granting them the liberty of acquiring even more extensive possessions." The Jewish communities of Aragon, clearly perceiving the nexus between their fiscal contributions and their general legal status, in 1354 petitioned the king not to mortgage to others his Jewish revenue. "Only if the communities pay their contributions directly to the royal treasury will they curry favor with the king and with his councilors and nobles."[21]

One of the main communal tasks consisted therefore in the collection of the royal revenue. Many extant tax lists show how deeply this fiscal administration of the community was woven into the entire governmental fabric of the Iberian Peninsula. In Sicily and Naples, Frederick II, the last Hohenstaufen emperor, although employing many Jews in the exploitation of general state monopolies, continued to place the burden of Jewish taxation upon the organized Jewish community. The same holds true of those Spanish and Portuguese rulers who, down to the eve of expulsion, still employed Jewish tax farmers and fiscal administrators for the country at large. The combined opposition of the Church and the cities was met by insincere promises, lame excuses (e. g. that Christian tax farmers were unavailable), or pointed refusals.

The rulers thus became deeply interested in strengthening the authority of the Jewish organs. They soon recognized that, although momentarily useful, informing, a perennial plague of minorities living in a hostile environment, introduced an element of instability and decomposition into the communal structure. Hence they repeatedly enjoined officials to lend to Jewish judges all possible assistance in the apprehension and execution of informers. In one case King Pedro III of Aragon actually forced two reluctant Jewish rabbis to sentence a hardened informer to death. On another occasion, Queen Leonore ordered the communal chiefs of Valencia to be excommunicated because they had yielded to official pressure in selecting their rabbi (1371). Portuguese law more generally prescribed that a Jew denouncing or summoning a fellow Jew before a Christian judge be fined the enormous sum of 1000 gold dublons. The chief rabbi was obliged to keep the offender in custody until the entire sum was paid. These extreme cases of respect for Jewish autonomy may easily be contrasted with government interventions in the inner management of the community which drew no reprimand of any kind. But such decrees and incidents, combined with the numerous special privileges extended to individual communities, reveal the general trend toward developing an efficient and orderly communal administration as part of the respective countries' government structure.[22]

Religious autonomy likewise went very far. Repeating the provisions of Roman and Canon law, many general and local privileges exempted Jewish parties from appearing in court on a Jewish Sabbath or holiday. "There are other days of the week sufficient to arrest and demand what may justly be demanded from them," state in unison the main medieval codes of Castile and Portugal. In some regions there could be no arrest of Jews for debts or tax arrears on Saturday. For even more obvious reasons, the archbishop of Toledo, moved by a petition of the Christian burghers of Brihuega, transferred the weekly fair in that city from Saturday to Wednesday (1386). Disregarding many canonical restrictions royal decrees and local custumals frequently extended far-reaching protection to synagogues and cemeteries, new as well as old. For instance, Infante Alfonso of Aragon, taking the Jews of Alcolea under his protection, decreed in 1320 that they could erect a synagogue in any part of the city, where they might "sing or recite their prayers in loud or subdued voices during the day or the night as they might deem fit." In his anti-Jewish crusade leading to the tragic outbreak of 1391 Ferrant Martinez often pointed to the existing synagogues as a sign of Jewish overbearance in the face of an old canonical prohibition. His contention that even the pope had no right to give a dispensation, although legally untenable, helped arouse the populace speedily to convert numerous synagogues into churches. In normal years, however, the authorities tolerated the erection of some of the finest architectonic monuments (e. g. the synagogue of Toledo by Samuel Abulafia in 1357) devoted to the worship of the Jewish God. Similarly, John I's prohibition for Castilian Jewry to recite the anti-heretical, and hence anti-Christian benediction of the 'amidah and his demand that it be expurgated from their prayerbooks (1380), were a wholly exceptional interference with the freedom of Jewish worship. As a matter of fact, the government had a direct stake in the orthodoxy of its Jewish subjects because of the manifold taxes on ritual meat and wine. Heresies within the Jewish group, moreover, were discouraged as symptoms of revolutionary disaffection with the established order. The thirteenth-century *Fuero real* of Castile included the provision that no Jew read or keep in hiding books attacking his own or the Christian religion. Prosecutions of heretical Jewry by the Inquisitorial courts were not altogether discouraged by the royal authorities. In 1352 Pedro IV merely reduced the amount of the fine to which an inquisitor had sentenced a Jew accused of the employment of magic to detect and recover stolen articles. The crime of sorcery, the king wrote, "is in various ways repudiated by our Catholic faith and, hence, is forbidden also by your law."[23]

Less uniform was recognition of Jewish judicial autonomy. The first Christian rulers of Aragon, Castile, Portugal and Sicily, confronted by a large and heterogeneous population, generally followed the principle, expressed in 1168 by Bishop Giovanni de Agello in his privilege for the city of Catania, that "the Latins, Greeks, Jews and Saracens shall be judged each according to his own law." While at times this principle could be interpreted to mean that litigations among Jews or crimes committed by Jews be adjudicated by a state or city magistrate in accordance with provisions of Jewish law, it normally led to recognition of a special Jewish judiciary. Some governments acquired a vested interest in Jewish courts by imposition of a special tax (called *bedinage* or *bedinaticum*) on fees collected in Jewish judicial proceedings. Legislative regulation vastly differed in details. Sometimes one monarch issued contradictory orders for different localities or in different years. On the whole, Jewish autonomy reached its peak in thirteenth-century Spain as the combined effect of the rapid "reconquest" of the Peninsula, the heterogeneity of the population and the absence of a powerful Christian middle class. Although even at that time royal arbitrariness occasionally led to interference with the due process of Jewish law, Jewish authority in both criminal and civil law was uncontested in principle. A first breach came when, in 1315, the Jews of Majorca were suddenly placed under the local civil law and judiciary. Before long Isaac bar Sheshet Profet, settling in North Africa, claimed that Majorcan Jewry had voluntarily abandoned the administration of Jewish civil law. Nevertheless, a large measure of Jewish criminal jurisdiction over acts "which are considered by Roman and Mosaic or Hebrew law as crimes or transgressions" committed by members of the community in and outside the *juderia* was still retained in Pedro IV's privilege of 1384 for the Jews of Majorca, although in 1377 the same ruler, apparently angered by the assassination of Joseph Picho, had curtailed similar rights long enjoyed by Barcelona Jewry. In 1380, King John I decreed for all of Castile that "no Jew of our kingdom, be he rabbi, elder, communal chief or any other person" shall undertake to adjudicate any criminal case. The growing anti-Jewish reaction throughout the Peninsula ultimately resulted in John II's decree of 1412 which, among other harsh provisions, contained the following article:

> That the communities of Jews and Moors in my kingdoms and dominions, shall not henceforth have among themselves Jews or Moors for judges, to decide civil or criminal causes that may occur between Jews or Moors; and I revoke any power that they hold in this matter from me or from the kings, my predecessors, through privilege or otherwise, and declare the same to be void. And I order that all causes, whether civil or criminal . . . shall be tried by the alcaldes of the cities, towns and places where they reside; but my pleasure is that in deciding civil causes, the said alcaldes shall observe the customs and regulations that have been observed among the said Jews and Moors, insofar as they appear authentic and approved for a long time.

This decree seems to have been allowed to sink into oblivion in the subsequent more tolerant period, but some of its severe restrictions were renewed, with even greater rigor, and extended to the entire united kingdom by Ferdinand and Isabella in 1476.[24]

In litigations between Jews and Christians judicial responsibilities and competences often strangely varied. In
twelfth-century Teruel the litigants chose a Christian and a
Jewish representative from among the native population;
two laymen of each faith served as a court of appeal. Later
such litigations were usually transferred to a higher state
official who, however, was often bound to apply the law of
the defendant. Sometimes, especially in Portugal up to
1473, both parties were expected to repair to the defendant's
ordinary court. It undoubtedly was for such use in general
courts, especially after 1380, that Pedro IV ordered the
communities of Barcelona, Gerona and Perpignan to prepare for him without delay a Catalan translation of the
Maimonidean Code. The rules of evidence were likewise
regulated differently in different times and localities. Frederick II of Sicily in 1310 could not understand why one of
his predecessors (Emperor Frederick II), in his privileges
for Trani and Syracuse, had declared all testimony of
Christians against Jews and *vice versa* as null and void. To
the Aragonese ruler this appeared as "the practice of a
depraved constitution or custom." But even in Aragon
Christian testimony alone was not regarded as sufficient to
convict a Jew, and witnesses of both creeds were usually
required to appear before the court. It was in the nature of
a reprisal for the alleged Jewish custom of excommunicating
Jews who testified against fellow Jews and for the annual
dissolution of vows (the legislator, evidently referring to
Kol Nidre, thinks that the prayer was recited on Passover)
that a royal decree of 1283 enabled Christian litigants of
Valencia to prove their contentions with the assistance of
but "two good and honest Christians." In Portugal, how-

ever, a Jew was generally required to submit evidence supported by at least one Christian, whereas a Christian could rely solely upon Christian witnesses. We also find exceptional regulations contesting the reliability of deeds issued by Jewish courts or notaries. In Portugal, in 1402, King John I forbade, on pain of capital punishment, the use of Hebrew in deeds issued by Jewish notaries. The penalty was modified by Affonso V to deposition from office and public flogging of the guilty notary, but the statutory insistence upon the exclusive use of "Latin and Portuguese" in deeds remained in force until the "Expulsion."[25]

Even in these cases, however, the medieval state rarely went the whole length of discriminating against testimony offered by "infidels," such as prevailed in both Jewish and Muslim law. Pedro I's refusal in 1351 to act upon a petition of the Cortes of Valladolid to subject the Jews to the jurisdiction of the ordinary courts because they "are a weak people and in need of protection and since, by appearing [with] their lawsuits before all the [ordinary] alcaldes, they would suffer great damage . . ." is typical of the attitude of the more benign and tolerant rulers throughout medieval Christendom. The superior state courts for Jews, like their frequent exemptions from general taxation, appeared to many Christians "as favoring the Jews and, in a sense, granting them a preference over Christians," as is freely admitted by a Portuguese king in the preamble to a privilege issued by him in behalf of these, his special subjects. This attempt at fair play, so astounding under the prevalent double standard of morals for adherents of the two faiths, can be explained only by its indispensability both to business and politics in a closed, highly integrated economy.[26]

4. NORTH OF THE ALPS AND PYRENEES

The position of the Jews in England, France, Germany and the Netherlands, although influenced by essentially similar social factors and Church doctrines, reveals a number of peculiar features and emphases. The differences between the northern and the Mediterranean Jewish communities do not quite coincide with the political, linguistic and geographic divisions which determined the course of European history. The Jews of southern France, for example, gravitated throughout the middle ages toward Spain rather than northern France. Their general culture, religious observance and community organization greatly resembled those of Castilian and Aragonese Jewry. On the other hand, northern Italy was increasingly drawn into the orbit of the Holy Roman Empire, and its Jewish communities maintained a lively intercourse with those beyond the Alps. Such Italian centers of learning, as Lucca, were the fountainheads of the famous Rhine academies. Being themselves offshoots of Palestinian rather than Babylonian Jewry, they impressed upon northern learning and ritual certain ancient traditions which greatly differed from those accepted by Babylonian-controlled Spanish Jewry. At the end of the middle ages the newly reconstructed North-Italian settlements received a larger influx of Germanic than of Sephardic Jews. In western Europe an even sharper line of demarcation must be drawn between the medieval period, in the proper sense, and the early modern period, the era of Resettlement. The former ended abruptly for the Jews with the expulsions from England (1290), from France (1394, followed by a few regional expulsions in the fifteenth century) and the Spanish Netherlands (1555). The resettlement of the Jews in these regions in the period of the Reformation and the Commercial

Revolution, mostly beginning with the arrival of scattered groups of Marranos who ultimately were legalized as communities of professing Jews, proceeded along such extraordinary lines that these groups in a large degree remained outside the range of the medieval community. It is characteristic of the persistence of Jewish folkways and organizational forms that this break in historic continuity did not result in a complete rupture with the established patterns of communal life.

On the whole, however, the northern countries and Jewish life in them were more typically "medieval" than the southern lands, where traditions of Roman and Muslim rule were constantly kept alive. Feudalism with its division of society into autonomous corporate groups was much more fully developed in the north. The influence of the primitive Teuton legal systems supplanted there more completely than even in Spain the theories and practices of Roman law. The question as to whether the status of the northern Jews was largely determined by the Teuton "law of aliens" is still subject to debate by scholars, but the "alien" character of the Jews was doubtless more pronounced in the north than in the more heterogeneous south. The Jewish corporate body, increasingly placed outside the framework of Christian society, became politically, more than in the south, a mere appendage of the royal power. It functioned economically primarily in the field of authorized moneylending — there was no such exclusive emphasis on the Iberian Peninsula, Sicily or the Balkans — at a price of large and frequent contributions to the chests of its respective, often mutually competing, sovereigns. Henry III's declaration in 1253, "that no Jew remain in England unless he do the King service, and that from the hour of birth every Jew, whether male or female, serve Us in some way," best describes the attitude of the powers that were. On the other hand, Archbishop Amulo's warning, as far back as 846, that the kings should not disregard the canonical regulations concerning Jews "because of the annual tributes and revenues paid" by the latter, sounded the keynote for deep apprehensions felt by many leading ecclesiastics.[27]

The growing prerogatives of Jewish moneylending, the ensuing economic exploitation of the masses by the Jews and the exploitation of the Jews by the kings, enhanced the respect for Jewish law and Jewish leadership. Notwithstanding the occasional prohibitions of Jewish "usury" (e. g. by Louis IX of France in 1254 and Edward I of England in 1275) inspired by canonical teachings, it was in the best interest of the Church to divert the opprobrium, in which was held the indispensable economic function of lending, to a group over which it claimed no jurisdiction. For centuries the Church opposed usurious transactions by Christian laymen and even ecclesiastics, but it was not always successful. The Nestorian patriarch, Dadhisho (about 520), practiced moneylending, and the clergy were among the chief moneylenders of twelfth-century Germany. By declaring that the Jews, who were not subject to Canon law, could make loans for profit, the Church automatically acknowledged their right to pursue economic careers in accordance with their own law. The effectiveness of tax collections likewise often depended on the control exercised by Jewish elders. That is why, like many other Christian kings, John II of France inserted in his charter of 1361 the provision that "the Jews and Jewesses may elect from among themselves one or two men in each town to impose the taxes upon them . . . and the aforesaid Jews or Jewesses, who would object or rebel, may be compelled to do so [pay the taxes] by the judicial authorities of the place under which they live." In England, King John and his successors chose to give entire control over Jewish tax collections to a Jewish *presbyter* appointed by themselves, but the authority of their appointees was not unchallenged. In 1241 Henry III was forced to convoke a Jewish parliament at Worcester, where more than one hundred representatives of the communities voted a heavy tallage of 20,000 marks. Similar attempts to concentrate Jewish tax collections for all Germany in the hands of a supreme Jewish officer appointed by the emperor, proved futile in the face of consistent Jewish opposition. The monarchs soon discovered that it was more to their advantage to entrust the task to elected chiefs enjoying the confidence of the taxpayers.[28]

The conception that the Jews belonged to the king fostered royal interest in every Jew and in his community. In 1286 Emperor Rudolf I ordered the Archbishop of Mayence to confiscate all property left behind by the Jews of Mayence, Worms, Spires, and so forth, who had emigrated "overseas" without permission. He also enjoined the Jewish chiefs of Mayence to lend assistance in the detection of such property. In France and Germany the dissolution into many feudal units obviously facilitated the movement of Jews from areas of greater to those of lesser fiscal pressure. To obviate competition, treaties were concluded between neighboring princes not to admit, or even to extradite, each other's Jews. Philip Augustus concluded such a treaty with Count Thibaut of Champagne in 1198, in the same year in which he decided to readmit Jews to his possessions. In the renowned convention of Melun of 1230 (1233) Louis IX severely prohibited Jewish emigration or removal within French territory.

"No one in the entire Kingdom," the king ordained, "shall be able to retain a Jew of another lord. Wherever a master shall find his Jew, he may freely seize him like his own serf, no matter how long the Jew might have dwelt under the dominion of another lord or in another kingdom." Louis IX further reinforced this convention by a series of treaties with individual barons. King Wenceslaus' treaty with the Swabian cities of 1385 provided for reciprocal extradition of Jews. Similar arrangements were made between Bohemia and Austria in 1360. To uphold the authority of the Jewish community, many local governments nevertheless cooperated with the Jewish chiefs whenever they wished to excommunicate and thereby economically ruin a member, or to banish him outright. The community also enjoyed far-reaching theoretical privileges, and broader ones in practice, with respect to the admission of new members. In his charter of 1361, John II of France promised to respect decrees of banishment issued by two rabbis and four elected chiefs, and not to allow royal judges or officials to inquire into the reason for these sentences. He demanded, however, in compensation for the loss thus sustained, that the community pay 100 Florentine guilders for each banished person, and that the latter's entire property be forfeit to the Crown. Confiscation, compensation or both are provided for in other decrees of the kings of France, England and other lands. Occasionally, individual Jews obtained charters exempting them from communal jurisdiction and insuring them against excommunication. Such an exemption, granted to one, Muschmann, by Frederick III in 1467, was the outgrowth of the imperial authority to suspend all decrees of excommunication. Frederick's successor, Maximilian I, further delimited the authority of the Jewish leaders to excommunicate fellow-members (1518). Few governments, however, not even that of France before 1394, went to the extreme of forbidding all bans by Jews, such as was postulated by the Parliament of Paris in 1374.[29]

Royal overlordship implied that the property not only of expatriate Jews, but also of those who died without heirs should devolve upon the king. What is more, since conversion to Christianity withdrew the Jew from the class of royal "serfs," the law frequently called for the confiscation of each convert's property. The Third Lateran Council vigorously protested against such discouragement of conversion. "If any, under divine inspiration, turn to the Christian faith, they should by no means be excluded from their possessions, since those who are converted to the faith ought to be in a better condition than before they adopted the faith." But a whole century was to pass before Edward I of England would, in 1280, decree that, for a period of seven years, only one-half the property be "given towards the maintenance of the poorer sort, who resided in the house of converts," and another century before Charles VI of France would agree not to despoil converts of their goods at all (1392, 1393). These were timely decrees, indeed, since only a few years after their promulgation the Jews were expelled from the two countries, leaving behind considerable remnants of those who preferred conversion to exile. As late as 1704, however, an English visitor to the Papal city was shocked to find the original "Scandalous Law" still in operation under the evidently flimsy excuse "that their estates being ill-acquired by usury, they cannot in conscience enjoy them." The Jewish community as such rather welcomed punitive laws against renegades, but undoubtedly resented the appropriation by the Crown of all heirless estates. It may be assumed, however, that either the absence of identifiable heirs was extremely rare — Maimonides in his *Code* completely discounts such an eventuality among Jews — or that the communal leaders found ways and means of evading the law.[30]

Jewish communal life in western and central Europe was regulated, with an infinite variety of detail, by the various imperial, royal, ducal, episcopal and municipal privileges extended to individuals or communities. From the Frankish Empire had come down a tradition of respect for Jewish autonomy in religious matters, which often extended to other domains of communal life. More complicated were the problems arising from business and social contacts between Jews and Christians. Here, too, except for fiscal exploitation, or rather, perhaps, because of it, we find a general trend toward fair play and the safeguarding of certain elementary principles of justice. The following provisions of Henry IV's 1090 privilege for the Jews of Worms which, confirmed by Frederick I in 1157, was extended to all Germany by Frederick II in 1236, well illustrate the protection extended the Jewish community by the Holy Roman Empire down to its extinction in 1806:

> Art. 1: Since we wish that in all judicial matters they should have to turn to us alone, we order, by virtue of our royal authority, that no bishop, chamberlain, count, bailiff, nor anyone else, except the person elected by themselves from their midst, shall presume to treat with them or against them in any matter or in any judicial proceeding. Only the person whom, in view of their belonging to our treasury, the emperor, following their own election, had placed at their head [shall be entitled to do so].

Art. 11: If a Jew should have a controversy with a Christian, or a Christian with a Jew, each shall, as the subject may require, institute proceedings and prove in accordance with his law. Just as any Christian may prove through his own public oath and that of a Christian and a Jewish witness that the guarantors placed by him in favor of the Jew have fulfilled [their duty], so may also the Jew through a public oath taken by himself, one other Jew and a Christian prove that the guarantors placed by him in favor of the Christian have fulfilled [theirs]. He shall be forced to do no more by either the plaintiff or the judge.

Art. 14: If the Jews should have among themselves a litigation or a matter for judicial decision, they shall be judged by their own peers and not by others. If anyone of them should desire to conceal the truth of what transpired among them, he shall be forced to confess the truth by the man who is their bishop [*episcopus*]. Should they, however, be incriminated in a major law-suit, they may bring the matter before the emperor, if they so desire.

Some time before 1242, England, as subsequently Majorca, joined Byzantium in subjecting Jews to general courts even in controversies with fellow-Jews. With these exceptions, however, European countries were, as a rule, satisfied to regulate litigations between Jews and Christians and such phases of criminal law in which the state, because of its responsibility for public order, had a direct interest.[31]

The enormous diversity of local legislation almost exhausted all theoretical possibilities in adjusting mixed Judeo-Christian law-suits. We find here the application of the ancient principle, *actio sequitur forum rei*, whereby a Jewish defendant could be sued only before a Jewish court.

This principle prevailed, as we have seen, in Worms; in
Spires, where the privilege of 1084 prescribed that the
authority of the bishop or his chamberlain might be invoked
only when the Jewish archisynagogus should be unable to
adjust a controversy; in Cologne after 1331; and in England
until the early 13th century. Another method was to let
both parties select as judges an equal number of coreligionists, these joint courts deciding by majority vote. Such a
court of *legales Christiani et Judaei* is recorded, for instance,
in England in 1204, in Würzburg after 1412 and in Augsburg
until 1436. Where general courts had exclusive jurisdiction,
the Christian burghers, naturally enough, wished to arrogate
it to their own city magistrates. Only few cities, however
(Paris in 1388, Strasbourg after 1263, Frankfort after 1337,
Nuremberg from 1331 on, Augsburg after 1436 and Worms
after 1406), succeeded in wresting such concessions from
their sovereigns. As a rule, the sovereign himself, or some
other high state official, was called on, since he was less
suspect of bias. In almost all cases, moreover, the prince
claimed appellate jurisdiction. In some localities, finally,
a special Christian *judex Judaeorum* was appointed by the
ruler, sometimes, as in Ratisbon, after nomination by the
Jewish community. This official's Christian biases were
expected to be counterbalanced by the state's interest in
the welfare of its Jewish taxpayers. Such justices of the
Jews existed in England; in France, except from 1291 to 1361
and for a few years before the expulsion of 1394; in Meissen
and other localities. In England, finally, the Exchequer of
the Jews had a special judicial section to adjudicate litigations arising from Jewish loan-contracts, fines, tallages,
etc.[32]

An enormous variety of laws regulated evidence in mixed litigations. Ordeals by fire and water or by arms were gradually eliminated. In the few regions where they were still admitted, the Jew was often to choose a Christian substitute, since judicial combat between members of different faiths might evoke the impression that the two Gods were also in combat. While Justinian's total disqualification of Jewish witnesses against Christians found but few emulators in the West (e. g., Louis IX in 1270, citing the *Code of Justinian*), several provincial Church councils, in contrast to the moderate demands of the universal Third Lateran Council, called for such discrimination. In England, on the other hand, in the interest of the Crown, Jewish moneylenders were favored against their non-Jewish debtors. To put an end to the constant recriminations, special "chirograph" offices were ultimately established in 1194 in six or seven cities. Here all loan-contracts were duly registered under the supervision of "two lawyers that are Christian and two lawyers that are Jews, and two legal registrars." Such evidence was considered final. Accustomed to innumerable forgeries even of state papers, however, the medieval mind was not easily reconciled to such preference of deeds over the testimony of living witnesses. Innocent III voiced, in 1205, to Philip Augustus of France a rather widespread grievance that the Jews "are given more credence because of the document which the indiscreet debtor had left with them through negligence or carelessness, than are the Christians through the witnesses produced." There was, of course, also ample opportunity for local legislators either to accept, with or without limitations, or to repudiate deeds issued by Jewish courts or notaries.[33]

5. The Resettlement Areas

The legal status of the Jewish communities in central and western Europe, as sketched here on the basis of medieval sources, remained basically unchanged in the early modern period in those regions where historic continuity was safeguarded by the more or less uninterrupted presence of Jews and by the continued validity of the medieval enactments, insofar as they had not been subjected to specific abrogation or modification. A new, wholly unprecedented, situation, however, confronted both the Jews and their Christian rulers in those western European areas where the Jewish settlements had been completely eliminated through successive decrees of expulsion and where, under the changed conditions of the Commercial Revolution and the early modern state, individual Jews were gradually readmitted under the guise of "Neo-Christians." The governments were primarily interested in the economic function of these Marranos, whom they were ready to treat as favored resident aliens and whose religious convictions were of little concern to them. The new arrivals, too, although often sufferers for their real faith, had long learned to conceal it and seldom wished to make of it a public issue. Hence the manifold problems of worship would probably have been left in abeyance by the respective administrations were it not for the coincident Reformation and Wars of Religion which made the profession of faith, attendance at Church services, and so forth, matters of urgent general concern. The sectarian clashes within the Christian Church thus deeply affected the position of the nascent and struggling Jewish communities in western Europe.

As in many other respects, Holland, emerging after the

Treaty of Utrecht in 1579 as a revolutionary political entity, could more readily afford to break with its past and embark upon a new policy toward the Jews. Even while still part of the Spanish Netherlands, the country had admitted a considerable number of refugees from the Spanish Inquisition. Although the agitation for the exclusion of Marranos had been quite vigorous under Charles V and culminated, despite the protests of the burghers of Antwerp, in the orders of expulsion of 1549–50, numerous individual Jews persisted under the guise of pious Christians. The liberation of Holland and the then revolutionary principle, proclaimed by the Treaty of Utrecht (Art. XIII), that no one be persecuted for religious belief, made it possible before long for overtly professing Jews to settle in Amsterdam. From 1597 on, regular groups of Portuguese Jews established themselves in the city. In the course of less than a quarter-century, three different congregations began functioning side by side, to be united in 1639. A Jewish burial ground, established in 1602 in Groet near Alkmar, because the Amsterdam authorities refused Jewish applications for a cemetery within their jurisdiction, was later transferred to nearby Ouderkerk (1614). For a time, Jewish funeral processions had to pay a special impost to every church by which they passed and were often subjected to chicanery and molestation by the population and local authorities. But in 1618 the government legalized the Ouderkerk cemetery and freed the Jewish community from the burdensome Church tax. It demanded only that the Jews bury their dead "in all quietness" and without public ceremonies.[34]

These government acts, however, did not imply any recognition of the legality of Jewish worship. In fact, the

sectarian controversies in the city of Amsterdam resulted
in repeated petitions by the oppressed "Remonstrants," or
the followers of Arminius, which contrasted the toleration
of Jews with the intolerance overtly practiced by the authorities toward Catholics and other dissidents. Yielding to
that pressure, the government actually prohibited Jewish
public worship in 1612. The Council of the Reformed Church
continued to denounce the Jews to the authorities, as when
in 1614 it informed the burgomasters that the Jews "possess
a school and a synagogue, perform circumcisions, keep
Christian servants and tempt Christians." But Jews continued to assemble quietly for private worship, and Rabbi
Abraham b. Joseph ha-Levi, commenting on the situation
in 1616, described prevailing practice as one approximating
liberty of conscience. "One must merely refrain from making
it obvious in public that one belongs to a religion different
from that of the rest of the inhabitants." Indeed, the
municipality of Amsterdam, in its petition of 1617 in behalf
of the Remonstrants, once emphasized that toleration had
been extended "even to the Jews who deny Christ, whom
the petitioners regard as their only Savior." These controversies led in 1615 to the appointment of a committee,
consisting of the Burgomaster of Amsterdam, Reinier van
Pauw, and the young but already prominent jurist, Hugo
Grotius, to review the entire status of the Jews. The two
commissioners submitted independent reports, that written
by Grotius being the more liberal. While denying that the
Jews were more privileged than the Catholics, Grotius
submitted a *reglement* of 49 articles providing among other
matters for the free exercise of Jewish worship and for the
employment of Jewish notaries for services exclusively on
behalf of Jews. The government, after due consideration,

refrained from issuing a nation-wide law, leaving it to individual municipalities to regulate the affairs of Jewish communities. Amsterdam soon took fairly liberal action. In 1622 it permitted the Portuguese Jews to use their own language in performing marriage ceremonies, provided that each marriage was subsequently confirmed in the City Hall in the presence of two city officials and a secretary. After unification of the community in 1639, moreover, a new statute, which will frequently be referred to below, gave extensive jurisdiction to the communal leaders. This regulation was officially confirmed by the city and thus given the authority of a municipal ordinance. It was this far-reaching cooperation of the municipal authorities, emulated in other cities of Holland, which subsequently enabled the Jewish communal leaders to rule their constituencies with an iron hand. These developments in the mother country affected also the status of the Jewish community in Holland's American colonies, although for specific local reasons the Jews of both Brazil and New Amsterdam were officially denied the right of public worship. In Surinam, however, the West India Company, in the privilege addressed to David Nassy in 1659, specifically granted the Jews "liberty of conscience and the public exercise thereof in synagogue and school, in accordance with the usage of these people in the city of Amsterdam."[35]

In England the Marranos who had gathered before the Cromwellian era, including the fairly numerous group of Elizabethan London, seem to have worshiped their Jewish God, if at all, furtively and in complete secrecy. Almost all of them continued to attend Catholic services in the chapels of the Spanish and Portuguese embassies, even though rumor had it that at one time the Portuguese ambassador himself was a Marrano. In the days of Cromwell, however, utilitarian considerations arising from the suspicions often aimed at Catholic Spaniards as conspirators against the safety of the kingdom, combined with the dramatic intervention of Menasseh ben Israel to inspire some neo-Christians to profess Judaism publicly. They soon organized the first more or less regular Jewish congregation to function in the British Isles since 1290. This congregation acquired in 1657 a house of worship at Creechurch Lane, in part replacing the private oratories theretofore used as the sole places of gathering. It also purchased a Jewish burial ground at Mile End. Some prominent members, to be sure, continued to pray in their private chapels. We have the deposition of an inquisitorial witness that in 1658, "upon several occasions he saw the said Don Antonio Ferdinando de Carvajal holding Jewish rites and ceremonies in a back room of the house where he lived." Before long, however, Carvajal seems to have loaned to the synagogue his two scrolls of law which his widow, Donna Esther, subsequently sold to the congregation for £30 (1670). These transactions clearly indicate the growing authority and unity of the young congregation named *Saar asamaim*. By 1703 its leadership felt strong enough to outlaw any rival organization of Spanish-Portuguese Jews in London and its suburbs, and to decree that if "any person or persons of what quality soever, that shall intent to divide this Union, by separating themselves to say Prayers with Ten in any place without the Synagogue, Althou it be not with the Title of making a new One incurs Immediately In Herem."[36]

The mere fact of the establishment of a communal synagogue and cemetery, however, did not signify public recognition. The Jewish leaders apparently derived their courage to defy existing law only from an obviously erroneous interpretation of the implications of their petition of March 1656 to Cromwell. In this sense one may, perhaps, say, as does one modern investigator, "that these proceedings — albeit discreetly conducted — were authorized and *publici juris.*" That the Jews were, however, well aware of the precariousness of their new institution and of the continued need of secrecy, may be clearly deduced from the well-known report of Revd. John Greenhalgh, written in 1662, about the great difficulties he had in obtaining admission to the synagogue, which was "strictly kept with three doors one beyond another." This vigilance was somewhat relaxed in the following year and Samuel Pepys seems easily to have gained admission for himself and two friends. The synagogue was speedily becoming a London curiosity. Jewish leaders, however, continued to look with misgivings upon visitors, whose going and coming added little to the decorum of the services, and in 1665 ordained that thenceforth no member should bring with him any ladies, nor rise from his place to meet them, nor make room for them, nor introduce any gentlemen without the express sanction of the *Mahamad.*[37]

Jewish apprehensions were fully justified. Stirred by the controversy aroused by Menasseh ben Israel's petition, anti-Jewish opinion was kept alive by the most fantastic rumors concerning the new Jewish houses of worship. A few months after the opening of the synagogue at Creechurch Lane, the Earl of Monmouth reported to his "deare Nan" that "the Jews' mouths, though not their eyes, are to be opened; whoe I do hear, are to have two sinagogs allowed them in London, whereof St. Paul's to be one." Especially after the passing of the Conventicle Act in 1664, the Jewish leaders were often threatened with prosecution by high officials. Charles II's favorable reply to a Jewish petition of August 1664 only partly clarified the issue and when, in 1670, the House of Commons discussed the position of the dissidents, it decided:

> that a Committee be appointed to inquire into the causes of the growth of Popery; to prepare and bring in a bill to prevent it, and also to inquire, touching the number of the Jews and their Synagogues, and upon what terms they are permitted to have their residence here and report it with their opinions to the house.

The Parliamentary Committee never reported on the Jewish question, but with the country becoming ever more conscious of it, the anti-Jewish faction made use of the cancellation of the Declaration of Indulgence in 1673 to bring about prosecution of the Jewish elders. The latter were indicted of a riot, for meeting together for divine services, and the London Grand Jury returned a true bill. They were saved only by the direct intervention of the king who ordered the Attorney General to stop the proceedings.[38]

These royal interventions of 1664 and 1674, gave a respite to the harassed elders but by no means legally established the rights of the community. In fact, under Charles' successor, James II, Parliament altogether contested the dispensing power of the Crown. James II, nevertheless, followed in his brother's footsteps. When, in 1685, forty-eight Jews were charged with recusancy and condemned to the enormous penalty of £20 a month for non-attendance at church services, the king, by a formal Order in Council, instructed the Attorney General to stop all proceedings, "His Majesty's intention being that they should not be troubled on this account but quietly enjoy the free exercise of their religion, whilst they behave themselves dutifully and obediently to his government." Neither did the famous Protestant Toleration Act of William and Mary (1688) in any way promote the legality of the Jewish community. The ambiguous status of the community, based upon repeated royal decrees of *nolle prosequi*, remained unaffected even by the gradual extensions of the Toleration Act to Catholics and Unitarians (1778–1832). Only from 1846 on was the Jewish community formally included in its provisions. Combined with the gradual repeal (1844–46) of many clauses in the Uniformity Acts and of the Laws of Recusancy, this inclusion finally established the legality of the Jewish communal organization. Curiously, Jewish leadership showed little concern about these legal uncertainties during the century and a half from James II to Victoria. "The synagogue was always open; its worshipers were not persecuted, and a considerable and increasing Jewish community gradually grew up both in London and the principal commercial centers. Every year the position became more secure, and premature attempts at legislation would have only endangered it." The absence of government regulation, indeed, seems to have interfered little with the effective communal control exercised by the elders on the basis of stringent, self-imposed rules.[39]

This equivocal position was naturally reflected in the British provinces and colonies. For many decades there was no other community on the British Isles, that of Portsmouth, probably the second oldest in England, being established no earlier than 1746. It was speedily followed by those of Plymouth (1752), Bristol (1754), Canterbury (1760), Cambridge (1774–78) and other cities. The situation was somewhat different in the British colonies in the New World. The earliest Jewish arrivals on the North American continent

appeared in force in then Dutch New Amsterdam (1654).
Coming from other Dutch colonies, they wished to worship
in the accustomed way and generally to develop community
life along accepted Dutch lines. But they encountered
considerable difficulties in obtaining permission for a burial
ground and public worship. In fact, one early settler,
Abraham De La Simon, was arraigned on a double charge
of having "kept his store open during the sermon [on a
Sunday] and sold by retail." In 1656 they finally obtained
a general decision of the Directors of the West India Company in Holland that they might enjoy in New Amsterdam
"the same liberty their nation enjoyed in Holland included
all the civil and religious privileges." The Directors soon
qualified the latter provision, however, by demanding that
they "be at liberty to exercise this religious worship in all
quietness within their houses."[40]

When the British took New Amsterdam and changed its
name to New York, the laws of Britain assumed validity.
To be sure, in the instructions issued by James, the Duke
of York, to Governor Andros in 1674, the latter was to

> permit all persons of what Religion so ever quietly to
> inhabit within ye precincts of yor jurisdiction wthout
> giving y^m any disturbance or disquiet whatsoever for
> or by reason of their differing opinion in matter of
> Religion: Provided they give noe disturbance to y^e
> publique peace nor doe molest or disquiet others in ye
> free exercise of their religion.

In several documents of the period, moreover, Judaism
is specifically mentioned among religions practiced in the
country. As late as 1685, when the Jews of New York applied
to Governor Thomas Dongan "for liberty to exercise their
religion," however, the Mayor and Common Council, to

whom the governor referred the petition, decided that public worship is tolerated by act of Assembly only for those "that profess faith in Christ, and therefore the Jews' worship not be allowed." This decision, may have been invalidated by a repetition of the clause of 1674 in new instructions to Dongan issued in 1686 by James, now King of England. In any case, it did not prevent the Jews from quietly maintaining a congregation. Apart from a general reference to the "separate meetings" of Jews, as well as of Quakers and Labadists in 1682, and the mention, in two reports of 1692, of the maintenance by various sects in New York, including Jews, of one "church" each, we have the important evidence of 1695, when Chaplain John Miller noted on his map of New York a synagogue on Beaver Street. The Shearith Israel Congregation on Mill Street was soon in full operation. Located in a private house owned by a Christian it was designated as "the Jews' Synagogue" in a deed of 1700. By 1705–6, a set of "Wholesome Rules and Restrictions" was adopted by the Elders to "Preserve Peace, tranquillity and good Government amongst y^m and those after them."[41]

With even greater ease the Jews pursued their independent communal career in Newport, R. I., which, in the course of the eighteenth century, developed into the largest Jewish community in the western Hemisphere. The first Jews seem to have settled there in 1658, and before the turn of the century opponents, such as Cotton Mather, were speaking of the city as "the common receptacle of the convicts of Jerusalem." Roger Williams, who had long argued for the readmission of the Jews to England, pleaded also for liberty of worship in the American colonies. "All these consciences (yea, the very consciences of the papists, Jews, etc. . . .) ought freely and impartially to be permitted their several respective worships and what of maintaining them they freely choose." Unhampered by legal restriction, therefore, the Jews of Newport seem to have organized a regular congregation soon after their arrival and to have acquired a burial ground in 1677. In the British West Indies, especially Barbados and Jamaica, Jews settled in large numbers and organized full-fledged communities. In Barbados, where they were officially admitted in 1655, they soon established the congregation *Nidḥe Israel* which, from its inception, tended toward the Spanish-Portuguese congregation in London. Although its first rabbi came from Amsterdam, its leadership subsequently depended largely on the London *Mahamad*. Curiously, on the occasion of an anti-Jewish riot in 1739, the synagogue was "pull'd down" and an unusual oath *more judaico* was adopted by the courts. In Kingston, Jamaica, the synagogue was dedicated in 1684, apparently without causing any public reaction. Here the Jewish elders were even in charge of the collection of state taxes from their coreligionists.[42]

In France, too, the incoming Neo-Christians were long forced to profess their religion in strict secrecy. Whatever communal life they had was completely devoid of legal approval. Even when, through annexation, France acquired Alsace-Lorraine and thereby took over many old and populous Jewish communities, the government still refused recognition to the growing groups of Jewish settlers in the other provinces. In Bordeaux, speedily developing into the main southern center of Jewish life, the Spanish-Portuguese community by 1734 possessed seven synagogues (in addition to a place of worship of the Avignonese Jews). In these institutions, according to a contemporary government report, they exercised their ritual in freedom and security, and even with ostentation. But the synagogues were in no way recognized by public law. Certain implications of several acts of government in the course of the eighteenth century, however, gradually removed the stigma of illegality. In the years 1706–52, for example, the government permitted newly composed Hebrew prayers to be recited on various patriotic occasions and to be published as part of the Jewish ritual. The aforesaid, rather biased report of 1734 also took cognizance of the fact that, since 1705, the Jews had ceased to be married according to Catholic rites, which theretofore they had used at least after being married by a rabbi, and pointed out that for many years past they had failed to present newly born children to the baptismal font but had them publicly circumcised. By 1728, moreover, they had been allowed to acquire a cemetery where "they perform their interments publicly, often in day time. When they fear that the populace might insult them, they arrange for an escort of an officer of the guard and soldiers." In submitting this anti-Jewish report to the government, De Boucher, intendant of the city, suggested that

> the King could without difficulty order the destruction of all synagogues and the prohibition for all Jews of whatever tribe to resettle here. As a result it will not be permitted to the Jews to congregate for worship under any excuse whatsoever, under the sanction of their expulsion from the realm, the confiscation of their property and even corporal punishments.

Although Chancellor D'Aguesseau approved of Boucher's proposals there is no evidence that drastic measures were carried out. As before, the Jews continued to pursue their communal activities, the government itself intervening in the disputes between the Portuguese and Avignonese

congregations and in 1760 approving a revised communal
ordinance for the former. In 1761 the Jews were given
permission to close shops and refrain from participation in
National Guard exercises on their Sabbath. In 1776, finally,
almost on the eve of the French Revolution, they were given
full communal recognition in the *lettres patentes* of King
Louis XVI.[43]

Basically similar were the conditions in the other communities founded in southern France by Neo-Christians, such
as those of Toulouse, Bayonne (St. Esprit) and Peyrehorade,
except that in the latter they were allowed to acquire a
cemetery as early as 1628. In Paris the legal status of the
community, as well as of its individual members, was more
precarious. Coming from both the Sephardic and Ashkenazic
regions, the few hundred Jewish settlers, living at best on
more or less temporary permits, succeeded in establishing
a number of private communal institutions in the course
of the eighteenth century. But wherever legal recognition
was required, the progress was extremely slow. Not until
1780 did the Sephardim of the capital obtain the right to
acquire a cemetery, their Ashkenazic brethren emulating
them in 1785. In contrast thereto, the communities not only
of Alsace-Lorraine, but also of Savoy, after their annexation
to France, continued to enjoy the full legal recognition
accorded to them by their former sovereigns. The sweeping
decree issued by the Duke of Savoy in 1648 retained its
uncontested validity to the days of the Revolution:

> We permit them the application in all Our States of
> their Hebrew ceremonies, rites, laws, customs and
> precepts, provided they inform thereof their conserva-
> teur. We also allow them to maintain a synagogue
> each in Nice and Villefranche [Villafranca], and to

> observe therein all their Hebrew ceremonies, precepts, rites and customs .... We forbid anyone to insult, oppress, molest or use violence against them, under the penalty of our displeasure .... [44]

In the French West Indies, on the other hand, an initial policy of toleration soon gave away to complete exclusion, moderated only by the persistence of occasional clandestine settlements. In Cayenne it was the Dutch West India Company which, before transferring the island to the French in 1664, insisted upon the maintenance of Jewish rights. The French had to pledge themselves that the Jews "will be given protection and assistance so that they may enjoy their possessions and property and freely exercise their religion." Since most Jews seem already to have departed for Dutch Surinam, this treaty apparently had little practical effect. In the other colonies, too, especially Martinique, after initial difficulties had been overcome, Colbert's liberalism, maintained by his mercantilist convictions that Jews would ultimately enhance the productivity of these islands, prevailed for a time. In 1671 a royal decree, counter-signed by the famous statesman, ordered the governor of Martinique and the other American islands

> to see to it that they [the Jews] enjoy the same privileges as those held by the other inhabitants of the said islands, and that they be allowed full liberty of conscience, only taking such precautions as may be necessary to prevent the exercise of their religion from causing any offense to the Catholics.

The latter, however, and especially the powerful Jesuit order, readily took offense and constantly agitated for suppression of the Jewish community. Their recriminations were reinforced in 1680 by the observation of the new governor, De Blénac, that "it seems that commerce is sufficiently established and matters generally in such a shape that they [the Jews] are not needed." These considerations induced the royal government to issue in 1683 a regular decree of expulsion affecting all Jews in the French islands of the New World. Reiterated in 1685, it prevented any legal recognition of a Jewish community until the Revolutionary era. Although, in the course of the eighteenth century, a fairly large number of Jews reappeared in the islands, some attaining positions of prominence, Paris refused more than *de facto* toleration. As late as 1776, it rejected the petition of Bordeaux Jewry — whose status had been regularized in that year — to convert this "simple" toleration into legal admission to the colonies.[45]

In short, the Jewish community in the major areas of early modern Resettlement and colonization had to reassert itself time and again against tremendous legal odds. Often subjected to fierce attacks by all forces of reaction, denied legal recognition by governments and, for the most part, ignored even by benevolent rulers, the Jews proved their mettle in establishing a vigorous, though self-imposed, communal control and in founding a number of flourishing communal institutions. Sooner or later, they succeeded in forcing recalcitrant administrations to acknowledge this uncontested reality of far-reaching Jewish autonomy and, in some cases, in enlisting their support for the maintenance of functional unity and effectiveness. If they were thereby aided by the existing variety of beliefs and disbeliefs and, hence, the growing necessity of mutual toleration, their main road to such noteworthy results was their adherence to age-old tradition and their undying will to survive and to retain identity in a rapidly changing world.

6. POLAND AND LITHUANIA

The dual monarchy, or as it preferred to style itself, the Republic of Poland and Lithuania generally followed the central European example. Its early legislation was borrowed, in some respects verbatim, from privileges granted Jews in neighboring Austria and Bohemia. The settlement of numerous German colonists, including German Jews, in Poland and the stimulus given thereby to the rise of Polish cities, introduced many German attitudes and legal concepts. Technically, Magdeburg law, chief model for the German cities in Poland, applied only to the Catholic and not to the equally numerous Jewish, Armenian, Greek and Tartar residents. But in the long run it necessarily influenced the legal status of non-German groups. The Jewish immigrants from Germany, on the other hand, brought with them the Judeo-German or Yiddish language, Judeo-German rites and observances, and the German communities' organizational forms. None the less, a few brief remarks on the specific Polish-Lithuanian phase of Jewish communal history appear justified here not only by the extraordinary role played by East European Jewry during the last centuries, but also by the numerous peculiarities of Polish society and government before the partitions of 1772–95, and by those of Polish legislation concerning the Jewish community.

The medieval Polish kings, wishing to attract Jewish settlers, extended to them increasing privileges. The decree issued by Boleslaw the Pious of Kalisz, in 1264, rather slavishly followed those of Frederick II of Austria (1244), Bela IV of Hungary (1251) and Přemysl II Ottokar of Bohemia (1254). These laws were, in turn, deeply indebted to the above-mentioned imperial decrees of 1090 and 1236 and the special privilege of 1238, issued by Emperor Frederick II in favor of Vienna Jewry. Boleslaw's decree was extended in 1334 to a much larger area and subsequently (1364, 1367) amplified in some points by Casimir the Great, the real founder of Poland. It was further elaborated in many significant details by Casimir IV in 1453. In this form it was invariably renewed by all Casimir's successors on the throne of Poland, becoming (together with the parallel privilege of the Lithuanian Grand Duke Vitautas for the Jews of Grodno in 1389), like the bull *Sicut Judaeis* for the Jews of Rome, the fundamental law for Polish-Lithuanian Jewry to the end of the country's independence. Like that papal bull, however, it was subject to interpretation and further elaboration by royal, parliamentary and gubernatorial enactments, and by judicial precedents which mirrored conflicting social forces, shifting attitudes toward the Jews and periodic changes in status. The basic constitution had, nevertheless, a modicum of historic continuity so sadly lacking amid the legislative vagaries of the kings of medieval Germany and France.

Although the kings of Poland did not use the official terminology of Jewish serfdom, beginning with Casimir the Great's statute of 1364 they frankly stressed the fiscal aspects of protection. They explained the exemption of Jewish owners of hereditary estates from military expeditions and military taxes by the fact that the Jews "belong to our treasury." In the same way they motivated their insistence on the rights of Jewish moneylenders to the estates of deceased debtors by the argument that "these Jews, as our subjects, ought to be prepared with their money to serve our needs." They also forbade provincial governors, to whom they otherwise entrusted supervision over Jewish

communities, to exact other than strictly voluntary payments, "because we reserve them for our own treasury."
Of course, this provision did not prevent the extortion of
manifold "gifts." By the eighteenth century, the Jews of
Cracow were paying some 7,000 florins, those of Lemberg
some 4,000 fl. annually to the local governors, whereas the
entire fiscal revenue from the original capitation tax did not
exceed, in 1578, 2127 florins for the two cities. Such emphasis
upon the special relation between Jews and the Crown,
never given the disparaging coloration of many utterances
of western popes, kings, thinkers and jurists, enhanced
rather than weakened the position of the Jews. The transfer,
in 1506, of the Inowrocław Jews by King Alexander to one
of his officials and the expulsion of Lithuanian Jewry in 1495
(revoked after eight years) are, each in its own sphere, an
exception proving the rule that the Jews of Poland suffered
but little from the adverse aspects of "serfdom." The
progressive weakening of the royal power, moreover, and
the gradual transformation of Poland into a republic of
nobles established a rival to royal control. In particular,
in the vast latifundia of southeastern Poland, owned by
territorial lords greatly resembling full-fledged western
feudal barons, the lord's right to regulate Jewish affairs was
fully recognized as early as 1539. The Polish Diet, consisting
of representatives elected by the upper and lower nobility,
became the supreme legislature for the entire country.
For a variety of reasons, Polish nobles utilized, much more
than did western feudal barons, the services of Jews in
estate management, collection of revenue from villeins
and crop marketing. Ultimately, this relationship led to
an unhealthy dependence of Jewish communities on noble
masters, some of whom issued ordinances regulating Jewish

community organization in their towns and hamlets in sovereign fashion. There was fostered a spirit of dejection, intrigue and petty tyranny on the part of a communal oligarchy, but the arrangement prevented, at least, large-scale discriminatory legislation. Despite constant anti-Jewish agitation by the Polish clergy and German burghers, the status of the communities was more consistently favorable in Poland than in any other medieval or early modern country with the exception of Holland.[46]

The fundamental privileges, supplemented by many special royal decrees and governors' ordinances in favor of particular communities (Cracow 1527, 1554; Poznań about 1550; Lublin 1556; Lwów 1569, 1604; Wilno 1633; Minsk 1681, and so forth) extended protection to Jewish religious and communal institutions. Desecration of cemeteries and stoning of synagogues were mentioned as especially heinous crimes. Under ecclesiastical pressure, to be sure, King Władysław IV reaffirmed in 1638 the provisions of Canon law forbidding the erection of new synagogues, at least when taller than, or hard by a church. Polish Jewry seems, nevertheless, to have but seldom (as in the aforementioned case of Łuck) encountered serious difficulty in obtaining, legally or otherwise, permits necessary for the building of houses of worship. Respect for the Jewish Sabbath was enjoined, even without any accompanying prohibition, so common in the western countries, of Jewish Sunday labor in public. The provisions concerning communal autonomy were likewise explicit:

> We also ordain that if any law-suit should arise because of discord or a controversy among Jews, no one except their own elders shall adjudicate it. Only

if they should be unable to establish the truth among themselves, they shall in such a case defer it to the lord governor [*palatinus*]. Furthermore, if any Jew should fail to obey his superiors, such a person shall pay to the lord governor a fine of three marks and to his superiors likewise a fine of three marks.

Intracommunal discipline was further reinforced by many special privileges, such as the great charter issued in 1551 by Sigismund II Augustus for the Jewish communities of Greater Poland and Mazovia. To secure full compliance with all communal and judicial acts of the Jewish leaders, the king decreed that "if any Jew should venture to take lightly the censures and bans imposed upon him by the rabbi, judge or other Jewish elders and make no attempt to extricate himself therefrom within one month, such a person, after being denounced to Us, shall be beheaded and all his property confiscated for our treasury."[47]

At first the kings arrogated to themselves the power of appointing regional rabbis. Jacob Polak, famous transplanter of rabbinic studies from Germany to Poland, was appointed by the king to serve as chief rabbi of Cracow (1503). Such appointments were made also in other important communities, e. g., Poznań and Lublin. The Jews resisted, however, and in 1551 obtained from the king the charter for the two provinces, whereby all lay and rabbinical offices were to be filled by regular elections within the respective communities. In 1569 a governor's ordinance in favor of the community of Lwów was announced at the famous Diet of Lublin, and thus invited widespread emulation. It established general electoral rights for all local rabbis and elders, subject only to confirmation by government organs. Other ordinances further enhanced the authority of these communal leaders. Since misdeeds of individuals often reflected on the entire community, King Jeremy Wiśniowiecki, in 1672, allowed the Lithuanian Jewish leaders to banish mighty individuals who, by inflicting losses on nobles or other Christians, embroiled communities in unpleasant controversies. In accordance with a resolution adopted by the Lithuanian Council, a privilege, granted Brześć Jewry in 1682, forbade nobles to lend money to Jews without the consent of the elders. Many local ordinances, beginning with that of Lwów, made tax farming by individual Jews contingent on the assent of the Jewish chiefs.⁴⁸

In their judicial relations with Christians, the Jews of Poland were exempted from appearing before either ecclesiastical or municipal courts, and were subjected directly to the jurisdiction of superior state organs, i. e., the king, his provincial governor, or a special *judex Judaeorum* appointed by him. Detailed ordinances (e. g., that of Lwów, 1692) regulated methods of selection of judges, secretaries and *instigatores* (a sort of prosecuting attorneys). Frequently the Jewish community had the right to protest appointments or to nominate two qualified noblemen, one of whom the governor then must appoint. Even where the deputy-governor (*podwojewoda*) regularly served as "the judge of Jews," the community delegated the Jewish *assessores* for each trial. Summons to Jews, moreover, had to be issued by Jewish communal marshals. Court sessions took place in the Jewish quarter, generally before the synagogue, and records were kept in the synagogue archives. Jewish convicts were incarcerated in Jewish prisons. Most sentences of lower courts were subject to appeal to the king; in some litigations exceeding the sum of 1,000 guilders the king's was the court of first instance. The rules of evidence followed the prevalent European model concerning mixed witnesses and oaths. The general privileges stated that two witnesses of each faith were required before any Jew could be condemned. The oath, which lacked in Poland some of the awe-inspiring features of the western oaths *more judaico*, was to be taken in the more solemn fashion on the scroll of law (*rodale*) only if the sum involved exceeded 50 marks. Otherwise, a simple oath was to be administered. In various ordinances Polish kings specifically objected to the placing of Jewish witnesses on a three-legged stool or a sowhide, widespread practices of the West which some Poles wished to see imitated. In a royal privilege of 1580, the courts were enjoined to interpret the term *rodale* in the basic constitution as referring to the scroll of law and not to a sowhide.[49]

The Polish Jewish communities cooperated also in tax collections for the state. Although the capitation tax, introduced in 1549, was not a discriminatory special tax for Jews, the communal organs were entrusted with gathering first 1.50 florins per family, then, from 1578 on, 1 florin and after 1613, 3 florins per capita of Jewish population. The importance of this revenue for the Polish treasury may be gauged from its yield which, due to immigration, an increased rate and, perhaps, more effective administration, rose from some 6,186 florins in 1569 to 80,000 florins in 1634, and to 220,000 florins from 1717 on. Numerous other and increasingly burdensome imposts made the fiscal contributions of the Jews and their communal administrators an ever more significant part of government revenue.[50]

7. Cities and Burghers

Besides Jewish traditions and interests, ecclesiastical teachings and state legislation, the rise of European cities had enormous influence on the legal status, mores and economic relations of the increasingly urbanized Jewish community. This influence came to the fore in three different ways. Wherever the city achieved full or partial sovereignty or even extensive autonomy, it utilized legislative powers to regulate the life of the Jewish group under its control. The concentration of the medieval city — unlike the ancient town economically more widely differentiated — upon industry and commerce, running parallel and often causally interrelated with the progressive elimination of the Jews from agriculture, led to manifold business contacts as well as economic rivalries between Jews and Christian burghers. Economic interests made of the burghers' class, even in the innumerable cities under royal, ecclesiastical or baronial suzerainty, a driving force which often determined the Jewish policies of western states. The struggle for liberation, finally, which characterized the entire history of the "third estate" until its ultimate victory under Capitalism and Democracy, and innumerable municipal constitutional experiments, stimulated emulation among Jewish inhabitants. Many a hue in the multicolored pattern of the Jewish community organization is due to such imitation, conscious or unconscious.

Full-fledged city states, such as the North-Italian republics, dealt with the Jewish question under general economic, rather than purely fiscal or religious, considerations. Of course, the revenue expected from Jewish taxpayers, who were allowed to engage in lucrative enterprises but lacked political power to resist fiscal exploitation, carried great weight in all considerations of admission or toleration. Religious prejudices, too, and the postulates of Canon law and Church doctrine deeply colored all trends toward excluding or lowering the status of these "infidels." The main consideration, however, was the extent to which their economic undertakings would accrue to the benefit of the dominant mercantile classes, or fulfill a necessary function by extending credit to a "needy" population. When Venice, Florence or Genoa felt that the Jews would prove effective mediators of trade with the Levant, they invited them to settle under advantageous conditions. Such invitations always included extensive safeguards of Jewish autonomy. Other Italian republics attracted primarily Jewish moneylenders, with whom they concluded treaties minutely describing the rights and duties of the Jews and the extent of communal self-government. These *condottas*, usually issued only for limited periods, were often allowed to expire when Christian charitable pawnbroking societies, so-called *monti di pietà*, seemed to make superfluous the services of Jewish bankers.

In all these city states the administration, naturally enough, wished more rigidly to supervise Jewish business than was customary in larger territorial states. Although for the most part maintaining the jurisdiction of Jewish courts over Jews, they placed judicial and other communal affairs under stricter control of city officials and mercantile associations. In Venice, for instance, the *Cattaveri* long controlled many phases of Jewish communal life and in 1671 took over supervision of Jewish excommunications, theretofore reserved to the Catholic patriarch. While the state recognized the jurisdiction of rabbinical courts in all religious and congregational matters, it strenuously objected to their role in civil disputes, except in cases of mutual agreement of the parties concerned. In Florence, even in the more liberal period before 1570, Jewish communal affairs were under the strict surveillance of the Eight *di Guardia e Balia*. A Jew wishing to appear before any other authority (including the ecclesiastical court in cases involving clerics) had to obtain special permission from these officials. The modicum of Jewish judicial authority preserved in litigations arising from Jewish laws of marriage and divorce could long be exercised by lay elders without the intervention of a permanent rabbi.[51]

In medieval England, on the other hand, the cities never succeeded in wresting even partial control over the Jews from the deeply entrenched royal masters. They bitterly resented not only Jewish competition and usury, but also the opportunity thus given to royal officials to intervene in controversies between Jews and burghers. Beginning with the abbot of St. Edmond who, in 1190, contended that "the Jews ought either to be of St. Edmond or be ejected from the town," many a city leader felt that complete exclusion of Jews was better than continued toleration under extraneous overlordship. In 1231–44 Leicester, Newcastle, Wycombe, Southampton, Berkamsted, Newbury obtained royal charters enabling them to exclude Jews, and in 1253 Henry III proclaimed the general principle "that no Jew be received in any town but by special license of the King, save only in those towns in which Jews have been wont to dwell." These restrictions were but a prelude to the ultimate expulsion of 1290.[52]

In their more effective struggle for liberation from imperial, ducal, or ecclesiastical sovereignty, the medieval

German cities frequently considered it more than a matter of prestige to subject the Jewish population to municipal rather than royal authority. Witnessing the ineffectiveness of imperial protection during the massacres of the Crusaders, cities assumed increasing responsibility for the safety of Jews. Although largely prompted by fear that rioters, as a Mayence chronicler put it, would "despoil not only the Jews, but all well-to-do persons," the city patricians usually demanded, as a counterpart to protection, the right to increased intervention in Jewish affairs. Here too, the claim to exclusivity was often interpreted to refer even to matters affecting Jews alone. Few cities went as far as Zurich which, taking advantage of the precarious position of the Jews, demanded that they take an oath to submit all their litigations to the burgomaster and city council. "As these shall judge to the best of their knowledge, so shall it remain for ever, and no Jew shall therein seek or receive from another the Jew law." Cities generally were satisfied, however, with jurisdiction over mixed cases, major cases of crimes committed by Jews (even against other Jews) and such non-contentious categories as the registration of real-estate transfers. The land register of Cologne includes many Jewish deeds. Most German cities sooner or later thus obtained the transfer of Jews to their direct protection and fiscal control, with all its adverse effects on Jewish autonomy. Many, whether sovereign or not, ultimately embarked on a policy of total exclusion. It was largely due to their initiative that a succession of local or regional expulsions in the course of the fifteenth and early sixteenth centuries wiped out all Jewish settlements over a vast area of the Holy Roman Empire. Some cities, such as Bremen, Lübeck or Glatz in Silesia, through their own legislative or administrative enactments, or through privileges, real or fictitious, which they obtained from their sovereigns, clung to that policy of extreme intolerance long after the American and French Revolutions.[53]

The Spanish, Portuguese, Sicilian, French and Polish bourgeoisie were long less inimical or successful. While occasional transfers of Jews are recorded in Aragon and France, the kings on the whole vigorously resisted curtailment of their fiscal rights. When the burghers of Palma, Majorca, in 1359, tried to force the Jews to contribute to an extraordinary war tax imposed by the king, they were promptly rebuked by Pedro IV because "the Jews are in no ways obliged to pay together with the [Christian] community of that city, but they make their own separate and distinctive" payments and contributions. We learn, however, of many successful interventions of Iberian cities in the inner affairs of Jewish communities. When the community of Saragossa issued, in 1331, an extensive tax ordinance, it succeeded in securing royal confirmation which expressly stated that these measures "in no way infringed on [the rights of] the said city or the Christians living therein." But the city objected and the community was forced to abandon or modify most provisions of the ordinance. In the course of time many Spanish cities acquired jurisdiction over Jewish markets, criminal offenses and mixed litigations. Tortosa, for local reasons, succeeded in subjecting the Jews to the local court even in Jewish cases. This was, however, not a city court but one of burghers and officials appointed by the king and the two feudal lords of the city. On the Iberian Peninsula the bourgeoisie acted, moreover, as the spearhead of all anti-Jewish movements. In the various Cortes it furnished the most insistent champions of anti-

Jewish restrictions, which often included considerable curtailment of Jewish autonomy. In alliance with a most intolerant branch of the Catholic Church, it finally obtained the complete elimination of the Jews from both Spain and Portugal.[54]

When the Aragonese rulers gradually re-established royal control over the Jews of southern Italy, many cities began demanding the participation of Jews in municipal contributions to the royal treasury from which, by virtue of their own even more burdensome special taxation, the Jews had been consistently exempted. In some cases, the Jewish communities, for the sake of promoting good will, voluntarily assumed a share in such imposts. In 1463 the burghers of Bari went further and demanded the segregation of the Jews in a ghetto and the invalidation of Jewish testimony against Christians. Such disqualifications of Jewish witnesses had, indeed, long before been proclaimed by the city laws of Palermo, "on account of the false testimony they had given against Christ." The kings resisted for a time, but finally yielded to the growing resentment of the cities, nurtured not only by religious intolerance and economic rivalry — the large and affluent Jewish community appeared indispensable even to most Christian burghers, the city of Palermo, for instance, sharply protesting in 1492 against the decree of expulsion — but also by opposition to extensive Jewish autonomy and the close alliance of Jews and the royal power. The burghers of Lecce seem to have voiced, in 1467, a fairly widespread objection when they said that, as a result of this alliance, the kings "had converted a single community into two communities in the same city."[55]

The Polish bourgeoisie was in a much more delicate position in coping with the Jewish problem. Largely sprung from German mass immigration of the fifteenth and sixteenth centuries, the burghers tried to inject the intolerant spirit of contemporary German cities into Polish politics. Between 1520 and 1600, in the period of the greatest expansion of Polish Jewry, at least eighteen towns secured royal privileges *de non tolerandis judaeis*. For a long time thereafter, the Jews were completely excluded from such important cities as Warsaw, Sambor, Drohobycz and Żywiec. But many Jewish communities, sometimes equal in age, populousness, culture and economic standing, reciprocated by obtaining similar rights to exclude Christians from their ghettos. If in a privilege granted by King Jan Sobieski to the Lithuanian city of Disne, in 1676, the Jews were debarred from organiz-ing a *kahal* or erecting a synagogue and, in their litigations with non-Jews, were specifically referred to the jurisdiction of the "Magdeburg" (burghers') court, this was an exception confirming the general rule of Jewish autonomy as enunci-ated by the same king soon thereafter in his confirmation of the privileges of the Jews in Lithuania. King and Diet cooperated also in issuing in 1678 a general decree against the citation of Jews to Magdeburg courts. The kings of the Golden Age of Poland and Lithuania, with fairly consistent impartiality, adhered to the principle that the Jews shall "be placed on a footing of equality with the burghers and shall be endowed with the same liberties." The economic conflict between the nobility and the bourgeoisie also long helped the Jews to resist the pressure of inimical municipal authorities. The progressive Polonization of the burghers, however, concomitant with Poland's general political and economic decline, strengthened anti-Jewish forces in the seventeenth and eighteenth centuries. By 1768, contends a

Polish author with some exaggeration, fully one-fifth of all Polish cities had no Jewish inhabitants. In that year the Polish diet, under pressure of the burghers, decreed that

> considering that Jewry causes intolerable injury to the cities and burghers, and takes away their means of livelihood . . . [we therefore ordain] that the Jews shall engage only in such business and in such larger and smaller towns as are open to them by their treaties with the cities . . . . They shall not enter commerce, serve as innkeepers or pursue a craft without such special treaties . . . under the penalty of 5,000 grzywień.

While this decree, in the growing anarchy of the decadent nobles' Republic, was largely observed in the breach, it undoubtedly added stimulus to the increasing diffusion of Jewish settlements over vast open spaces, especially in southeastern Poland. The combined pressure of this anti-Jewish agitation and the growing dispersal of Jewry, strengthened external and inner forces of disintegration within the great self-governmental agencies of the Polish Jewish community and helped undermine their effectiveness both for the Jews and the country at large.[56]

8. Precarious Balance

Among these conflicting forces of state, city and Church the Jewish community had to pursue its steady course. While frequently allied with the royal power, it had to pay all sorts of regular and extraordinary taxes as a price for royal protection. The price often became unbearably high, and many a community found itself in inevitable bankruptcy. At the same time, enforced alliance with the monarchical power augured badly for the Jews in revolutionary periods, when the opposition often found it most convenient to strike at the Crown's most defenceless allies. The chaotic complexity of political forces operating in the medieval scene, and the inherent dangers of betting on the wrong horse, stimulated the withdrawal of Jews behind ghetto walls and strengthened inner bonds of solidarity.

The Church professed a mainly theological interest in Jewish survival to the end of days, and secular powers occasionally paid lip service to this messianic expectation. The latter, however, generally admitted more or less frankly that their main interest was in the Jew's economic functions, particularly his fiscal contributions. That is why legislation concerning Jews was aimed mainly at regulating economic activities, settling controversies among Jews and Christians, and strengthening the authority of communal organs which served as the state's most effective tax collectors. Provisions for the maintenance of public order and protection of Jewish persons and property, as well as safeguards of freedom of religious observance, merely supplemented these primary norms. It may be said that the legal recognition and support of Jewish autonomy was in more or less direct ratio to Jewish fiscal contributions. It was at its highest where Jewish taxes played the most significant role in the state's budgetary system, as in north-central Europe during the middle ages, and at its lowest in the Byzantine Empire or the areas of Resettlement where the Jews paid little more than did their Christian neighbors. By emphasizing the fiscal and judicial functions of the community, western legislators helped to shape it, even more than any other corporate body, into a powerful approximation of a "state within a state."

CHAPTER VIII

SUPERCOMMUNITY

LIKE THE medieval city, the Jewish community usually had definite boundaries. For the most part, they did not spread beyond the city limits. Sometimes the community extended over the entire city area, but more frequently it was confined to a special quarter, the ghetto. Whether self-imposed or compulsory, such a Jewish quarter resembled a miniature town, often being separated by a wall from other sections of the city. Sometimes, however, the community transcended city boundaries, embracing also Jews living nearby and too sparsely settled to organize a community of their own. Such Jews participated in the benefits of the larger community, frequented the communal synagogue at least on high holidays, made use of the community's schools, courts and cemetery. The cemetery was, indeed, the most frequent criterion of communal allegiance. Since the possession of a graveyard was contingent upon a special privilege, usually extended only to larger communities, the Jews of an entire district, often a whole province, were forced to belong to such a central community.

Such affiliation need not have been exclusive. For example, the Jews of a large part of Bavaria possessed only one central cemetery in Ratisbon. Containing the remains of many generations of pious and learned men, it became the focus of legends and the center of pilgrimages from the entire province. Nevertheless, local communities possessed a large degree of independence, and individuals owed their principal loyalty to local leaders. This situation, incidentally, explains the existence throughout the middle ages of numerous privileges granted various Jewries, exempting them from the payment of general or specific tolls for the transportation of their dead. In other cases, especially in smaller or less densely populated areas, ownership of a cemetery often determined the choice of the communal center and its leadership.

Concentration of communal powers was fostered also by the fiscal interests of the state. Since one of the main reasons for the toleration of Jews under medieval Christendom was their financial contribution, and since the communities were generally held responsible as such for the total amount of taxation, it naturally appeared advantageous to the state to concentrate the task of taxgathering and the responsibility for its satisfactory operation in ever fewer hands. The Jews, too, found it to their advantage to possess superior organs for the supervision and unification of communal endeavors, for the establishment of courts of appeal, for the appointment of authoritative persons to negotiate with the government, and often also for the issuance of ordinances enjoying more widespread acceptance. Thus evolved those regional organs which, extending over the area of a province or of a whole country, left their permanent imprint upon the entire structure of Jewish autonomy. The forms of such super-communal cooperation varied. Often, as in the Orient, single chiefs, Jewish or Christian, were entrusted with some or all communal responsibilities. More characteristic of European regional leadership, however, were the loosely organized synods and occasional rabbinical or lay assemblies. Under favorable circumstances the latter developed into permanent representative councils of rabbis and laymen.

1. Regional Chiefs in the South

In Portugal Jewish communal authority was more centralized than in any other European country. Whether or not Kings Affonso III and John I consciously followed Muslim examples, their constitutional enactments regulating the Jewish community organization, the statute of 1402 in particular, established a decided Jewish hierarchy with most of the powers vested in the chief rabbi (*arraby moor*). Appointed by the king, probably after consultation with the Jewish leaders, this supreme officer of Portuguese Jewry resembled the Babylonian exilarch in having responsibility both for the revenue due the state by the Jews and for the orderly management of the Jewish communities. Unlike the exilarch, however, he found no constitutional checks in the recognized authority of the academies. He appointed seven overseers (judges) in the seven major communities of the realm; these in turn controlled the selection of the local elders. These district overseers also served as the intermediary courts of appeal, while the chief rabbi, assisted by a special overseer, chancellor, secretary and sheriff, passed final judgment in all civil litigations among Jews. He instituted criminal proceedings and, except in certain minor transgressions which were the competence of local authorities, arrested lawbreakers. All elections of local rabbis and teachers depended on his confirmation and, when necessary, he forced the community to employ such officials "in accordance with custom." He could also order an unemployed teacher or rabbi to accept a call from a congregation even if it was unable to pay the prevailing salary. In order more effectively to supervise the administration of the individual communities and to gain first-hand acquaintance with the local conditions, the chief rabbi was expected to pay an annual visit to each community. In submitting to such overwhelming state control, Portuguese Jewry seems to have yielded to pressure. It is notable that extant Jewish records of the fifteenth century mention the official chief rabbis with decreasing frequency and appreciation, while often referring glowingly to services rendered by private scholars and royal councilors, such as Don Isaac Abravanel until his flight to Spain in 1483.[1]

In the Spanish kingdoms, too, regional concentration for fiscal purposes became an early necessity. At an early date taxes were imposed in a lump sum upon the Jewries of an entire district, and in Aragon each such *collecta* became the basic Jewish regional unit. Communal agreements, special royal privileges or ancient customs decided the extent of control exercised by the district center. Frequently, for example, the ban could be proclaimed only in the chief synagogue of the district. In an interesting responsum of Ibn Adret (after 1270) we read:

> Know ye that we [the community of Barcelona] and the communities of Villafranca, Tarragona and Montblanch possess a common chest and treasury for the payment of taxes and imposts. Whenever the government imposes upon us a certain amount, or whenever we wish to make new agreements concerning tax appraisals and declarations [for the payment] of what our master the king demands from us, we never give them orders, although our community embraces the majority [of the Jews in the district] and leads in all matters. If we were to do anything without their advice, they would not listen to us. Sometimes we send men to them, and sometimes their delegates arrive here with their consent. Should they refuse

to do either, we would force them through the arm
of the government to come to us or to adopt in their
own locality the same measures and proclaim the
same bans as we do. There are, however, other
regions in which the main community gives orders
to its daughter communities and enforces its will,
since in all these matters various regions observe
different customs.[2]

As a matter of fact, when Barcelona once tried to force
Montblanch to do its will, the latter successfully appealed
to the king.

From time to time delegates of all Jewish communities
in one or all provinces (Aragon, Catalonia, Valencia, the
Balearic Islands and the County of Roussillon) were called
together by the king, for the most part in order to redis-
tribute a total tax. They disbanded immediately after performing the specific task for which they had been assembled.
The only major attempt to establish a permanent diet and
executive for all Aragonese Jewry was undertaken in 1354
at such a general conference in Barcelona. Although fairly
successful in some of the immediate political tasks, it was
a complete failure organizationally. According to the pro-
posed constitution delegates of all communities were to
meet at five-year intervals, discuss matters of common
concern, and elect a permanent executive committee of
six members (*nibrarim*), two each from the provinces of
Aragon and Catalonia, and one each from Valencia and the
Islands. This committee was to conduct all negotiations
with pope, king and Cortes, seek redress against rapacious
government officials, interfering clergy and hostile mobs,
stamp out informing and help regulate the inner life
of the communities. If necessary, it was to invoke the

assistance of the government against recalcitrant constituents. The Barcelona conference also adopted various resolutions concerning legal and taxation problems, protested against the encroachments of the inquisitorial courts upon inner Jewish affairs, which it regarded as justified only in the case of Jews denying the existence of God or the revealed character of Scripture (two dogmas common to Christianity and Judaism), demanded vigorous prosecution of the rioters during the massacres occasioned by the Black Death, and petitioned the king against the increasing transfers of Jews from royal to baronial jurisdiction. From the outset the gathering was attended only by representatives from Catalonia and Valencia. It nevertheless successfully initiated diplomatic negotiations which resulted in several favorable papal bulls and royal decrees. The Aragonese and Balearic communities, moreover, soon approved the Barcelona proceedings and endorsed the resolutions adopted there. Evidently indifference and petty jealousies rather than overt opposition were responsible for this failure of Aragonese Jewry to establish a permanent "democratic" representation which, in all likelihood, would have anticipated much of the glory of the famous Polish Councils.[3]

The kings of Aragon, like their confreres of Castile and Navarre, seem to have preferred to entrust responsibility for entire provinces or the country as a whole to individual chief rabbis who, appointed by themselves and combining spiritual with secular means of enforcement, were more likely to execute their wishes willingly and effectively. Freely elected representatives of the Jewish communities might at times have showed the same unbending spirit which caused the kings so much trouble at the Cortes. Castilian district chief rabbis are recorded, for instance, in

Burgos as far back as 1255. In 1401 the Burgos rabbis still enjoyed the right of appointing and deposing local elders (e. g., in neighboring Sahagun) and also served as the court of appeal for the entire region. In the fourteenth century the archbishop of Toledo appointed a chief rabbi for his entire diocese, apparently subject only, as in 1389, to royal confirmation. In 1395, after years of bloodshed, the archbishop reappointed the "alcalde and chief judge of the Jews" in the person of his physician, Maestro Pedro, who like many others seems to have embraced Christianity under duress. The majority of Jews meekly surrendered.[4]

There were also chief rabbis of the entire realm, usually distinguished by the title "rabbis of the court." The designation of the famous cabalist, Todros ha-Levi Abulafia, as "the prince of the Spanish captivity" by Abraham Bedershi in the middle of the thirteenth century may not be absolutely conclusive. But in 1383–85 David ibn Yaḥya (Negro) is officially described as the *Raby mayor de toda Castella*. The Council of Valladolid of 1432 was not only led by Abraham Benveniste, "rabbi of the court," but in one of its decisions referred also to the widow of a former Chief Rabbi, Don Meir Alguades. In 1465 Samaya Lubel, the court physician, is candidly styled "rabbi, chief judge and tax distributor of all the Jewish communities of my kingdoms and dominions." Finally, after the unification of Castile and Aragon under Ferdinand and Isabella, the jurisdiction of this threefold office was extended over all the communities of united Spain and entrusted to the court banker and tax farmer, Abraham Seneor. He is mentioned in this capacity in various records dating from 1476 to 1492. Unwilling to leave the country, he ended his startling career as the accredited leader of Spanish Jewry by conversion to

Christianity, the royal couple and the primate of Spain acting as sponsors. As chief rabbi, he adjudicated civil litigations among Jews, often serving as their court of appeal (from which, however, one could still appeal to the king). He protected Jewish interests wherever threatened, invoking, for example, royal protection against a Dominican preacher and a local magistrate in his own residence of Segovia (1485). He took a leading part in the redemption of Jewish captives in Malaga. His major function consisted, however, in supervising the distribution and collection of Jewish taxes.[5]

In Aragon, too, we indirectly learn of the appointment, before 1258, of Solomon Alconstantin (Alfaquim), King James I's secretary, as the chief judge of Aragonese Jewry with the right of appointing deputies in the various provinces. When one such appointment was contested in 1271, the king personally intervened with reference to his own earlier authorization. In 1304–5 James II, "confiding in the industry" of Ismael de Portella, entrusted him with the decision in all judicial appeals of Aragonese Jewry. Other officers of this kind are recorded in the fourteenth and fifteenth centuries, although vacancies seem not always to have been speedily filled. By far the most prominent among these chief rabbis of Aragon was Don Ḥasdai Crescas, the well-known philosopher and apologist. A similar *rabi mayor de los judios del reyno* is also recorded in 1394–1401 in Navarre, when the office was held by the king's physician, Joseph Orabuena.[6]

The attitude of Spanish Jewry to their chief rabbis, despite a certain studious avoidance of this subject in the Hebrew letters of the period,[7] apparently was not altogether unfriendly. If David Messer Leon, speaking as an outsider, summarily condemned Abraham Seneor's administration, he was undoubtedly prompted by Seneor's apostasy rather than by the alleged mismanagement of his office. In general he considered the title "rabbi" ill-chosen for a governmental appointee, undistinguished by learning or piety; he would have preferred the Egyptian designation, *nagid*.[8]

While resenting the extensive governmental control over their autonomous institutions, the Jews of Spain doubtless realized the benefits of a unified fiscal administration — which was not always an unmitigated blessing, however — and the advantage of having a permanent representative at the royal court. Aragonese Jewry especially, after learning through bitter experience how the post of the official aristocratic "spokesman," appointed at their instance by Pedro IV, was converted into one more costly royal sinecure, greatly appreciated the services of influential fellow-Jews like Crescas. In fact, the Barcelona conference of 1354 specifically petitioned the king to abolish the tax for the maintenance of their princely "spokesman," because "although we are his [the King's serfs], there is no point in" the continuation of this office. Nevertheless we find Pedro IV in 1367 still insisting upon the payment of Infante John's salary "as the protector of the Jewish communities of our entire country." These mixed feelings are well illustrated by the decisions of the synod of Valladolid, convoked and presided over by one such *rab de la corte*, Abraham Benveniste. In this significant gathering of 1432, a number of resolutions were adopted which, although having little immediate effect, well characterize the outlook of Spanish Jewry. Apart from defining many of the judicial, fiscal, educational and general administrative functions of the chief rabbi, the ordinances then issued included the following provisions:

> No person of Israelitic stock shall have the right to avail himself of any decree, letter of grace, privilege or any other mandate, whether written or oral, issued by our lord the King, or our lady, the Queen, or any other lord or lady, so as to have himself commissioned to serve as rabbi, obtain an agreement or emolument from any of the communities, be appointed scribe, slaughterer, reader, teacher, court messenger, investigator, or secure any other communal office . . .without the permission of the communities or the community to which appertains this particular appointment . . . . This rule shall not apply, however, to the aforementioned Rabbi Don Abraham, because it was and is the desire of all the communities that he shall serve as their highest judge and tax distributor, and he accepted this position at the instance of the rabbis and the call of the communities. Whoever happens at present to be in possession of some such letter of grace, we ordain him to submit it to the right honorable Rabbi Don Abraham for examination within the next six months, so that those of them which ought to be executed shall be carried out. During this period he may, if he so desires, carry on the functions of his office, as he is accustomed to do by the authority of the said letter of grace, but his salary shall be determined by the aforementioned Rabbi.[9]

In Sicily and Naples, too, the Aragonese kings tried to introduce centralized control along Spanish lines, but after a while encountered a great deal of opposition. To be sure, the Jews themselves are said to have suggested, in 1396, the appointment by King Martin of a Jewish chief justice (*iudex universalis*, in Hebrew misspelled as *dienchelele*) in all civil and criminal matters, in the person of Joseph Abenafia. But the royal decree is rather vague and fails to mention the communities which made the suggestion. On the contrary, the reiterated decrees in Abenafia's favor, issued in 1397 and 1399, indicate a good deal of opposition. In 1406 the king had to enjoin the community of Palermo, which fourteen years previously he had himself designated as "the head and uppermost of all the Jewries in our entire Kingdom of Sicily," to respect Abenafia's jurisdiction, whereupon the Christian municipality, perhaps instigated by Jews, requested the king to exempt the local Jewish community from the control of the Jewish supreme judge. The matter may have remained in suspense when Abenafia died. The king then ordered the Jewish communities to pay all arrears of his salary to his widow, Falcona (February 1408). Neither are we informed about the appointment of his successor, Rais of Ragusa (perhaps identical with Raysius, whom Martin in 1399 had appointed proto of Syracuse "for life"). On Rais's death in 1414, we are told, Queen Bianca appointed Isaac b. David of Marseilles as chief justice. A few months later the Queen strictly forbade the Christian officials to interfere with Isaac's administration, but in 1418 two Jews were specifically exempted from his jurisdiction. Isaac's successor, Moses de Bonavoglia, enjoyed a longer tenure of office, but was also the subject of more outspoken attacks. A royal favorite exempted from all taxation by the king in 1413, he was appointed chief justice in 1420. For some reason this appointment evoked a storm of protests, the two leading Christian municipalities of Palermo and Messina claiming that it violated their ancient privileges. Upon investigation, the king revoked the appointment in June 1421, but renewed it in November

1422 "at the request of all the Jewish communities" of the
realm. For an unspecified reason the Jews changed their
mind ten years later and offered the royal government a new
tax as a price of abolishing the office of chief justice. When
the community of Messina failed to pay its share of 100
ounces, it was sharply rebuked by the king for ingratitude
(1433). Moses was, nevertheless, restored to office in 1439
and seems to have retained it until his death, despite
instantaneous protests of the Palermo municipality. His
successor, Joshua Bonartino, evidently likewise elevated to
office because of his services as court physician, was less
fortunate. His appointment in 1446, followed by the
squashing of some inquisitorial proceedings against him,
evoked such concerted opposition that the king, accepting
an offer of 600 ounces by the united Jewish communities,
definitely abolished the office in 1447 and substituted for it
a parliament, as suggested by the Jews.[10]

Thus went out of existence the chief rabbinate of south
Italian Jewry, whose influence upon the life of the communities during the half century of its existence must have
been greater than may be perceived through the few extant
government decrees. While its state function must have
been primarily fiscal — a fact proven by the taxes offered as
a price of elimination — it furnished the Jews a central
agency both for the administration of justice and for political
action. In 1399 Abenafia, whose salary, incidentally, was
fixed at 36 ounces annually, obtained from the king the
confirmation of certain general ordinances adopted by the
Jewish communities. In 1403 he acted in behalf of the
communities in the redemption of Jewish captives in Malta
and Gozzo. Moses de Bonavoglia, whose journeys to King
Alfonso in order to obtain privileges for Jews are repeatedly

mentioned in the sources, secured in 1430 the revocation of a royal decree imposing upon Sicilian Jewry attendance at the conversionist sermons of Fra Matteo of Agrigento. Nevertheless, the disadvantages of centralization and the appointment by the chief justice of often undesirable local judges, seems to have outweighed the advantages, and Sicilian Jewry, which was, perhaps, originally responsible for the creation of the office, ultimately had to pay dearly for its abolition.[11]

2. NORTHERN CHIEF RABBIS

The Jews in the northern countries were confronted by similar cross-currents in the states' and their own fiscal and organizational desires. As far back as 828, Archbishop Agobard of Lyons complained of Everardus, the *magister Judaeorum* who, together with the royal "messengers," interfered with his pious endeavors to segregate the Jews. Although Agobard's references to this officer are far from explicit, he seems to have been appointed by the emperor to protect the interests of Jewish subjects. He apparently had few executive powers, but in each case had to invoke the assistance of the royal commissioners. Much more extensive were the powers of the chief officials serving during the French reunification of the thirteenth and fourteenth centuries. In two royal decrees of 1276 we find the first mention of *procuratores* of the Jews in the Provence and their apparent chief, Bentifac. But we learn little about their position and functions. Nor are we informed what, if any, relations existed between these officers, who occasionally travelled as far as Sicily to plead the cause of Provençal Jewry before the king, and the two Jews of Tarascon who had been entrusted by the king in 1270 with the collection of 6,000 Turonian pounds over a period of five years and the distribution of this impost among the various Jewish communities and households.[12]

Two decades later, however, in a document of 1297, reference is clearly made to a Jewish *procureur général*, Kalot of Rouen, who a year previously had already served as intermediary between the Crown and the Jews. In 1297 he and another Jew, Joucet of Pontoise, arbitrated a dispute between the king and his brother, Charles of Valois, concerning the control over 43 Jews. They assigned 12 to the king and the rest to his brother. In 1359 or earlier, Louis d'Evreux, Count of Étampes, of royal parentage, was appointed by the king *gardien général des Juifs et conservateur de leur privilèges*. As such, he had general supervision over civil litigations between Jews and Christians and, assisted by a Jewish and a Christian commissioner, adjudicated conflicting tax claims. This office, whose jurisdiction was subsequently altered by special ordinances, lasted until the eve of the general expulsion of Jews from France in 1394. Simultaneously, Manecier of Vesoul, the Jewish banker and chief negotiator for the return of the Jews to France, was entrusted with the task of collecting revenue from them. Finally, a chief rabbi and chief judge, in the person of Mattathiah Trèves, Manecier's relative, was elected by the French communities and confirmed by the king. When, after the death of this first incumbent, a controversy broke out over the succession, the French Jews, apparently unable to agree on various fine points of the law, consulted several prominent scholars abroad. While Meir ha-Levi of Vienna sided with the opposing candidate, Isaiah b. Abba Mari of Savoy, Mattathiah's son, Joḥanan, was confirmed in office by the legal decision in 1391 in the shape of responsa by the three leading Spanish rabbis of the period, Isaac b. Sheshet Profet, Ḥasdai Crescas and Moses Ḥalawa of Tortosa.[12a]

In England, King John appointed, in 1199, Jacob of London to serve as the "presbyter of all the Jews throughout England with all that pertains thereto for the rest of his life." Addressed in flattering terms such as *dilectus* and *familiaris noster*, this official became thenceforth the main tax collector of English Jewry. Usually he was selected by the king from among the richest bankers in the country and was held personally responsible for the taxes arbitrarily imposed upon the royal "serfs." At times, as in 1254, the exactions became so unbearable that Arch-presbyter Elias l'Eveske and his associates dramatically requested that permission be given to the Jews of England to leave the country. In 1241, during the regime of Elias's predecessor, Aaron of York, Henry III, the most ruthless of these royal exploiters of the Jews, attempted to secure additional funds by assembling a Jewish "parliament" in Worcester. The larger communities sent six delegates each, the smaller ones two each. Their only order of business was to vote new revenue for the king. For similar reasons the king consented in 1257 that the Jews "shall have free choice in the election of whomever they want as their new *sacerdos*," subject only to royal confirmation. Contrary to a widely held opinion, superficially supported by official designations such as that just quoted, these presbyters had no spiritual function whatsoever. They were but fiscal agents, having an official residence at the exchequer of the Jews, but with no spiritual or judicial functions in either purely Jewish or Judeo-Christian relations. In addition to rabbis attending to Jewish judicial procedure, Richard I appointed two "justiciars of the Jews" for mixed cases. It is characteristic of the king's protective attitude toward his Jewish moneylenders, the main parties in such mixed litigations, that the first two justices so appointed were Jewish. Their successors, however, were always Christian officials of high standing.[13]

The progressive political dissolution of the Holy Roman Empire militated against any centralization of Jewish leadership. Emulating their western neighbors, several emperors attempted to establish a central authority for German Jewry but, in view of its different historical development, they soon tried to combine spiritual-rabbinic with the strictly fiscal features. After a futile attempt of Charles IV, immediately frustrated by the massacres of 1348, King Ruprecht at first chose, in 1400–4, two laymen (Elias of Weinheim and Isaac of Oppenheim), charging them with the collection of the entire revenue accruing to the Crown from the Jewish *Opferpfennig* and fines. He then turned, in 1407, to a rabbi, Israel allegedly of Krems or Kremsier but living in Rothenburg, and appointed him to serve as "Our and the Empire's Jewish chief master [*Hochmeister*] over each and every Jewish master, Jew and Jewess of the German lands." Although the emperor partly camouflaged his motives behind a shower of praise for his candidate, "an old and recognized authority in the field of Jewish studies and enjoying among the Jews a fine reputation of never having wronged anybody," and his professed intention to stem the numerous abuses in the proclamation of bans by unauthorized rabbis, the Jews clearly sensed the main fiscal objectives. The majority of the German rabbis, invoking the old injunction against accepting government appointments to Jewish communal offices, speedily excommunicated the new appointee. Ruprecht reciprocated by publicly declaring this excommunication null and void, and by threatening with severe fines all who recognized its validity. Less successful was the attempt of Emperor Sigismund nineteen years later to have three Jewish masters appointed by his trusted Jew, Ḥayyim of Landshut, although the old and revered Rabbi Jacob Moelln of Mayence (Maharil) was among Ḥayyim's choices. Sigismund and his successors, Frederick III, Charles V, Ferdinand I and Maximilian II, reverted to the selection of single leaders. Their recorded appointees were Anselm of Cologne (1435), Seligmann Oppenheim of Bingen (supported by a large synod convoked by himself at Bingen, about 1456), Samuel b. Eliezer (1521–52), and Jacob b. Ḥayyim of Worms (1559–74), respectively.[14]

In view of the evidently lukewarm cooperation of imperial Jewry with these government officers, the less official position held by Josel (Joseph) of Rosheim in the days of Maximilian I and Charles V (the designation "chief rabbi of all Jewry in Bohemia and Germany" applied to him by the Burggraf of Prague in 1534 was, perhaps, but a lapse of an overzealous official), more closely approximated that sort of all-German Jewish leadership which the emperors desired to establish. Although the resonant title of "Ruler of Jewry in the Empire," which Josel once assumed, brought him into conflict with the courts, in whose opinion this designation was reserved for the emperor alone, he was described in an imperial privilege of 1544 as the "commander of all our Jewry in the Holy Empire." He often preferred this military-sounding title for his communications to the Strasbourg Senate and others. Nevertheless his actual sphere of influence did not seem to extend much beyond southwestern Germany. Apparently the emperors after Maximilian II abandoned all centralizing efforts, whose futility must have become ever more obvious as imperial powers suffered further eclipse in the subsequent religious wars. In the seventeenth and eighteenth centuries we find most provincial leaders, such as existed in Moravia and several minor western states, exercising their authority side by side with representative councils. All these provincial chief rabbis, however, were elective officers, generally chosen by the provincial councils for a limited period. Even if they required government confirmation, they did not appear to the Jewish communities under them as chiefs imposed from above.[15]

Neither did the kings of Poland-Lithuania succeed in permanently establishing an appointive country-wide or provincial rabbinate. Mention has already been made of the appointment of Jacob Polak as chief rabbi of Cracow with jurisdiction over the bulk of Lesser Poland. Even earlier (1389–93), one Pechno was *episcopus Judaeorum Poznaniae*, very likely the first appointive provincial rabbi in Poland. King Sigismund I, in his appointment of Moses Fischel as tax farmer of the Polish communities in Greater and, perhaps, Lesser Poland, in 1499, laid the ground for a considerable extension of the powers of the regional chiefs. A few years later (1514) the king, undismayed by Fischel's extortions which were checked only by the intervention of the Poznań governor, appointed Abraham of Bohemia, Franczko (Ephraim) Fischel and Michael Ezofowicz, a brother of the influential convert, Abraham Ezofowicz, to serve as general elders (seniors) of Greater Polish and Mazovian, of Lesser Polish and of Lithuanian Jewry, respectively. No attempt was made here to conceal the fiscal objectives, and the Jewish opposition engendered thereby forced Fischel and Ezofowicz to resign after but one year in office. Abraham, who at first agreed to substitute for Fischel in Lesser Poland as well, was likewise forced to yield.[16]

Jewish pressure was kept alive until the king consented to confirm the choice of regional leaders by the Jewish communities. This compromise was first expressed in 1518–19 in the royal confirmation of Poznań Jewry's own selection of two new chief rabbis for the province. It was followed by the decree of 1527, in which the king ratified the unanimous election of Rabbi Samuel Margolies and authorized him,

> as long as he may live, to judge in matters pertaining to law, to recognize, bind or absolve, to impose censures and bans, in accordance with the ritual and custom of Mosaic law, and to exercise all other forms of authority in spiritual matters with respect to all the Jews residing in the lands of Greater Poland and the Duchy of Mazovia. It is hereby expressly stated, and, as the said Jews have declared before Us, has been observed as an ancient usage that, if any Jew should venture to take lightly the censures and bans imposed upon him by the aforementioned Doctor [Rabbi] Samuel and make no attempt to extricate himself therefrom within one month, such a person, after being denounced to Us, shall be beheaded and all his property confiscated for Our treasury.

The royal confirmations of Judah Aaron as chief rabbi of the provinces of Lublin, Chełm and Bełz in 1522, and of the famous Shalom Shakna of Lublin and Doctor Moses Fischel (a grandson of the former tax farmer) as joint chief rabbis of Lesser Poland in 1541, extended this practice to the other provinces of the Republic. The aforementioned royal decrees of 1541, 1551 and subsequent years, evidently modelled after that of 1527 but going much beyond it, finally established the general principle of free elections to Jewish communal leadership. The smoldering conflict between the Crown and the Jewish communities was thus ended by mutual concessions, which ultimately led to the establishment of the elective general and provincial councils of Polish and Lithuanian Jewry.[17]

The provincial chief rabbinate, now purely at the discretion of the Jewish electorate, remained a feature of Jewish communal organization in independent Poland. The constant redistribution of the Jewish population, on the other hand, the ensuing growth of new self-assertive communities and the territorial changes in the country at large necessarily affected also this spiritual and judicial leadership and, to an ever greater extent, the organizational and fiscal management of the various provinces.

The community of Cracow which, until 1648, held undisputed leadership over the provinces of Cracow and Sandomierz and alone elected the regional chief rabbi, constantly yielded ground to the increasingly independent northern district, where Pinczów and Opatów long struggled for supremacy. After 1692, the former capital became increasingly isolated. In contrast to purely administrative organs, which from 1717 on had their main seat in Pinczów, the chief rabbinate permanently remained in its ancient celebrated seat. The provincial communities, however, assumed a more decisive role in the selection of the regional rabbi, who simultaneously served as the local rabbi of Cracow. Similar developments also caused the gradual loss of status by the community of Poznań in Greater Poland.

After 1736, the tragic year of the Poznań blood accusation, the provincial leaders could no longer agree upon the selection of a chief rabbi. The seat remained vacant despite express orders of the governor in 1752 that it be filled without delay. When the district of Podole was ceded by Poland to Turkey in 1672, the provincial chief rabbis of Lwów naturally lost their control over the Jewish communities of that district. After its reversion to Poland in 1699, Podolian Jewry fought tooth and nail for independence, and in 1713 established a separate provincial rabbinate in Satanów. At the same time, Lwów was forced to retreat in the remaining districts of Red Russia (roughly Eastern Galicia). In 1735, King Augustus III personally rebuked the local Jewries of that province for their *novitates* in attempting to separate themselves from the Lwów rabbinate. Despite this censure, the local leaders proceeded in the same year to elect the rabbi of Żółkiew as their provincial chief. From that time until the annexation of Galicia by Austria in 1772—indeed, even long afterwards—there was constant intercommunal strife, often resulting in a partition of the chief rabbinate. Since Lwów itself had two increasingly segregated Jewish communities (the urban and the suburban), the possession of but half of the chief rabbinate by the local rabbi, and the constant mutual recriminations between partisans of the respective officers, greatly damaged the prestige of the office. Despite all these shortcomings the provincial chief rabbinate of the eighteenth century was the backbone of the Jewish communal structure and the most stabilizing factor in the midst of overwhelming forces of dissolution affecting Polish-Lithuanian Jewry and the country at large.[18]

3. INTERTERRITORIAL COOPERATION

Cooperation of many communities could also be obtained
by methods more closely corresponding to their desire to
maintain their independence both of the state and of each
other. Whenever the occasion arose accredited representatives of several leading communities could meet more or
less informally, debate the outstanding issues of the day
and devise concerted action. Records of such intercommunal
and even international cooperation of medieval and early
modern Jewries are fairly numerous, although far less
numerous than one might expect in view of their far-reaching
cultural and economic interrelations and the great similarity
of their external status under western Christendom.

In view of the international position of the papacy, the
Roman community, as in the days of the Caesars, was
frequently in a position to render valuable services to coreligionists in other lands. It was undoubtedly due to its
influence that Gregory I sharply ordered the discontinuation
of forced conversions in southern Gaul and wrote several
of his famous epistles in favor of Jewish groups living outside
the nascent Pontifical State. Roman Jews must also have
brought to the attention of Pope Nicholas IV the plight of
German Jewry, when the emperor persisted in keeping
Meir of Rothenburg imprisoned. It was not their fault that
the papal intervention long proved ineffective. The famous
humanist, Johannes Reuchlin, faced in 1513 by a dangerous
trial in Rome on account of his controversy with Pfefferkorn,
addressed a Hebrew epistle to Bonetto de Lattes, the head
of the Roman community and papal court physician, with
the request that he "influence his Holiness, our lord, the
Pope, that no power or permission be given to compel me

to appear before any judge except the judges of my province, as is required by our statutes and laws." As in antiquity, Roman Jewry entertained and diplomatically supported delegates from other communities, such as the Lorraine rabbi, Jacob b. Yeḳutiel, when he arrived in Rome in 1007 to protest against anti-Jewish persecutions in his country, or the deputation dispatched to Rome in 1215 by an assembly of southern French notables under the leaderships of Isaac Benveniste. Among the other delegations which received moral and political support from their Roman coreligionists, were that sent by the Jews of Carpentras in 1762–64; Jacob Zelig's (Elyakim b. Asher Zelig), dispatched in 1758 by Polish Jewry to obtain a renewal of the papal condemnation of the ritual murder accusation; and the envoys of the Portuguese Marranos, who were long successful in preventing the establishment of the Inquisition in their country. When Bohemian Jewry was facing sudden expulsion in 1744–45, Jonathan Eibeschütz, then rabbi in Metz, appealed to the community of Rome to use its good offices to obtain papal intercession with the Austrian Empress. At the same time, he solicited financial assistance for his Bohemian coreligionists from the wealthy Sephardic communities of Bayonne and Bordeaux. Even such an adventurer as David Reubeni was lavishly entertained by his Roman hosts and given an official residence to suit his fastidious tastes. On the other hand, Roman Jewry was frequently forced to appeal to other communities for financial assistance. The recurrent burnings of the Talmud in the sixteenth century and its subsequent, more or less permanent outlawry in Rome — in 1759 a visitor failed to secure there a single copy — which were bound to have repercussions throughout the Catholic world, furnished a particularly appropriate occasion for such an appeal. In 1784, the Roman community turned to coreligionists in distant Berlin and London in its search for political and legal assistance in the emergency which speedily developed from the unlawful conversion of two Jewish boys.[19]

Problems of relief or religious conformity and intracommunal discussions often stirred communities of many lands to united action. When the first hosts of Crusaders began threatening the Jewish communities in France in 1095, the French rabbis dispatched messengers to the Rhenish communities asking them to order general fasts and prayers in their behalf. The Mayence elders immediately proclaimed a day of fasting and assured their French coreligionists of their deep sympathy. Although at first glibly believing that they themselves were not menaced, the Jews of Mayence, shaken in their confidence, before long sent delegates to Emperor Henry IV imploring his protection. The emperor's alleged circular letter to the princes of Germany may have proved unavailing at the moment, but it undoubtedly had some bearing upon the steps which he took in favor of the Jews in the following years. About 1547 the historian, Joseph Hacohen, addressed an appeal to the community of Salonica to send contributions for the redemption of Jews captured by Andrea Doria and Cigala Visconti. When the Moravian community of Kremsier suffered severely from the invading Swedish troops in 1643, Samuel Aboab, residing in Verona, was asked by the Portuguese community of Amsterdam to forward 200 thalers to the victims via Vienna. Aboab added 40 thalers collected among his Sephardic coreligionists in Verona, and also induced the heads of the Ashkenazic community in that city to call a meeting for the consideration of further relief action. To forestall a threatening expulsion of Silesian Jewry in 1558, the Polish Council of Three Lands decided to disburse 400 florins. Relief activities in behalf of stricken German communities and the numerous German emigrés during the Thirty Years' War engaged the constant attention of the Polish and Dutch communal leaders. On the other hand, numerous appeals were issued by the Polish communities in their own emergency, beginning with the Cossack rebellions as far back as 1642. In 1674 they sent a special representative to enlist the interest of the communal leaders of Amsterdam. They had to appeal again in 1677 to their wealthy coreligionists in Holland, "in whose eyes money does not count when it comes to spending it on the fulfilment of a commandment." They also sent messengers to Italy. The Italian communities were approached, on the other hand, directly by the communities in Turkey upon whose shoulders rested the main burden of redeeming the captives brought from Poland. In 1648 a special messenger, David Carcassoni, was sent from Constantinople to Italy and Holland to solicit money for the redemption of captives. Western communities, such as London and Amsterdam, likewise communicated with each other about means of relieving the widespread distress. We also find records of several communities cooperating in the redemption of a single captive (e. g. in Mantua, in 1708).[20]

The anti-Maimonidean controversy, although directly involving only the communities of southern France, likewise had deep repercussions throughout the Mediterranean basin. Two wealthy and learned Jews in Rome, we are told in a contemporary undated report, succeeded in influencing the pope (perhaps Nicholas IV, 1288–92) to issue a proclamation, subsequently read in the synagogue, highly praising Mai-

monides' efforts to prove creation *ex nihilo*. The Pope is
supposed to have forbidden any interference with the study
of the *Guide* under the penalty of 100 silver pieces. To
prohibit the reading of the *Light of the Eyes*, a distinguished
historical work written by Azariah de' Rossi, by immature
and untrained readers to whom, in their opinion, the author's
critical acumen might do more harm than good, the communities of Venice, Pesaro, Ancona, Cremona, Padua, Verona,
Rome, Ferrara and Siena issued in 1574 an ordinance
demanding that, before studying the book, each reader obtain
a rabbinic authorization. Characteristically, the rabbinate of Azariah's native city, Mantua, which had licensed
the work before it was sent to the press, failed to join in this
united action. Far more important was the Shabbetian
movement which, for over a century, divided Jewish groups
all over the world and provoked communal bans and counter-
bans from the Netherlands and Poland to the Near East.
The Emden-Eibeschütz controversy, but an incident in
this anti-Shabbetian struggle, stirred up the communities
from Hamburg to Constantinople.[21]

Cases of intercommunal appeals to help settle local
conflicts fill the annals of late medieval and early modern
Jewish history. Reference has already been made to the
intervention of the Spanish and Austrian rabbis in the
controversy over the occupancy of the chief rabbinate in
France. In 1518 another such *cause célèbre* began to haunt
the rabbinic offices in northern Italy and Germany. Josel
of Rosheim records in his *Memoir* an extended controversy
between the Bohemian communities of Prague and Horowitz
(1534). Various German and Polish rabbis intervened,
whereupon he and Abraham b. Avigdor were elected arbiters.

The Jews of Horowitz, however, were dissatisfied with their decision and threatened Josel's life, until various leaders of Austrian and Italian communities interceded in his behalf. Of some consequence also was the conflict over the reintroduction of the ancient "ordination." Initiated in sixteenth-century Safed by Jacob Berab, but speedily controverted by the rabbis of Jerusalem, it assumed for a while universal Jewish significance through the organizational and legal issues involved and through its underlying messianic expectations. And it was Menasseh ben Israel's negotiations with Cromwell for the admission of the Jews which opened a new period in their history in Anglo-Saxon countries.[22]

4. FRANCO-GERMAN SYNODS AND CONFERENCES

Instances of such collective action far transcending the bounds of an individual community, or even of a regional super-community, could easily be multiplied. Action was usually effected through correspondence. But some of the geonim, confronted by the problem of widely scattered Jewish settlements seeking their advice, had complained of the inadequacy of correspondence[23] and now it was often felt that more considered and effective steps could be expected from a meeting of responsible leaders. A conference of rabbis and laymen would also lend greater authority to the ordinances. The medieval Jewish communal leaders merely had to emulate the example of the Catholic Church whose synods, provincial as well as universal, had a venerable tradition. Few of these Jewish gatherings, however, could be rabbinical synods in the technical sense. Generally, in accordance with the significance of the lay element in the Jewish community, they had to include representative laymen and to deal with all sorts of political, organizational and relief matters, as well as with religious and legal enactments.

These conferences and synods, naturally enough, were a primary necessity only in countries whose Jews had no country-wide or regional leadership. Most of them are recorded in France after the period of the Carolingian *magister Judaeorum* and before the reunification of Jewry under their fourteenth-century *gardien général* and chief rabbi; in Germany after the first Crusade; and in Italy, where full political sovereignty of the various republics, combined with their cultural interdependence under the aegis of the papacy, compelled frequent cooperation among the Jewish communities. The "mystic urge" toward ethnic-religious survival and the development of self-governing Jewish institutions was no less vigorous in the Muslim lands or in Spain, but the existing permanent central or regional agencies guaranteed sufficient continuity of common action. The assemblies of Barcelona in 1354 and Valladolid in 1432, referred to above, were called principally for specific purposes: the former to replace (or supplement) the appointive chief rabbi by a freely elected all-Aragonese executive committee; the latter, summoned by the "rabbi of the court," to buttress the sinking prestige of the Castilian chief rabbinate. Although both met with royal approval and, incidentally, adopted a series of other highly significant resolutions, their effect upon the subsequent organizational destinies of Spanish Jewry was practically nil. Similarly, a conference convoked in 1455–56 by the newly appointed chief rabbi of Germany, Seligmann Oppenheim, for the evident purpose of reinforcing his authority among the Jews of Germany, broke down because of the opposition

of several rabbis. Curiously, the final blow to Seligmann's
authoritarian ambitions was delivered by Israel Isserlein,
rabbi of a relatively small community in Austria (Wiener
Neustadt), who was a recognized juristic authority. In
England, whose Jewry generally followed in the footsteps
of the Franco-German communities, we find hardly any
records of regular synods. Largely obviated by the existing
arch-presbyterate, however non-ecclesiastic in character,
they were expressly forbidden in 1242 by Henry III, the
same monarch who only one year before had convoked a
Jewish parliament at Worcester.[24]

The earliest Jewish synods on record are those of the
northern French and the Rhenish communities. Their
origins, like those of most important institutions, are
shrouded in darkness. Various ordinances ascribed to
Gershom "the Light of the Exile," founder of the famous
Franco-German schools of learning, are occasionally styled
"excommunications enacted by the communities." Beyond
this slender evidence, however, and the generally reasonable
assumption that the legislator had some sort of understanding with the communal chiefs of his own city and
perhaps also of some neighboring towns, there is no proof
that he ever presided over a gathering of Jewish leaders.
Similarly, a less far-reaching decree, associated with the
name of Solomon Yiṣḥaḳi (Rashi), is vaguely described
as issued by "the inhabitants of Troyes together with the
communities in its environs." Very good reasons have been
advanced against dating these ordinances in the eleventh
century, the period of Gershom or Rashi.[25]

The first full-fledged synod known in the annals of Jewish
history is, therefore, that convoked at Troyes by Rashi's
grandsons, Jacob (Tam) and Samuel b. Meir (about 1150).

The introduction to the decisions, extant in several texts, describes its constituency:

> Therefore have we taken counsel together, the elders of Troyes and her sages and those of her vicinity; the sages of Dijon and her environs; the leaders of Auxerre, Sens and her dependencies; the elders of Orléans and her environs; our brethren the inhabitants of Châlons[-sur-Marne]; the sages of the Rheims district; our masters in Paris and their neighbors; the scholars and councilors of Melun and Etampes; the inhabitants of Normandy and the coast; of Anjou and Poitou; the leaders of our generation living in Lorraine. Of those mentioned here some have already agreed, but from some we have not yet heard, though the matter was urgent. We have relied, however, upon our knowing them to be "great men listening to their inferiors" and upon the truth of our decision which, if it were not written down, would have deserved to be written down.

Although the signatures attached are rendered diversely in the various extant versions and are evidently incomplete in all, we may assume that a large group of northern French (and possibly western German) rabbis participated in the deliberations — according to one version 150 elders were present — or subsequently ratified the decisions. The only ordinance recorded, perhaps the only one adopted, was a prohibition against repairing to Gentile courts or invoking the aid of Gentile officials without the consent of the opposing party. A second synod of Troyes (after 1160), less representative in attendance, issued ordinances reinforcing the authority of the Jewish courts while safeguarding the rights of individuals within the community. Subsequent synods were held mainly in the Rhineland, under the leadership of the three strongly allied communities of Mayence, Worms and Spires (known under their joint Hebrew abbrevation *Shum*). The most important were the two synods held in 1220–23 in Mayence and Spires under the guidance of the leading jurists, Eleazar b. Judah ha-Rokeaḥ and Eliezer b. Joel ha-Levi. They issued a number of significant ordinances regulating many phases of religious, economic, family and community life. While gatherings during the fourteenth, fifteenth and sixteenth centuries made a less permanent impression, the rabbinical assembly of Frankfort in 1603, undoubtedly stimulated by intervening developments in Italy and Poland, surpassed all predecessors in the number and boldness of its enactments. Many of these synodal regulations deeply affected Jewish communal life in central Europe and will frequently be referred to in our subsequent discussion.[26]

The primary purpose of the early French and German gathering evidently was juristic and organizational. The later conferences more frequently pursued defensive and political aims. The conference held in Mayence about 1307 seems to have had as its only objective the raising of the sum of 30,000 marks demanded by the emperor for admission to Germany of the numerous refugees from France. Similarly, the Nuremberg meeting of 1476 considered only the means of raising a substantial sum in order to secure Emperor Frederick III's good will in the face of the alleged ritual murder in Trent. Curiously, the leaders in Nuremberg, probably fearing, as indeed did the Frankfort conferees of 1603, an accusation of encroaching on the prerogatives of the imperial treasury, did not venture to start their own collections, but asked Joseph Colon, rabbi of Mantua, to issue the appeal in their behalf. Colon did not hesitate to reinforce his appeal by threat of excommunication so that "they shall not disobey the decision of my masters assembled at Nuremberg in all that they may impose upon each community, to pay, severally or conjointly, and contribute toward the expenses [for the combatting] of the false accusation." At the instigation of Frankfort Jewry, which in 1509 could not obtain full cooperation of the other communities in its struggle with Pfefferkorn, Maximilian I issued in 1510 an order to all the Jews in the Empire as well as in his Hereditary Estates to appear at, or send representatives to, Worms on a date to be set by five specified Jewish commissioners. The meeting was delayed until 1513 and had little practical effect. Perhaps the absence of the most powerful Jewish individual in the Empire, Josel of Rosheim, accounted for this failure. Josel himself got together a fairly large and representative assembly in Augsburg in 1530 to meet the challenge of the historic Diet then in session. Here, too, however, deliberations were unduly dragged out and, although significant resolutions were finally adopted primarily against Jewish usury, they came too late to have any practical effect on the Diet. Perhaps equally incidental was the renewal, by a "synod" in Worms in 1542 attended by 3 delegates from Frankfort, 2 from Worms and one each from Landau and other cities, of the old prohibition of rabbinical bans issued against non-residents.[27]

The emperors, on the other hand, ever impecunious and awake to the fiscal opportunities arising from their relations with the "serfs of their chamber," soon realized that conferences of Jewish leaders could be utilized to good advantage, to substitute for, or to reinforce, the faltering authority of their imperial tax farmers and official chief rabbis. Emperor Sigismund, dissatisfied with the results of his previous appointment of a central committee of three rabbis, ordered the Rhenish Jews to appear before him at Nuremberg in 1431. Each community was to send at least one rabbi and one other delegate. Noticing that the Frankfort community had failed to send representatives, the emperor threatened the recalcitrant leaders with a renewed cancellation of debts owing to Jews. In 1434, he extended a similar "invitation" to numerous communities in Austria, Switzerland, Württemberg, Baden, Saxony, Thuringia and the Rhineland to send delegates to Basel, where he eventually obtained his desired "testimonial gift." Four years later, despite the intervening appointment of Anselm of Cologne to the chief rabbinate, Albrecht II once more ordered the Jewish communities throughout the Empire to send deputies to Nuremberg. These "Jewish diets," in all respects resembling the extortionist "Jewish parliament" of Worcester in 1241, were convoked again by the friendly but needy Emperor Frederick III in 1453 and 1471. In these assemblies, however, the conflict between the interests of the imperial and the ducal or municipal treasuries became ever more obvious. The latter, trying to reserve for themselves the financial resources of their Jewries, encouraged their passive resistance to exaggerated imperial claims. The emperors, after 1471, abandoned these clumsy attempts at enlisting the cooperation of the Jewish taxpayers through the decision of their own freely elected "diets."[28]

5. ITALIAN ASSEMBLIES

Political and fiscal aims dominated also most of the Italian synods and conferences, although the idea of their first meeting seems to have sprung from pro-Maimonidean interests. It was the most distinguished Jewish philosopher in medieval Italy, Hillel of Verona, who about 1289 suggested a meeting to discuss the philosophic writings of Maimonides. This conference was to have been convoked at Alexandria, and apparently was to have consisted mainly of the oriental Jews known to be sympathetic to the philosopher's point of view. Representatives of that Council (va'ad) were then to call on the communities of Germany and France to send to Venice, Marseilles or Genoa delegates who, after submitting their grievances against certain Maimonidean doctrines, should ultimately accept the decision of the Egyptian and Babylonian rabbis.[29] This religious world Jewish congress, of course, never met. The later Italian synods, however, likewise utilized the occasion of their political and fiscal deliberations to issue religious ordinances and to try to remedy certain social and organizational evils.

In southern Italy, assemblies of representatives of the major communities must have coexisted with the office of the Sicilian chief rabbinate. The impetus to both the establishment and abolition of this office seems to have come from some such assemblies. So was the formulation of ordinances, the royal approval of which was subsequently sought by the chief justices. The significant capitoli, confirmed by Alfonso in 1421, were submitted to him "on behalf of all Jewish communities in the realm," apparently during the intermission between the deposition and reappointment of Moses de Bonavoglia. In 1447 the Jewish envoys to an all-Sicilian conference, which obtained the removal of Chief Justice Joshua, were given the right to appoint local officials in conjunction with local elders. The conference was thus invested with executive functions. Four years later another conference obtained renewed royal confirmation of Jewish privileges, including the free use of synagogues and schools and taxation on a par with the Christian communities, i. e. on a relative population basis. Another set of significant privileges, including royal protection for the observance of Jewish law and communal autonomy, and a general exemption of the Jews from inquisitorial investigations and attendance at conversionist sermons, was granted in 1459 at the instance of two Jewish ambassadors representing all the Sicilian communities, which in return obligated themselves to pay a new royal tax. In behalf of another conference, Benjamin Romanus of Syracuse secured in 1466 royal approval for the establishment of a central Jewish college in Sicily.[30]

While these conferences may have been primarily due to Jewish initiative, others were called by royal officials for explicit fiscal purposes. Although the *colletta*, or grouping of entire communities for purposes of more efficient tax collection, was abolished by Parliament in 1443, instructions were issued by the viceroy in 1469 to the communities of 18 Sicilian districts to send one or two delegates to Palermo to receive communications concerning their expected services to the king. Similar orders given the tax collector of Calabria in 1488 probably reflected a custom widespread throughout the kingdom: "You shall choose a locality which shall be most convenient to all the Jews in the province; through proclamations and mandates you shall issue orders to the said Jews, that on a day fixed by you they shall all appear before you in the said locality." In conjunction with the other communities, Jewish taxes were thus to be allotted among settlements and families.[31]

One of the most remarkable sessions of the Sicilian Jewish "parliament" was called, "upon certain knowledge and mature deliberation" by the viceroy in 1489. Every community was instructed, under pain of a severe fine of 1000 gold regali, to send in June of that year one or two delegates to Palermo, or to give proxies to the delegates of a neighboring community. Palermo, because of internal dissension, despatched six delegates, who conjointly could cast only the one vote allotted each community. The proclaimed aim of this session was two-fold: to provide for the king's service and to benefit the Jews. Resolutions advocating favorable legislation were accepted by the viceroy merely for investigation or, at best, recommendation to the king, although their essence did subsequently obtain royal approval. On the other hand, a decision that all Jews contribute to a *donativo* for the king was immediately confirmed. This large subsidy of 6,000 florins for the eventful Spanish expedition against Granada was thereafter collected with great ruthlessness. It appears that this Jewish parliament as well as its predecessors, had permanent officers, such as a treasurer instructed to disburse "from the moneys of the Jews of this realm" 4 ounces in payment of the expenses incurred by two representatives. Other expense accounts of Jewish delegates are also recorded. In the fateful year 1492, the parliament first met merely to pass tax legislation. When the Spanish decree of expulsion was extended to Sicily, however, it instantly despatched envoys to Ferdinand to plead for revocation, the viceroy allowing them to raise 150 gold ducats in Rome for their expenses. All efforts to stay execution of the decree having failed, the Jewish "ambassadors" turned their attention to the organization of an orderly exodus. Regulations enacted by them were confirmed by the viceroy on August 18, 1492, exactly two months after the promulgation of the decree of banishment.[32]

Despite its great influence upon the destinies of Sicilian

Jewry, particularly after the elimination of the chief
rabbinate, this Jewish parliament, like its predecessor
of Worcester, met too irregularly and was too much under
the direct control of the government to stand comparison
with the later Polish and Lithuanian Councils. In the
annals of Jewish intercommunal assemblages, however, it
ought to occupy a much more prominent place than has
hitherto been given to it by Jewish historiography.

Even more loosely organized were the conferences of the
northern and central Italian communities — a clear reflection
of the divided political sovereignties throughout this section
of the peninsula. Only the gatherings of the elders of the
various communities in the Papal States, devoted to the
adjustment of state-wide taxes, bear some resemblance to
the Spanish *collectas* and the Sicilian parliament. Although,
according to the papal privilege of 1402, the community of
Rome was entitled forcibly to collect the assessed contributions of the provincial Jewries, it usually preferred amicable
agreements on quotas. We possess the Hebrew text of one
such agreement, dated 1443. It is also likely that the first
recorded conference of the peninsular communities, which
seems to have met at Rimini in 1399, had been convoked by
the community of Rome for the purpose of reaching an
agreement even before it had secured the papal decision.
The sessions of representatives of communities of Candia,
beginning in 1238, which were the oldest conferences in
Italian-speaking areas, were limited to one geographic sector,
but had broad agendas.[33]

In matters of more general interest the cooperation of
many communities throughout the north and center of the
peninsula was sought. Unfortunately we do not possess
the records of the first large Italian conference, held in

Bologna in 1416 and attended by delegates from the Papal
States, Tuscany, Padua and Ferrara. We know, however,
of its selection of a "vigilance committee" which met two
years later at Forli. The immediate purpose of these meetings was to devise means of counteracting the effects of the
extremely anti-Jewish bull promulgated in 1415 by Anti-
Pope Benedict XIII, and of obtaining favorable legislation
from Martin V, elected to the Holy See in 1417. To secure
the necessary funds the committee at Forli imposed a
combined property and capitation tax (1½ per 1,000 florins
of property and ½–1½ ducats per family) on its constituent
groups. At the same time, it issued a series of ordinances
aimed at excessive luxury, gregariousness in public thorough-
fares, and card games, all of which practices seem to have
given offense to the Christian population. Severe penalties
were to be meted out to every Jew who failed to denounce
a card player to the communal authorities. Encouraged by
its successful negotiations with Martin V in 1419, the
vigilance committee seems to have met again in Perugia in
1423. Its original ten-year term, expiring in 1426, was
evidently renewed, to enable it to call another general conference in Florence two years later. Martin V's levy on the
communities of Ancona and Venice, in retaliation for the
alleged intention of the Muslim administration in Palestine
to convert the Franciscan chapel on Mt. Zion into a synagogue, was the primary object of that conference. In addition, however, it issued a regulation against usury. The
hostile bull of Eugenius IV issued in 1442 had as a sequel
the rabbinical assemblies of Tivoli and Ravenna which,
besides considering means of obtaining revocation, seem to
have entered into diplomatic negotiations with the Duke
of Mantua. They tried to induce the Duke to grant the

right of settlement to prospective refugees from the Pontifical State, "to give them permission publicly to observe
the Mosaic law, to adjust their litigations in Jewish courts,
and freely to engage in all occupations." Six years later
John Capistrano's anti-Jewish agitation (the renowned
preacher is supposed to have offered the pope a fleet to
transport all the Jews of Rome to a distant locality) and
Nicholas V's prohibition of interest charges by Jews — a
reversal of traditional papal policy, which encouraged Jewish
moneylending — induced the community of Recanati to
call a general assembly of the leaders of neighboring communities.[34]

The most important Italian synod, meeting at Ferrara
in 1554, was occasioned by the burning of Hebrew books
throughout Italy in the preceding year. To obviate future
difficulties, the synod decreed that "printers shall not be
permitted to print any hitherto unpublished book except
with the permission of three rabbis, each ordained by
three rabbis, and the consent of the heads of one of the
communities nearest the place of printing." It adopted a
number of other resolutions which, remaining in force to
the eighteenth century, exercised great influence upon the
communal evolution of Italian Jewry. The more liberal
policies of Sixtus V with respect to Hebrew books caused
the establishment of a commission of one member each
from the communities of Rome, Venice, Mantua, Ferrara,
Modena, Reggio and Padua to supervise pre-censorship, and
stimulated the Padua community to call a conference with
those of Piedmont, Mantua, Milan and Ferrara to consider
means of obtaining a papal permit for the reprinting of the
Talmud (1586). We hear less of such all-Italian gatherings
through subsequent periods of Italian Jewish history which,

until Italy's unification in the nineteenth century, were relatively "dark."[35]

The main reason for the discontinuation of the Italian, as well as the German regional assemblies undoubtedly lay in the governments' growing doubts of their efficacy in increasing public revenue. In general it may be stated that governments reciprocated Jewish suspicions of royal appointees by viewing unfavorably any freely elected or self-appointed regional Jewish leadership. The early meetings, to be sure, were often called with royal permission. Such permission is expressly recorded in the decisions of the Barcelona Conference and may be taken for granted in the case of the semi-official synod of Valladolid. Likewise, the resolution of the second synod of Troyes begins, "by order of the king." The Champagne fairs were chosen less for the understandable fear of suspicions which otherwise might have arisen from such a concerted gathering of strangers in a medieval locality, than because of the greater convenience and security of travel for delegates. In Poland, as we shall see, the businessmen who constituted the majority of each council also found it to their mutual advantage to meet at an annual fair. These conferences were, none the less, often suspected of hatching Jewish secret plots. The Inquisition had to be placated by the community of Rome in 1443 through the submission of a Latin translation of its agreement with other communities of the State. The German conference of 1493 aroused widespread Gentile suspicions, while the Frankfort assembly of 1603 led, three years later, to a protracted trial in which delegates were accused of high treason. Three different German translations of the resolutions prepared for the court are extant. The proceedings evidently ended with the liberation of the accused,

but in 1623 the emperor ordered the Jewish community
to pay prosecution costs to the Archbishops of Mayence and
Cologne who had acted as the imperial commissioners, and
an additional fine of 30 gold marks to the latter. These
never-ending suspicions combined with internal acids generated by the Commercial Revolution, which began to dis-
solve the cohesiveness of the Jewish communities, and discouraged the convocation of further Italian or German
conferences until the Emancipation era.[36]

6. POLISH-LITHUANIAN COUNCILS

A far more satisfactory solution was obtained by the
Polish-Lithuanian and, to some extent, the Moravian and
some western German communities through the establishment of permanent councils recognized, but not controlled
by the government. These, too, evolved much less from a
mystic urge than from sheer force of circumstances. The
Polish state, guided almost exclusively by fiscal considerations, wished Jewish tax collections effectively concentrated
in the hands of a few leaders. On the other hand, the Jews
coming for the most part from Germany, brought with them
a fairly deep-rooted opposition to strong government control. At the same time, mass immigration from varied
German territories, each of which had its own set of customs,
observances, economy and organizational methods gave rise
to numerous legal problems calling for adjustment by
authorities transcending any one locality. Talmudic law
persistently excluded local leaders from sitting in judgment
on litigations which involved the interests of their own
community. This made a superior instance increasingly
indispensable. Moreover, the defense of Jewish rights in the
midst of conflicting interests of nobility, clergy, munici-

palities and a steadily declining monarchy; negotiations with influential officials and leaders of the central and provincial diets; the prevention or revocation of contemplated hostile measures; common action to meet the ever-present menace of blood accusations which, however local in nature, always threatened to involve the country's entire Jewish population; the defense of traveling Polish-Jewish merchants, especially those visiting the fairs at Leipzig and Breslau — these and other political necessities called for a pooling of the resources of Polish Jewry. Finally, there were numerous difficult questions of economic and cultural adjustment which could effectively be regulated only by some superior authority. Certainly the perennial struggle of Jewish craftsmen against city guilds and the dangers emanating from the competition of Jews with nobles in tax farming and the exportation of grain, as well as the growing intercommunal problems of Jewish book publishing, education and social welfare increased the need for concerted action.

The early decades of the sixteenth century witnessed the beginnings of inter-communal collaboration. Just as the great Polish diet, the *sejm*, had grown out of the nobles' provincial gatherings, the so-called *sejmiki*, so were the foundations for the Polish-Jewish councils laid by gradually evolving provincial semi-parliaments. As far back as 1334, Casimir the Great confirmed the general privilege of the Jews in Greater Poland (the district of Poznań) at the request of "worthy men, our faithful Jews from our lands." Two centuries later Sigismund I, disappointed with the results of his experiments with individual tax farmers and general elders, convoked a provincial gathering of Greater Polish Jewry at Włocławek in 1519 to obtain increased revenue. Similar concentration of rabbinic and lay power was proceeding in other provinces of Poland and Lithuania. In 1533 there was in the latter a nation-wide Jewish tribunal. In Poland, too, such a tribunal must have been established at an early date, since Sigismund I confirmed in 1540 the existence of an all-Polish court of two rabbis each from Cracow, Poznań and Lwów, and presided over by the rabbi of Lublin. Lublin was selected as the seat of this supreme court not only because of the great reputation of its rabbi, Shalom Shakna, but primarily because its fairs, visited by Jewish merchants from all over the country, made it convenient for communal lay elders. For the same reason Jarosław, centrally located in Lesser Poland, likewise frequently served as the Council's meeting place. The promulgation, in 1549, of the new general poll tax, although it introduced no new specifically Jewish impost, created new problems concerning the Jewish quota and its distribution and forced on Polish-Jewish leadership more regular consultation. The political successes culminating in the abovementioned decrees of 1551 and 1569, which definitely guaranteed free election of communal officers and rabbis, and the printing of the first Polish Talmud edition (1559–77), which was introduced into all Polish schools and academies, undoubtedly were also the effect of some such united action.[37]

Out of all these groping attempts at unity, there finally evolved the Council of Three, then of Four Lands (*Va'ad arba' araṣot* or *Congressus generalis judaicus*), so called because its early regular sessions were attended by representatives of Lesser Poland (principally the elders of Cracow and Lublin), Greater Poland (Poznań), Red Russia (Lwów) and Lithuania (Brześć, etc.). In 1623 Lithuania seceded and its chief communities organized a separate body, called briefly the Council of the Province (*Va'ad ha-medinah*).

Thenceforth Volhynia (chief city usually Ostrog) often figured as the fourth Polish land and the established name of the large Council persisted. As a matter of fact, however, there were constant subdivisions, partly due to local demands for independent representation, partly to increasing fiscal decentralization. Ultimately no less than twelve distinct fiscal districts were represented. The separation of Lithuania, too, was largely due to fiscal considerations, inasmuch as the two countries, although united under one king, had different internal organizations and treasuries. The Jews of Lithuania, being separately assessed, preferred separate responsibility for their taxes, usually less than half the Polish quota. From time to time, delegates of the Lithuanian Council continued coming to Lublin or its vicinity to discuss problems of broad scope. As far as can be seen from the few extant records of these united gatherings during the years 1633–81, the Lithuanian Council contributed only about one-seventh of the common budget, largely for defense and anti-defamation. Constant recriminations about finances between the two councils, however, and the specific protective measures demanded by the Lithuanian section, stimulated the desire for complete separation. When the capital of Poland was transferred to Warsaw which, unlike Cracow-Kazimierz, had no large and affluent local community, the task of safeguarding the nation-wide political interests of Jewry was entrusted to a permanent "Warsaw Committee" of eight special *syndici* (*shtadlanim*) appointed by the two councils. The problems arising from the failure of one Lithuanian community, Tykocin, to join the exodus of 1623, and its ensuing abnormal position within the Polish system, led to bitter debates between the two councils as well as within the Polish Council. The session

of 1681 settled the conflict on the basis of the decision of
the supreme rabbinical tribunal in Poland,

> that the leaders of the Four Lands have no suprem-
> acy, hegemony or dominion over the province of
> Lithuania, be it in financial matters, or questions of
> honor, or in anything that the mouth can utter and
> the heart can think of. Neither shall there ever be
> any kind of united action or partnership [of the two
> councils] in whatever matter, not even in the expendi-
> ture necessary for the prevention of an actually im-
> pending general expulsoin of the remnant of Israel.

In such a case, however, the leaders of the two councils
were expected independently to take the necessary steps
in their respective provinces.[38]

Due to the fact that the original minute book of the
Council of Four Lands, kept at Lublin, was largely destroyed by several conflagrations, information concerning
organization and activities largely depends on chance copies
of decisions in the minute books of constituent congregations. The protocols of the Lithuanian Council, however,
have been well preserved in three slightly differing copies.
The Polish *Va'ad* seems generally to have consisted of some
thirty delegates elected by provincial councils. They included the seven leading rabbis, representing four major
communities and organized as a supreme tribunal for Polish
Jewry. The Lithuanian Council was smaller, at first consisting of some six to nine members and gradually, after the
admission of Wilno in 1652, increasing its membership to
some twelve or fifteen. The Polish group met more or less
regularly in the Spring and Fall at the fairs of Lublin and
Jarosław. In the eighteenth century, with the growing
emphasis on fiscal functions, it frequently held sessions in

one of the small towns belonging to the private estates of the respective aristocratic chancellors of the Polish exchequer. From the outset the Lithuanian sessions were far less frequent and regular. At first all meetings were at Brześć or another city in the same district. In 1644 the three constituent communities agreed to meet in fourteen-year cycles, so arranged that two sessions were to be at Brześć and one each in Grodno and Pinsk. As a matter of fact, the seasons and places of the meetings varied greatly. Minute books and other records indicate a total of 43 sessions in the first 108 years of the Council's existence (1623–1730). They were at intervals of one to four years, except when the session of 1713 was followed, apparently, by a lapse of eight years. After 1730, sessions became ever more irregular: none is recorded between 1731 and 1738, but there was one each in 1739 and 1740. These were the last until 1748, 1751 and the final, dramatic gathering of 1761. This irregularity was an obvious foreshadowing of dissolution.[39]

The two central councils, as well as the provincial councils, chose their own officers. The chairmen, called marshals (in Hebrew *parnasim*), in emulation of the Polish central and provincial diets, were salaried officials. They were, nevertheless, selected only from among the leading patrician families, thus greatly contributing to the increasingly oligarchic character of communal leadership throughout the country. Assisted by a staff of syndici, secretaries, treasurers and other officials, they wielded great power over all Polish Jewry. In Lithuania the first presiding officer was a rabbi, Meir of Brześć (son of Saul Wahl, the legendary one-day king of Poland), but only laymen occupied the chair in the Polish Council. Bitter strife between candidates supported

by rival communities and families ultimately helped undermine the institution. In particular, the controversy between
Abraham of Lissa, chairman for the years 1740–53, and
Abraham of Lublin, his successor for the years 1753–61,
greatly marred the Council's record during its last two
decades.

This record otherwise is very impressive. As the main
fiscal agency, the Polish Council furnished ever increasing
sums to the state treasury. Responsible only for a total
tax of 15–20,000 florins ((złoty) when founded, its burden
increased to some 100,000 in the course of the seventeenth
century, and was fixed, in 1717, at 220,000. This increase
was wholly incommensurate with the growth of the Jewish
population and certainly failed to take into account the
frightful economic decline, which, indeed, it greatly accelerated. A series of economic regulations helped adjust
Jewish economic activities to the new requirements. Not
only did the Council try to obviate the disastrous competition between Jews and nobles in the farming of state revenue — it adopted stringent measures in its early session of
1581 — but it also regulated various aspects of moneylending, such as interest rates, forms of loan deeds (1607,
1681, 1707), and receivership proceedings. A series of
ordinances adopted in 1607, under the chairmanship of Rabbi
Joshua Falk Kohen of Lwów, was published in 1692 under
his name. Of special interest here are regulations adopted
in the sessions of 1583 and 1595 concerning elections to local
communal boards and the latter's rights and obligations.
Zealously guarding the privileges inaugurated by the decrees
of 1551 and 1569, the Polish Council decided in 1583 that

it is forbidden to install rabbis, elders, chiefs, members
of committees or any other office-holders save through

elections in the Jewish street. The officers must be
called to serve on the basis of an agreement between
the elders and chiefs and the committee as well as in
accordance with the provisions of our Torah. Concerning this matter we possess privileges from the
kings and from all the nobles and rulers of the country. . . . Anyone guilty of a transgression, shall pay to
the governor 100 złoty, to the judge 50, to charity 50,
and to the community 100 złoty.

The Lithuanian Council added the provision that no Jew
shall cite a Gentile before a state or local court without the
permission of his communal chiefs, whose advice must also
be strictly followed by Jewish defendants in mixed litigations. In 1671 the Council of Four Lands, endeavoring to
re-establish law and order in the Polish communities dis-
organized by the ravages of Cossack massacres and foreign
wars, issued the following brief but expressive proclamation
for reading in all Polish synagogues:

Announcement is herewith made and a warning
issued with respect to persons engaging in debasing
[metals], whether in goldsmithery or in any other
trade. Such persons shall be handed over to the
authorities and shall be severely fined in order to
eradicate the thorns from the vineyard, the vineyard
of the Lord of Hosts. Similarly those who purchase
stolen goods, who serve as brokers between two
Gentiles, as well as those who reveal Jewish secrets
to the uncircumcised, or show or teach the uncircumcised Jewish trades [and thus undermine the competitive power of the Jewish community], woe unto them
and unto their souls! The great and fearful ban
issued with the blowing of the horn and all candles
extinguished . . . shall rest upon these lawbreakers
and also upon those who seek [communal] appoint-

ments from the [Gentile] authorities and who try to obtain tax immunities from the authorities. They cause much expenditure, and the Lord shall not consent to forgive them. Such persons shall be excommunicated from the two worlds, their property shall be free for all, and when they suffer reverses no one shall assist them, but on the contrary shall remove them to the "lowest hell," and segregate them from the community of the dispersion.

Finally, to uphold their own authority, the Councils made such local officials as the Wilno *shammash* insert a clause into their oath of office binding them never to affix their signature to a local enactment running counter to any resolution of the Council.[40]

The Polish Council, often acting in behalf of both councils, maintained relations with Jewish communities abroad. It prosecuted fugitive criminals and defaulting debtors from other lands; extended financial, political and moral assistance to foreign communities; intervened, when requested, in communal quarrels abroad (for instance, that about David Lida, the Ashkenazic rabbi of Amsterdam, and the more renowned Emden-Eibeschütz controversy). It issued bans on Shabbetians within and without Poland (1676, reissued in 1722) and several times debated the Frankist issue. It expressed its approval or disapproval of books, often giving authors and publishers a sort of copyright by means of bans on reprinting by unauthorized outsiders within a specified period. It supervised schools and charities and in general exercised supreme control over the communal life of Polish Jewry. Although legally restricted to Poland, its decisions carried great weight throughout Ashkenazic Jewry. Jacob Emden, during the last years of the Council's existence, recorded that, in earlier times, its leaders "could issue orders to distant countries for the congregations in exile, their words were listened to by all our people, and even in Turkey, Jews were wary of counteracting their wishes, for they were considered on a par with the Sanhedrin and the High Court of Jerusalem. Disobedience to their commands was a mortal sin similar to that of the 'rebellious' elder. . . ."[41]

The foundation underlying the two central councils were the provincial councils and chief rabbinates which, with their often varying destinies and constitutional experiments, deeply affected the evolution of Polish-Jewish autonomy. The provincial council of Poznań and Greater Poland, whose extant records have been assembled and thoroughly studied, is a more or less typical example of the operation of provincial units. Headed by a permanent provincial chief rabbi and a provincial "marshal," this council distributed among individual communities the tax burden assigned it by the central council, adjusted difficulties within the province through its own judiciary, carried on diplomatic negotiations which sometimes extended to Breslau and other foreign cities, issued its own approbations of Hebrew books, and adopted a number of independent ordinances.[42]

Even less than the Lithuanian Council, which from time to time passed resolutions against foreign Jews or those immigrating from Poland, could it escape the characteristic limitations of the prevalent local "patriotism." It objected, for example, to two Italian brothers, Zacuto, "dwelling here with us, in order to trade like any of us, which is unlawful, since they are aliens and from a distant country." These Italian merchants were, in fact, informed by the Poznań community that their stay in the city should not extend beyond one month, that they might sell their merchandise to Jews only, and must not proceed to the Lublin fair

without a special communal permit. Having disregarded the
latter injunction, they were expelled on short notice by the
provincial council and forbidden to return to the city
except at fair periods under pain of a severe fine of 1,000
Hungarian guilders (1620). Ironically, half a century later
Moses Zacuto, apparently a son of one of the two exiles
and a rabbi in Venice, supported representatives of the
Greater Polish Council then trying to raise funds in Italy
for the relief of needy Poznań Jewry (1672). On the other
hand, to eliminate local collusion, the Poznań communal
board moved that the council prohibit the election of a
native as provincial chief rabbi. When this rule, confirmed
by the king in 1556, was first broken by the election of
Simon Wolf Auerbach, a Poznań resident (1621), the provincial elders bowed before the accomplished fact, but
suggested that a more stringent bar be inserted in the
statute books.[43]

The glory of both the central and the provincial councils
ended in the catastrophic decade of Cossack massacres and
Swedish-Muscovite invasions (1648–57), which inflicted
wounds from which Polish Jewry has never completely
recovered. Supreme fiscal power, originally the prime factor
in establishing the councils' authority, was also largely
responsible for the ultimate ruin. The growing burden of
taxation, often substantially increased by extralegal payments to influential officials of the Crown, Diet, Church or
city, forced debts both on communities and central and
provincial agencies. True, the Lithuanian Council had, in
its first session of 1623, far-sightedly adopted a resolution

that no community shall assume any [permanent] indebtedness. Should there occur a temporary shortage
forcing the communal elders to borrow money, they

may do so provided they pay back the loan within a
year, under the sanction of a penalty and fine in the
discretion of the provincial chiefs.[44]

But this pious resolution failed to stem the tide of annual
deficits, perennial scourge of public taxing bodies, and the
avalanche-like effects of long-term indebtedness at high
interest.

At first Jewish communal credit was sound and their
bonds sought after, especially by Christians, burghers,
nobles and, above all, monasteries and diocesan chapters
possessing idle funds. The papal nuncio, Mgr. Lascari,
explained in 1751 the large proportion of Jews in the Polish
population and their favorable status by the fact that both
secular and monastic clergy had lent them money on interest.
The inducement of a 10 per cent interest rate proved
stronger than the fear of investing on the slender security
of a synagogue. The nobles imitated the clerical example,
and the constant fear of losing their investments was largely
responsible for the protection extended to Jews and their
synagogues by both clergy and nobility.[45] The prevalent
rate of seven to ten percent for Jewish loans, though quite
low for the capital markets of the day, caused outstanding
loans to quadruple in less than a quarter century.

The communities, however, frequently unable to service
debts from regular revenue, assumed ever new ones which
ultimately reached staggering proportions. Time and again,
a community or provincial council was unable to meet its
obligations, whereupon numerous Jews and their goods were
seized by the powerful creditors. Five years after the sus-
pension of payments by the provincial council of Greater
Poland in 1694, the Council of Four Lands had to overhaul
its entire revenue system, and reorganize the tax distribution

in the seven new districts. This reform, however, proved
ineffective in preventing another breakdown which came
fourteen years later. The Poznań council's credit sank so
low that when, in 1759, the provincial elders issued a note
on 3,000 florins in favor of one of its constituent communities, nobody would cash it. Similar conditions prevailed
in other provinces. Rises in interest rates to 10, 15 and even
30 per cent, which, of course, only aggravated the evil,
were common. The effect was that, by 1764, the better
managed central council owed the moderate amount of
188,843 florins (including 17,345 florins in interest arrears),
while the accumulated debts of the twelve provincial councils amounted to 2,312,746 florins. To these sums must be
added over 1,000,000 florins for the debts of the chief provincial communities, and several more millions for those of
the numerous smaller settlements. Some estimates of the
total communal indebtedness of Polish Jewry (without
Lithuania) in 1764 run as high as 10,000,000 florins. Assuming an interest rate of but 7 per cent, which is very much
lower than reality, interest charges without any amortization aggregated three times Polish Jewry's total direct fiscal
contribution of 220,000 florins. This paradoxical situation
could not possibly escape the notice of the Polish nobles,
and the enemies of Jewish autonomy among them effectively
and repeatedly wielded this weapon in Diet debates.[46]

The vices of Polish parliamentarism, which ultimately
undermined the state's political and economic power, also
crept into the Jewish public agencies. Emulating the noto-
rious *liberum veto* of the *sejm*, which incidentally long helped
the Jews forestall legislation hostile to their autonomy,
individual Jewish delegates often remained away from or
quit sessions, thus preventing action, which usually required

unanimity. Increasing concentration of power in the hands of a small financial oligarchy led to extensive favoritism and other abuses. Growing mass disaffection, particularly in the vast, predominantly rural expanses of southeastern Poland, ultimately produced those semi-revolutionary currents of Frankism and, on a different plane, of Ḥasidism, which greatly undermined the communal control of the established leadership.

As in the Polish structure, the signs of disintegration were first discernible in the provincial councils, e. g., the protracted inability of the Greater Polish communities to elect a new chief rabbi. Communities, on the periphery of a province, such as Przemyśl or Rzeszów, often obtained a sort of "free cities" status under the direct jurisdiction of and with a seat in the Central Council. They thus resembled some of the *Immediatstände* which so vastly complicated the constitutional life of the declining Holy Roman Empire. The effectiveness of the provincial councils was further reduced by the breakdown of leading centers. In 1762 the elders of Lwów complained to the authorities that "not one Jew of the entire Lwów synagogue is still to be found among the Jewish chiefs of the province." In the same year the community of Lublin obtained from the Council of Four Lands complete separation from its provincial delegation. Signs of dissolution had by 1764 become so obvious that, after several unsuccessful attempts, the enemies of Jewish autonomy at the Diet obtained a unanimous decision ordering the dissolution of both the central and the provincial councils. The Jews, or at least their leaders, mourned the passing of the once effective institution, which was hallowed by a bicentennial tradition. On the seventh day of Passover in the Poznań synagogues it was announced that "all the ties and belts are broken wherewith we have been girdled ever since the organization of our community."[47]

The organizational decomposition of former Polish-Lithuanian Jewry was further accelerated by the partitions of Poland. For a time, semi-official committees in Warsaw watched over the interests of Jewry, particularly during the momentous deliberations of the Quadrennial Diet on the contemplated overhauling of the entire government and social structure of Poland. More permanently, liquidating agencies were busy adjusting claims against the councils, distributing them among the communities and arranging amortization. Indeed, the problem of Jewish communal debts, inherited from the Polish era, baffled the bureaucracies of Austria, Prussia and Russia for many decades. For the Jews, the continued payment of debts of defunct organizations was but a bitter reminder of the glory that was passed. None the less, they were increasingly inclined to visualize these institutions of a bygone era only in their brightest aspects and ready to condone their many all-too-human shortcomings.[48]

7. OTHER CENTRAL EUROPEAN COUNCILS

While the Polish Council focused the attention of world Jewry, and at times served as a sort of central legislative and judicial body for neighboring Ashkenazic communities, similar councils in Moravia and other parts of the Holy Roman Empire had a decidedly local character. Nevertheless, in the life of the respective provinces they, as well as the provincial chief rabbinates, played a very significant role.

Information concerning the beginnings of the two institutions in Moravia is unfortunately even more limited than that concerning the origin of the Polish councils. Known under the same Hebrew name, *va'ad*, the Moravian council, too, seems to have existed much earlier than 1653, the date of the earliest records of its regular sessions. Then and afterwards it adopted resolutions and issued ordinances similar in content and style to those of the Polish councils, which, indeed, it may have tried to imitate. The origin of the chief rabbinate which, by 1651, likewise appeared to contemporaries as of hoary antiquity, seems to date back to Maximilian I. Bendit Axelrad Levi is designated in 1519 as "chief of all Moravian communities." The office was then occupied by Mordecai Moses Eles before 1553. Among their successors, down to 1925 when the office was abolished, were many shining lights: Judah Löw b. Bezaleel (1553–73), Yom Tob Lipmann Heller (1625–26), David Oppenheim (together with Gabriel Eskeles, 1690–1718) and Samson Raphael Hirsch (1847–51), to mention only one name for each century. Under the leadership of these rabbis, there gradually grew up a body of constitutional law governing Moravian Jewish community life. Compiled in 1651–52 by Chief Rabbi Menahem Mendel Krochmal in cooperation with the provincial elders, the constitution consisted of 311 articles, and was frequently called the *shia* (311) *takkanot*. A century later, however, the Austrian government, headed by the "enlightened absolutist," Maria Theresa, demanded greater control over the Council. The Empress personally insisted on certain amendments in the constitution, which had been translated for her by the famous convert, Alois von Sonnenfels. After the inclusion of these and other amendments, likewise suggested by the Austrian authorities and designed largely to curtail autonomous rights, the statute was published under imperial sanction as the *General Polizei-, Prozess- und Kommerzial-ordnung für die Judenschaft des Markgraftums Mähren*.[49]

The Council's vitality was, nevertheless, soon demonstrated again. It adopted a series of educational reforms, which were included in the so-called *takkanot ha-medinah* promulgated by Chief Rabbi Moses Lwów (Lemburger, 1754–58). Although characterized by rigid provincialism and severe exclusion of impecunious foreign students, the new regulations insisted on the maintenance of a central academy in Nikolsburg with a minimum of 25 enrolled students, and of at least two other academies in each of the six districts which must provide for the education and support of not less than 10 students each. Thus they were an important step forward in the organization of Jewish higher education. Buttressed by strong local communities, which long maintained their peculiar semi-municipal character, and by a foundation (*Landesmassafond*) established by Joseph II in 1787–88, the Council and its chief rabbinate weathered the successive storms of the Revolutionary era and the Austrian Emancipation, to re-emerge in 1918 as the "Union [*Landesverband*] of the Jewish Communities in Moravia" in the newly constituted Czechoslovakian Republic.[50]

Quite different were the provincial council and chief rabbinate in neighboring Bohemia. The "Jewish city" in Prague long held undisputed leadership and its communal organs automatically represented all Jewry of the province. The organizational anarchy which set in during the Thirty Years' War, however, undermined the authority of the Prague chief rabbinate, in which four occupants followed one another between 1619 and 1636. The post was not filled again until 1640, when Simon Spira-Wedeles was elected. Six years passed before his re-election obtained government confirmation. Not long thereafter the provincial communities broke away and organized an independent council of ten elders (2 chiefs, 5 ordinary members and 3 associates) which was functioning as early as 1659. Later reorganized to consist of delegates of the twelve districts of Bohemia, this provincial council dealt with the Prague elders on a basis of equality. The assessment and distribution of taxes was the object of frequent agreements between the two bodies. Unity, for a while precariously maintained through the person of the chief rabbi, broke down after the death of Simon Spira in 1679. The provincial communities, unable to agree on a single candidate, elected two provincial chief rabbis who served side by side with the chief rabbi of Prague. The breach was temporarily healed under the vigorous leadership of David Oppenheim who, in the years 1713–36, served with distinction as chief rabbi of both the capital and the province. He alone could venture to issue, in 1717, an order demanding from every newly elected district rabbi that he first obtain the written approval of the chief rabbi and the provincial elders. A semblance of unity was also maintained in the administration of his successor, Isaac Spira-Wedeles (Simon's grandson, in office 1738–49), the last chief rabbi of Bohemia. Not even the great authority of Ezekiel Landau, whose fame as a jurist restored some of the glory of Prague's rabbinic center, sufficed to re-establish the communal unity of Bohemian Jewry.[51]

The Jewish provincial assemblies of certain German principalities were also of decidedly local importance. The Frankfort conference of 1603, to be sure, had made a signal attempt to establish a central organization for German

Jewry built around provincial centers along the lines of the
Polish Council. A uniform system of taxation was to be
administered from eight district cities (Frankfort, Worms,
Mayence, Bingen, Hamm, Friedberg, Schneitach, Waller-
stein and Günzburg), while five district courts were to be
established in Frankfort, Worms, Fulda, Friedberg and
Günzburg. The conference evidently did not take cognizance
of the numerous Jews in the Austrian hereditary estates,
perhaps because the strong chief rabbinates of Prague and
Nikolsburg obviated the necessity of any organizational
reform. In any case, the efforts of the Frankfort assembly,
even if they had not had the ill-luck of being immediately
frustrated by protracted government investigation, would
have been doomed to failure through the growing disintegration of the Empire.[52]

On the other hand, the rising power of the German
princes, and their increasingly absolutist regimes stimulated
the regional unification of Jewish communities in at least
some western German principalities, such as Hesse (both
Cassel and Darmstadt), Paderborn, Münster, Bamberg,
Mecklenburg-Schwerin, Hannover, Wied-Runkel, Fulda, the
electorates of Mayence and Treves, Kleve, the Mark, Silesia
and Lower Austria. Typical of all these are the provincial
assemblies and chief rabbinates of Cassel and Kleve.

The Cassel assembly was not a representative council
but rather a plenary meeting of all heads of Jewish families
in some 45 towns and 150 villages of that section of Hessia
who, under pain of severe penalties, were obliged to meet
triennially in a locality designated by the government. From
its inception under William the Wise (1567–92), or at least
from its session of 1626 which voted a substantial contribution to the government treasury, drained by the Thirty

Years' War, to its abolition by the revolutionary government
of Westphalia in 1807, this assembly served principally the
needs of Cassel's fiscal and police administrations. Its
object was impressed on the minds of members by the
landgraf's proclamation, usually handed to each member
before the meeting and read aloud at the opening of the
session. "All the Jews," the proclamation read, "are to
behave quietly, modestly and peacefully, must not show
undue zest in speech . . . they have to follow in everything
without reservation the orders of the [government] com-
misioners." One of the avowed aims was to check every
family's right of settlement and its behavior during intervening years. Another was the issuance of new privileges to
men of twenty-five who, as the eldest sons of native, "protected" Jews, wanted to establish new families. The assembly, furthermore, elected six provincial elders (one each
from each of the six districts), a chief and fourteen assistant
collectors of revenue, a treasurer for the school fund and
another for the collections for the Holy Land. Perhaps the
most important officials were the tax assessors. Each district having nominated six candidates, the chief rabbi drew
by lot seven of the 36 names. These men became, for three
years, undisputed masters of the Jewry of the state, due to
their power to assess beyond appeal the contribution due
from each family. A resolution of 1690, nevertheless, reaffirmed the full independence of the individual communities.[53]

It is, indeed, a sign of the vitality of Jewish self-government that, even under these unfavorable circumstances,
the assemblies often adopted sound measures regulating
Jewish education and social welfare. They were therein
actively supported by the permanent provincial chief rab-

binate which, although initiated by the prince under strict
government supervision, could not but strengthen autonomous forces. In his curious decree of 1625, Landgraf Moritz
wrote that

> he had learned that the Jews of his principality sub-
> mitted their litigations to foreign rabbis — previously
> in Fulda, now in Friedberg — and that the fines
> thereby imposed accrued to the benefit, one-half each,
> of the burggraf and the Jewish community there.
> This state of affairs can no longer be tolerated, since
> it not only causes the Jews much peregrination and
> expense, but also involves the loss to himself of *regalia*
> and *jurisdictionalia* due him. Without prejudice
> for the penalty to be imposed upon them for having
> hitherto concealed the above situation, the Jews are
> herewith ordered to engage a rabbi of their own in
> the Principality.

The Jews obeyed, although as late as 1655 they had to
petition the government for the right to elect a chief rabbi.
Until 1772 this officer was forced to reside in Witzenhausen,
allegedly because he would thereby be "equally near to all,
easily secure a satisfactory lodging and live in quiet sur-
roundings," but undoubtedly primarily because Jews were
not admitted to the capital except during fairs. It may be
noted, nevertheless, that despite the legally recognized
right of appeal to the Cassel government against sentence
of the rabbinical court, state organs allowed the Jewish
provincial assembly to subject such appeals to a fine of 10
thalers (1690). The treasury's half of such fines may well
explain this deviation and shed some light on the government's refusal, in 1772, to act on the suggestion of the
Hessian diet to suppress the rabbinic judiciary altogether.[54]
  Little government control is noticeable, on the other

hand, in the earlier years of the Jewish provincial assembly in Kleve. The central government, located in Berlin, was relatively remote, and most local congregations of the province were mere offshoots of the Kleve community. Even in the eighteenth century they usually consisted of only a few families. Although these may have established small synagogues and cemeteries, for all major communal affairs they remained attached to the community of Kleve and its rabbi, the provincial chief rabbi. Government taxes, especially, were permanently assessed for the entire province. With or without direct government interference, these were a strong link to resist centrifugal trends. Under these circumstances, the assemblies of Kleve (as well as those of the neighboring Mark), sometimes acting in unison, resembled the plenary membership meetings of a large local community of Poland or Moravia much more than they did the great *va'adim*, with which they shared this rather vague designation. Like that of Cassel, they were totally submerged in the new consistorial organization of the Kingdom of Westphalia during the Napoleonic era.[55]

Varying degrees of government pressure and of the Jewish urge to more effective self-government are reflected also in the evolution of the other German provincial assemblies and chief rabbinates. It was, clearly, at the government's behest that representatives of the Lower Austrian communities assembled in Vienna in 1669 (such deputies are recorded already before 1652) to elect twelve tax assessors for the following three years. In the principality of Bamberg, on the other hand, where "protection" over the Jews was divided between the bishop and the barons, the bulk of Jewry united in 1619 to elect a common chief rabbi. Later

the two sections established a council with delegates from
four main districts. Having adopted a memorable constitution in 1678, this council continued to exercise great
influence on the affairs of Bamberg Jewry, even after the
annexation of the bishopric by Bavaria during the Napoleonic wars. It was finally suppressed by a Bavarian decree
of 1813. A number of local communities, however, supported
on fiscal grounds by baronial suzerains, one of whom claimed
in 1736 that he was "enough of a rabbi" for them, refused
to submit to the jurisdiction of the council or the chief
rabbi. The Münster triennial Jewish diet which met from
1735 on was obviously a joint product of the Jews' resentment against mismanagement by the bishop's "commander
of the Jews," — an office which, ever since 1651, had been
held by influential and autocratic court Jews — and the
government's desire to deal with a central Jewish agency.
It required three decades of persistent efforts for the Jews
to secure the establishment of a regional chief-rabbinate in
1771. The first Jewish assembly of Mecklenburg-Schwerin
met in 1752 without any government authorization, but it
was not until 1764 that government approval enabled the
provincial leaders to silence opposition and adopt a constitution of 66 articles. The city of Schwerin, however,
retained a measure of independence, resembling that of
Poznań in the Council of Greater Poland, and merely contributed to the expenditures of the chief rabbinate which
was established in 1763. Less is known about the propelling forces in the organization of the regional council of the
County of Wied-Runkel, except insofar as they are reflected
in the successive layers of its remarkable statute, published
a few years ago.[56]

8. EUROPEAN INNOVATIONS

In this great variety of Jewish supercommunal organs developed in the European middle ages and early modern times, we find considerable departures from the patterns evolved by the talmudic and geonic sages. While generally accepting the Talmud as its ultimate authority and bowing reverently before the Babylonian and Palestinian expounders of ancient wisdom, European Jewry shaped its communal destinies in accordance with its own social and political requirements. Since its socio-economic and political status had, to a large extent, been determined by developments under the Christian Roman Empire, it is not astounding to find more direct survivals of the free, egalitarian structure of the Graeco-Roman diaspora community than of the more hierarchic forms of the Palestinian and Babylonian groups.

Hereditary leadership, reminiscent of the patriarchate or exilarchate, was practically unknown in medieval or early modern Europe. Heredity occasionally may have influenced the choice of a communal leader. It may have established even legal preferences in favor of certain candidates against others. But it never became a dominant constitutional principle. In fact, concentrated leadership in the hands of individuals became less and less frequent as Jewry was allowed to develop its autonomous organs without or with little state interference. In the Mediterranean countries, under the combined influence of Muslim traditions and royal insistence, the Jews still accepted without demurrer a single provincial, or even national chief rabbi. But he was far from playing the role of an exilarch or gaon. At best he was tolerated as a government, rather than a community appointee, and was largely judged on his personal merits.

Whatever his fiscal and judicial prerogatives may have been, the Jews often discarded his leadership in favor of that of others with superior legal acumen, erudition or piety. They flocked into the academies of rabbis of their own choice, addressed their inquiries to authorities recognized by themselves who might hold no public office, and freely accepted the writings of any distinguished author as authoritative guidance for private and communal life. Wherever they could, they altogether abandoned the centralized leadership of individuals subject to state control, and turned to synods and conferences of rabbis and laymen or, if at all feasible, to permanent councils.

These conferences and councils, too, developed in the course of time many of the imperfections inherent in human institutions. Reflecting, in particular, the shift of forces inside and outside individual communities, they often were subject to the same corrosive forces of oligarchy and economic exploitation which undermined the strength of their constituent bodies. But by focusing the attention of the Jewries of an entire province or country, and by endowing them with a certain singleness of purpose and unity of action they frequently stemmed the tide of communal anarchy and served as a stabilizing factor in the dark ages of permanent insecurity.

CHAPTER IX

LOCAL SOCIETY

TO THESE various forms of provincial or nation-wide supercommunal control may be contrasted numerous smaller societies (*ḥebrot*), especially those which constituted mere subdivisions of local communities. Where, as in the larger Turkish communities after the mass immigration of Spanish-Portuguese refugees, there existed no fully organized and unified local community, voluntary associations often served as unifying links among disparate congregations. The famous Talmud Torah association of Salonica, for instance, with a building which housed educational institutions from grammar school to academy, was, from its foundation in 1520, the center of many community-wide undertakings. Thirteen individual congregations, including ten founded by refugees from Spain, Portugal and southern Italy in the difficult years between 1492 and 1535, served more specific needs. Memorial services for distinguished leaders and other city-wide assemblies were held in the Talmud Torah. Moses Almosnino there submitted his report on negotiations undertaken with the Porte on behalf of the entire community. So proud were the Salonican Jews of their educational institution, which in more than one respect anticipated the best of the American Jewish center, that one sixteenth-century rabbi, Isaac Adribi, claimed that "even those inhabiting distant lands have their eyes and hearts turned toward" it. Indeed, legacies were left to it not only by local citizens, but even by the rich of other communities, from Angora to Budapest.[1]

Usually, however, such free societies were but cells within a larger communal organism, subject to a more or less rigid control by an established local leadership. As a rule they enjoyed no power of taxation but were dependent on their members' voluntary contributions. Hence they lacked some of the public law attributes of organized communities. Nevertheless, they often possessed statutes of their own, whose violation was punishable by severe fines or even expulsion. While expulsion did not necessarily mean as complete a loss of status as would communal excommunication, its effects on social and occupational standing could be extremely serious. Relying primarily, however, on deeply-rooted loyalties, and specializing in communal activities closest to members' hearts, they fostered the communal spirit among the mass more effectively than could the official community, so often burdened with domineering cliques and so rarely holding popular assemblies. Of course, some associations likewise developed influential coteries, but by constantly offering an opportunity for the formation of new factions and the secession of dissatisfied minorities, they opened a broad field to the energies of all public-spirited citizens. Women, in particular, rigidly excluded from active participation in official communal management, found in these associations an outlet for charitable propensities and organizing abilities.[2]

These associations may be classified into four main groups on the basis of purpose, aimed at religious, educational, charitable or occupational needs. Lines were not sharply drawn. Some associations, particularly in smaller communities, offered a variety of services. Many professional guilds, for example, maintained a synagogue and other religious and educational institutions. On the other hand, in some large communities, specialization was highly developed. Some functions connected with funerals, for instance, were performed by one, others by a second society. That there was much duplication of effort goes without saying, but it was largely compensated for by the benefits of the division of labor and the stimulation of interest among many members.

1. Religious Confraternity

Among religious associations, those maintaining synagogues and constituting separate congregations were to be found in practically all communities so large that a single building could not accomodate all worshipers. Differences in ritual, frequently arising from the confluence of streams from diverse countries of origin, necessitated separate divine services and often led to the formation of separate congregations. Sometimes ritualistically diversified congregations shared one edifice. When the Spanish refugees began to arrive in large numbers in Rome, the native congregation added a story to its synagogue, assigning the ground floor to the newcomers. Later, other congregations were set up; and the main communal structure of Roman Jewry, ultimately housing five distinct congregations, came to be known as the *cinque scuole* (five houses of worship). Since, on the other hand, Jewish law prescribed merely the participation of ten adult male Jews in any full-fledged divine service, individuals could with greater or lesser regularity easily assemble a congregation at home.

This pulverization of congregational life made rapid progress at first in the Turkish communities after the mass immigration of the Spanish and Portuguese exiles. Moses Capsali, the first *ḥakam bashi* of Constantinople, may have tried to stem the tide of this communal separation, and for a time succeeded in preventing "innovations" on the part of immigrant scholars. Neither he nor his successors could, in the long run, prevent formation of the forty-four independent congregations which so deeply impressed a German visitor in the mid-sixteenth century. As stated above, ten new congregations were formed in Salonica alone after 1492, organized according to the country of provenance. Five were Spanish (the *Gerush Sefarad*, Castilian, Aragonese, Catalan and Majorcan), three Portuguese (from "Portugal," Lisbon and Evora), and two south-Italian (Sicilian and Calabrian). To prevent further subdivisions, many of these congregations pledged themselves against separation. The futility of some such agreements, however, is demonstrated by a responsum of the famous Egyptian rabbi, David ibn Abi Zimra. The majority of a newly-founded Salonica congregation, we learn from his decision, dissatisfied with the management of the owner of the building, resolved to form a new association only twenty-three years after agreeing not to separate for at least a century.[3]

In central and eastern Europe, too, an increasing number of private associations and even individuals maintained places of worship for particular neighborhoods or social or cultural groups. To save face, some communities of Central Europe adopted the compromise that one synagogue, erected by the community at large, was to be invested with the full sacred character of a "little sanctuary," while other places of worship, which usually accommodated in fact the overwhelming majority, were to be regarded as semi-private dwellings. Needless to say, informality enhanced

the popularity of the latter type. Ezekiel Landau, commenting on the situation in eighteenth-century Prague, typical
of all central and eastern Europe, complained bitterly that,
although private dwellings were full of uncleanness and
profanity, "the slave girl has inherited the place of her
rightful mistress, and the private gatherings are filled, while
the synagogues remain unattended." The spread of the
ḥasidic movement in the Russo-Polish areas, in particular,
accompanied by lively struggles between the ḥasidim and
their opponents as well as among the various ḥasidic groups,
stimulated the rise of such small religious associations. They
were inclined, by virtue of partisan fervor, to magnify ritual
minutiae and infinitesimal doctrinal divergences into basic
issues. Soon every distinguished ṣaddiḳ boasted congregations of followers in many townships and villages. The
unity of communal life, nevertheless, remained largely
unimpaired, inasmuch as, above all these congregations in
Austria, Prussia and, until 1844, in Russia there stood the
generally recognized leadership of an official community.[4]

More specialized religious functions were performed by
burial societies which soon arose in most large communities.
Possibly going back to talmudic and geonic prototypes,
such organized societies arose independently in Spain and
Germany. The earliest extant statutes of such fraternities
date from the beginning of the fourteenth century when
we find them fully established in Huesca (1323) and, in
modified form, in Miltenberg near Mayence (1329). The
Huesca statutes were confirmed by the government after
the elimination of provisions which "appeared to be in
conflict with the royal jurisdiction." This Huesca society
of "grave-diggers" (ḳabbarim or cavafuessas) had, however,
a semi-professional character, inasmuch as members were

paid for services, even though a special article prohibited charges to mourners. Divided into seven sections, the fraternity was directed by a board of seven elders, each elected by one section for seven months, with no right of re-election within two years. Admission of new members was by vote of the board plus fourteen special representatives also chosen by the seven sections. Special privileges were extended to sons of members. Moral and religious conduct and strict discipline were enjoined with considerable attention to detail. A confraternity of *cavadores* is also recorded in the tax ordinance of the Saragossa community of 1331 as the only association enjoying certain tax immunities. Similar societies are mentioned about the same time by Nissim b. Reuben, rabbi in Gerona, in connection with legacy laws, and by Asher b. Yeḥiel of Toledo, in replies to inquiries concerning the rights of leaders and hereditary members in one such *ḥaburah*.[5]

Later, these societies became increasingly philanthropic in nature, offering services gratuitously to both rich and poor. They generally came to be designated as "holy associations of loving-kindness," a reference to the *ḥesed shel emet* of the well-known homily on Gen. 47.29. All large and many small communities soon possessed such a "holy association" or *ḥebrah ḳadishah*, whose members were increasingly recruited from among the wealthiest and most learned groups in the ghetto. Their services began at the bedside of the dying, where they recited special prayers, such as those collected by Aaron Berekiah of Modena in the *Ma'abar yabboḳ* which first appeared in 1626, and were concluded by the offering of sympathy to the mourners after the funeral. They were often assisted by special societies and foundations for "the covering of the dead";

by male and female *lavadores* (in Hebrew *ḥebrat reḥiṣah*) for the required ablutions of the corpse; and by *levayat metim* who specialized in the proper arrangement of funerals. Even in modern Poland and Lithuania some funerary associations retained semi-professional features characteristic of the Huesca "grave-diggers." Evidently to eliminate extortionism, the Lithuanian Council ordered in 1761 that funerary guilds should not delay burial when mourners offered security rather than cash for services, or when it appeared doubtful whether a particular burial should be at the association's expense or at that of the communal chest. Maximum fees were fixed at 200 florins for the middle-class, and 600 florins for the wealthy.[6]

Other religious associations met for nightly or early morning services. Numerous special prayers were composed for these services. Recorded in 1378 in Saragossa under the name *lelezmuroz* (apparently the equivalent of *lel ashmorot*, the night of watches), such fraternities under similar names (*shomerim labboḳer*, etc.) spread particularly in Italy during the seventeenth and eighteenth centuries.[7]

Rather special in nature were the mystic associations of Cabalists and Shabbetians devoted to the promotion of an "initiated" mode of life and the cultivation of mystic lore. They, too, had antecedents in the ancient *ḥaburot*, which undoubtedly had been nurtured from the great syncretistic and gnostic wave of the declining Graeco-Roman civilization. They were continued in open and secret conventicles of adepts of the rising medieval cabala under Islam, and soon also in Christian Provence. Information concerning their organization, the rights and duties of members, relations with State and communal organs is naturally exceedingly scanty. But there is little doubt that, in a religiously fermenting environment, they added a distinctive hue to the multicolored pattern of the Jewish community.

Records of three such groups which have come down to us from sixteenth-century Safed show that their secrecy was prompted by a desire to avoid the populace rather than by any need of concealing obnoxious doctrines or practices. Instructions given to one group by its foremost leader, Moses Cordovero, merely enjoin extreme saintliness, moderation and ritualistic devotion. Only three of the forty-one articles refer to the members. They advise each

> to associate daily with one of his fellow-members and to discuss with him the problems of worship. On every Friday to discuss with that same fellow-member all one had done during the entire week and thence-forth proceed to receive the "Queen Sabbath"... and to converse with fellow-members all the time exclusively in Hebrew.

Of great interest are the statutes of the mystic Paduan association *Or Torah* (the light of the Law) led by Moses Ḥayyim Luzzatto during the years 1730–32, and those of the society *Ahabat Shalom* (The Love for Peace), founded in Jerusalem in 1754. The "Association of the Ḥasidim," however, a Shabbetian organization operating in Germany around 1700, concealed behind a similar other-worldly and ascetic façade, strong propagandist aspirations of a powerful movement which had been driven underground. Such missionary fervor was generally combined with mystic speculation. In the later "ḥasidic" associations of the Beshtian kind, the so-called ḥasidic *shtubels* which, soon assuming the character of a mass movement, fought their battles in the open with growing popular acclaim, there appeared also a wholehearted affirmation of this-worldly reality. Mass appeal, however, coupled with a few ritualistic peculiarities, often tended to transform such groups of the elect into ordinary public congregations, or even majority groups.[8]

2. EDUCATIONAL ASSOCIATION

Beginning with medieval Spain, societies called *Talmud Torah* (the Teaching of the Torah)[9] belonged to the most significant educational institutions of Jewish communities. Although from talmudic times the provision of educational facilities was considered a general communal responsibility, the task was often delegated to semi-private associations. While, for the most part, the latter limited themselves to establishing schools for the children of the impoverished who could not afford private tutors, a few such groups pursued more ambitious programs, offering primary, secondary and higher education for children and adults regardless of financial standing. Advanced and adult education was generally entrusted to special societies, maintaining schools of higher learning, if not to the communal rabbi. Others arranged for group study of assigned sections of the Talmud (the so-called *ḥebrot shas*), and otherwise stimulated study among members or the public at large.

Most of these associations had formal statutes, some of which were printed soon after adoption, outlining aims of the founders, the competences of officers, the educational and administrative policies set by the members. One of the oldest and fullest collections of European Jewish statutory provisions is that known as the *Ḥuḳḳe ha-Torah* (Laws of the Torah). Although extant in several manuscript versions, this collection can neither be dated precisely nor ascribed to any definite locality. We know only that it considerably antedates 1305, when one manuscript was copied, and that it most likely was composed somewhere in northern France or the Holy Roman Empire. It is equally uncertain whether it was enacted by a particular association, by the leaders of a community or by representatives of several communities, although its tenor suggests a minority reform movement. The absence of citations from this collection in subsequent medieval letters and educational reforms makes it also very plausible that this reform trend never became a mass movement. Its postulates, in fact, may never have found practical application. Especially its demand for a semi-monastic segregation of teachers and students in a *midrash* near the synagogue, with permission to visit families only on Sabbaths and holidays, is so clearly a deviation from established usages of the Jewish street, so unmistakable a mark of Christian influence, that the communities' failure to act on such suggestions is easily understandable. None the less, some provisions of this statute, to which reference will be made in our analysis of communal education, seem indirectly to have influenced subsequent attempts at educational reform, and many statutory regulations of later groups.[10]

While these provisions delegated responsibility for management of the school largely to communal leaders, there were certain family foundations in which the original donors tried to reserve all rights to themselves and their descendants in perpetuity. They, too, had to accept some communal supervision. In 1332, for instance, one Joseph b. Ephraim ha-Levi established an educational foundation in Ecija, Castile, by donating some land and 5,000 maravedis in cash (equal to 500 mar. in gold). This foundation was to maintain a school in the city under the combined management of the communal elders and the founder or the oldest of his progeny. "Such shall be the practice in all coming generations to the end of the world." The physician Hélias of Valence, a native of Arles, went even further; in 1407 he decided to endow the local school in Arles which had just been compelled to close for lack of funds. As was not uncommon, he forced the hard-pressed communal elders to accept a considerable part of the endowment in communal debentures and extracted a promise of prayers, to be recited by the precentor, on every *Simḥat Torah* in perpetuity, in his and his family's behalf. Moreover, he provided that the administration of the school must be in the hands of governors to be designated by him (including his own grandchildren), and thereafter their descendants to the end of days. With an imperturbable serenity typical of medieval Jewry, Joseph and Hélias, heedless of all previous warnings, overlooked the possibility that, within a few generations, the entire communities of Ecija and Arles would be wiped out by strokes of intolerant royal pens.[11]

Far more typical of the medieval and early modern statutes of educational associations is that adopted by the Talmud Torah society of Venice which, for a time, enjoyed a very high reputation in the entire Sephardic world. One of its pupils, David Pardo, upon assuming the rabbinical office in Amsterdam, took the Venetian statute as a model for that of a similar association which he founded in his adopted city. Very interesting are also the successive statutes adopted by the Talmud Torah society in neighboring Verona, as well as the revised statute of the Modena association dated in 1758, which was largely based on regulations and practices in force from the association's establishment in 1597. Its objectives are defined in Art. 1 as follows:

To assign a place for study, i. e. a two-story house, each story containing at least two rooms, and to establish there a school for public use and a meeting place for the scholars. There shall be gathered all the boys of our city who desire to study any subject taught in any grade as described below. There shall also be flats for two teachers so that they be readily available at any time to impart knowledge to the people. They shall be obliged to teach the Torah to the boys who will come to study the Lord's perfect Law. They shall also teach them writing in both Hebrew and Gentile [Italian], and all that without any reward and payment [on their part]. Excepted are the small boys of the first grade who are to be taught by the woman teacher in her house, as shall be explained in Art. 9. In order that they [the teachers] be able to live with no other employment and to devote their undivided attention to their God-ordained calling, the members of the Association shall fix for them a monthly salary as they shall see fit, according to the time and the heaviness of the burden resting upon them. Our house shall be wide open not only for these children, but for everyone desirous to approach the sanctuary, to partake of the Torah and to study it; be he a native of this city or of another city, a stranger or a citizen, "He who is hungry shall come and eat."

There follow 28 other articles, equally wordy and studded with biblical and talmudic phrases. They describe the election of directors; administrative and educational management; the appointment of teachers, two men and one woman, two or three assistants, and a janitor; their respective tasks; the division of grades; subjects and hours of instruction; textbooks; required attendance of pupils at synagogue services, especially to hear the semi-annual sermons; the management of the school library; and various disciplinary measures. Of special interest is a warning to parents or guardians who might wish to send children to work at an early age; by enrolling in the institution, each student would assume the obligation to attend until the age of fourteen, unless he could secure a special dispensation from the directors. Violators of this rule would be denounced to the communal authorities, who might stop relief payments to the parents or guardians.[12]

3. PHILANTHROPIC SOCIETY

Stimulated by the Crusades, a large number of charitable organizations began to spring up all over Europe, undoubtedly owing in part to the Muslim example. Even more important were the impact of increasing economic differentiation among the classes, the speedy transformation of methods of production, and the general rise in the standard of living, all of which contributed to the steady growth of a variety of underprivileged groups. Charities theretofore were administered almost exclusively by the Church and would have proved woefully inadequate even if ecclesiastical leaders had adhered to a program of a *quarta pauperum*, *i. e.* of assigning one-quarter of the revenue of the Church — its entire property had once been designated as the *patrimonium pauperum* — to the support of the poor. As a matter of fact, however, these leaders, absorbed in careers of political and economic expansion, entangled in worldwide and local power politics, delegated more and more of their charitable functions to special monastic orders, such as the Franciscans, and to private groups of burghers. The

Jewish communities, too, although offering no counterpart
to the sharp division between the Catholic clergy and the
laity and, hence, between the ecclesiastical and secular
charities, were stimulated by the same basic socio-economic
trends to form an ever increasing number of philanthropic
societies and foundations.[13]

Specialization among charitable organizations went far,
even too far for their own good. They often had no reason
for existing but the ambitions of a founder. Through a
legacy, in particular, one could create any new organization
providing for real or imaginary needs. Wills were usually
literally observed, and rabbis — even those who, like Jacob
Tam, tried to facilitate the shifting of communal funds in
accord with changing needs — had compunctions about
transferring legacies provided with a specified aim. The
decision rendered by Jacob Weil of Erfurt (15th century)
concerning a legacy left by a woman providing for the
distribution of weekly allowances to the poor of the city
reflected dominant rabbinic opinion. He forbade to utilize
these funds for the support of students arriving to study
at the local academy by arguing that, "although, had the
testator known that education is preferred to charity, she
might have devoted the fund to educational matters, here
we cannot exercise our discretion, because the local poor
had already acquired a right in the foundation."[14]

Similar foundations and societies are frequently mentioned
in medieval Spain, although it is not always easy to grasp
their structure and function. As far back as 1266 we find
the record of a Jewish "house of mercy" in the small community of Jerez de la Frontera. Records of charitable organizations in the last century of Jewish settlement on the
Peninsula are more common. In Saragossa, also distin-

guished for its Christian guilds and fraternities, we find a Jewish society for the visiting of the sick, named *bikkur holim* (1382, 1397), which became the standard designation for associations of that type. Saragossa also possessed a general charitable society for the poor, especially for orphan girls, called in Spanish *Hoce Hece*, evidently a corruption of the Hebrew 'ose ḥesed. According to a privilege granted by Alfonso V in 1425, it had the right of adopting its own statutes and ordinances and freely electing officers who were authorized to enforce payments of dues by members. This society existed as late as 1476. What its relations may have been to another charitable society, recorded in 1467 as the *rotfecedi* (*rodfe ṣedeḳ*), which designation was likewise destined to become extremely popular, is not certain. In Toledo, one of the largest communities in medieval Europe, a contemporary poet, lamenting the ravages of the "holy war" of 1391, decried the dissolution of societies devoted to funeral rites and education, marriage and circumcision ceremonies and general social welfare. On the occasion of the liquidation of Jewish communal property left in Spain by the exiles of 1492, we often hear of associations "for the clothing of the poor," "of the hospital," and the like.[15]

The number of such charitable organizations grew by leaps and bounds in the early modern period. Italy soon took the lead in the Jewish, as it did in Christian charities. In Rome, where a communal decision of 1617 referred to but eight associations, there were a few decades later more than twenty, engaged in diversified activities. No less than seven provided clothing, food and shelter to the poor, some specializing in the support of women and captives. Two other societies supplied a minimum dowry and trousseau to needy brides. Another organization offered assistance in cases of sudden death, another cared for the sick. Apart from members, the population at large often contributed through public collections. To obviate excessive competition, the regulation of 1617 prescribed that only two representatives from each of the eight recognized societies be allowed to make collections in front of the synagogue on Purim and the Ninth of Ab. On the other hand, refusal by a citizen to stand with the box and publicly to solicit donations was punishable by a fine of 5 giulii. This impressive record of the community of Rome was, none the less, far outstripped by that of Amsterdam. The will of one B. Cohen, who died in the early 1800's, included bequests for no less than 210 philanthropic and educational associations, to which he had been a more or less regular contributor in his lifetime.[16]

This extraordinary expansion of Jewish philanthropic societies in the eighteenth century was undoubtedly due to the combined influences of growing rational humanitarianism, new emphases on free associations of citizens, the decline in the power of the churches and the growing sufferings from wars and speedy transformations of life in the Commercial and Industrial Revolutions. The "glorious" eighteenth century has not unjustifiably been styled by a modern authority a "century of beggary." If in the Paris of Louis XIV some 40,000 inhabitants (one-fifth of the population) were dependent on public or private charities, if the rich province of Flanders in 1772 had to support as public charges one-seventh and Berlin, at the end of the Seven Years' War, fully one-third of their respective populations, it is not astonishing to find nearly bankrupt Jewish communities of central and eastern Europe forced to strain their resources to the utmost to alleviate the misery of

impoverished members either directly or through charitable
societies. It must be borne in mind, however, that some of
these associations were primarily, if not exclusively, the
members' mutual benefit societies. The renowned Venetian
association for endowing orphan girls, with ramifications in
Pisa, Hamburg, Amsterdam, Lyons and even Belgrade and
Safed, gave preference to daughters of impoverished members. The association for the visiting of the sick in Fürth,
according to its statute printed in 1818, was designed to
extend aid only to members of several years standing. It
is interesting to note that this statute definitely excluded
all communal officials, honorary as well as salaried, from
holding office in the society.[17]

4. THE PROFESSIONAL LEAGUE

Economic self-interest was clearly the main motivating
power in the formation of those numerous occupational
associations of Jewish craftsmen which, sometimes organized
along the lines of medieval guilds, were found in most
countries of Jewish mass settlement, especially Poland.
Their antecedents went back to remote antiquity, to the
villages and city quarters of Israelitic Palestine inhabited
by people of a single craft. In the talmudic period, such
associations of craftsmen and shippers regulated admission
to the craft, also fixed prices for services, establishing, e. g.
regular zone tariffs for the shipment of goods. The rabbis
of both Palestine and Babylonia countenanced these self-
governing bodies and recognized the legitimacy of their
agreements affecting the public at large. We have also
seen how the special sections assigned to various crafts in
the great synagogue of Alexandria fostered in them the
esprit de corps and facilitated the placement of more recent

arrivals. From an inscription found in Hierapolis, Asia Minor, and dating from the second or third century, we learn about two apparently wholly Jewish guilds of dyers and weavers. The Theodosian Code specifically regulated the services to be rendered the state by the Jewish association of shipmasters (*navicularii*) in Alexandria.[18]

The continued development of the guild system in the Byzantine Empire, particularly as reflected in the legislation of Leo VI (about 895), inevitably stimulated the Jews, increasingly affected by governmental intolerance and segregation, to organize along occupational lines. Not only the guilds of dealers in bullion and moneylenders and those of bankers and money-changers, but also the numerous craft associations in the clothing industry either had to admit Jewish members — which in view of their pronounced religious character seems unlikely — or allow Jews to establish competing corporations. Such are, indeed, clearly implied in Benjamin of Tudela's description of the Jewish craftsmen in Constantinople and elesewhere in the Balkans.[19]

Whether or not the spread of Islam interrupted the continuity of the Byzantine and Persian guild system is debatable, although no conclusive evidence for such interruption has been forthcoming. In any case, from the ninth century on, partly in connection with the religious propaganda of the Karmatians, trade associations of all kinds spread throughout the Muslim world, until Turkish Istanbul (Constantinople) in 1640 counted some 1100 guilds in its numerous bazaars. Due to the Muslim canonical prohibition of usury, which included all profits in credit and exchange transactions, banking, money-changing and trade in bullion were largely delegated to "infidel" Christians and Jews, who often formed such independent corporations. Occasionally even Jews converted to Islam were excluded from the regular Muslim guilds which, as frequently elsewhere, tried to preserve trade monopoly for old members. Unfortunately, extant Hebrew sources from Muslim areas are rather inarticulate in regard to Jewish trade or craft associations. We must be satisfied with incidental references, such as are contained in a responsum of Simon Duran to a League of Jewish Merchants meeting in a sort of Chamber of Commerce in fifteenth-century Algiers.[20]

More direct references to Jewish professional confraternities, with a strong social and religious coloring, are found in the available records from medieval Spain and Italy. The large Jewish population of these countries, in order to subsist, had to utilize all occupational opportunities left open by the state laws which, in fact, were more liberal there than in northern lands. Wherever the number of skilled Jewish craftsmen in a particular branch of industry warranted it, they organized, under the prevailing economic regimentation, a sort of closed shop to keep out undesirable competitors, to reduce competition among members, to regulate the admission and number of journeymen and apprentices and, occasionally, to combat threatening large-scale production and to supervise quality of output. While too few statutes of medieval Jewish guilds are extant to vouchsafe any broad generalization, it appears that all these economic motives which dominated the formation of Christian medieval guilds in their classical era of evolution, operated also in the field of Jewish industrial crafts, except that the latter had to adjust themselves to varying pressures from Christian rivals. In Europe north of the Alps and Pyrenees (except for early modern Poland and Bohemia-Moravia) this pressure, coupled with the relative numerical

weakness of the Jewish population which required but a
few specialized artisans for its own needs, prevented the
formation of regular craft associations. Here the community,
utilizing its extensive jurisdictional powers over Jewish
autonomy, and particularly the newly developed instrument
of the *ḥerem ha-yishub* (the ban of settlement, which often
involved permission to ply some craft), was in a position
fully to protect the acquired rights of the few local master
artisans without reference to special corporative statutes.
The small size of the communities also obviated the need
for the provision of those social and religious services which
often occupied an important place in guild functions in more
populous areas. These secondary motives of medieval guild
formation, as well as those which might perhaps be styled
tertiary and which tended to secure to members the benefits
of independent guild jurisdiction, civil and criminal, and
certain advantages in the frequent class struggles and local
power politics, were present also in the Jewish craft corporations, though perhaps to a lesser degree.[21]

As in the case of the Jewish religious brotherhoods, the
earliest records of Spanish Jewish occupational associations
go back to the fourteenth century. Pedro IV in 1336 not
only confirmed the statute of the Jewish guild of cobblers
in Saragossa, but allowed Jewish shoemakers throughout
Aragon to organize a fraternity. It is perhaps not too far-
fetched to assume that the king was induced to the extension
of this unusual privilege by some influential Jewish cobbler,
such as Juce Arrueti who is recorded as having served as
royal shoemaker later on (1367–1370). If, under pressure of
anti-Jewish sentiment, the Castilian government in 1412
prohibited Jews and Moors from plying a series of crafts for
Christian customers, this decree seems soon afterwards to

have sunk into oblivion. In fact, in 1443 King John II took special pains to protect the Jewish artisans against similar provisions of the papal bull of 1442. As late as 1486 Ferdinand and Isabella effectively intervened with the city of Burgos, which wished to restrict the activities of its Jewish craftsmen to the Jewish quarter. At times the power of the organized guilds was such that, as in many medieval cities, they became a prime political factor in the Jewish community. In the difficult years of reconstruction after 1415, they seized the reins of government in Saragossa, evoking Solomon Bonafed's caustic remarks about "tailors serving as magistrates and cobblers as judges," as well as King Alfonso V's complaint that communal administration had fallen into the hands of those more apt "to be governed than to govern" (1417).[22]

In southern Italy, too, Jewish craftsmen had held a prominent position ever since King Roger transplanted a large number of Jewish silk workers from Thebes to Palermo (1146). Frederick II made excellent use of Jewish collaborators in the exploitation of his newly established monopolistic enterprises for the manufacture of silk and dyed stuffs. Caschisi, the head of the Jewish carpenters' guild in Palermo, collaborated with distinction in the building of the royal palace in 1451. Even in the intolerant period of 1492–1539, the Jews were well represented in the building and metal crafts and the production of arms. In Rome a list of 385 Jewish families, compiled before 1527, indicates the occupations of 91 heads of families. Among these were no less than 20 tailors and 30 other craftsmen. In 1541 the Jewish tailors' guild, approached by the Christian, concluded with their confreres an agreement concerning the manufacture of "Romanesque" cloth. Like the guild of Jewish bankers, this association operated under the supervision of the communal organs; the pact was confirmed by the signature of the communal secretary and entered into the communal minute-book.[23]

The highest development of Jewish guilds — often actually so styled — came about in Poland as the combined result of the rapid increase of the Jewish population which necessitated great economic differentiation; its relatively favorable legal status; the considerable political weakness of its chief competitors, and the progressive elimination of many Jews from certain fiscal and commercial occupations reserved for the nobles. Largely excluded from the Christian guilds on competitive as well as religious grounds, since every guild was at the same time a religious fraternity with its own chapels and patron saints, the Jews began organizing their own associations, often in open defiance of existing Christian corporate bodies. Supported by the authorities — King Sigismund I, for instance, decided in favor of a Jewish guild in 1539 — and a vigorous communal leadership, they succeeded in overcoming all outer and inner resistance and formed powerful guilds throughout Poland. In the eighteenth century Lissa possessed Jewish guilds of tailors, goldsmiths, lace-makers, plumbers, tanners, barbers, weavers of goldcloth and furriers. The statute of the latter guild, like that of its confreres in Cracow (of 1613) and those of several other guilds in these two cities, Lwów, Przemyśl, Poznań and Płock, have been printed. Charters of many other associations are known to exist in various manuscript collections, and their publication in the near future would help clarify a significant phase in both the communal and the economic history of the Jews. The following excerpts from the provisions of the constitution adopted in 1639 by

the then newly formed guild of Jewish barbers and surgeons
in Cracow may serve as an illustration of such organic laws:

1. First, they [the master barbers] are obligated to
make a weekly collection for charity among their
members. . . . 2. No barber may keep in his shop
more than one apprentice to teach the trade to.
This apprentice must bind himself for three successive
years. . . . 3. Each barber may, as is the custom, engage another apprentice as a partner who is to get
one-third of the profit. . . . 4. . . . all the apprentices. . . are compelled, first of all, to obligate and
record themselves in the minute-books of the Jewish
community to the effect that they will not marry a
local girl, in order not to cast additional burdens on
the people of this community. . . . 5. The above-
mentioned barbers have also bound themselves not
to raise prices. . . . On the other hand, they will not
cheapen or lower — God forbid — their fees by being
too liberal. . . . 8. The barbers have also agreed that,
if a competent barber who does not belong to our
community should settle in our midst, and even
though he be acceptable to the entire community,
but if he should not be willing to bind himself by a
hard and fast pact to accept all the rules above
recorded, then the barbers are bound to uphold one
another in opposing that man.

These regulations were incorporated in the official minute-
book of the community and thus obtained the full sanction
of the community at large.[24]

This type of sanction, or even more effective communal
control, existed in most of these professional or other associations. As far back as 1383 Infante John issued a privilege
for the community of Perpignan, enabling it to establish
confraternities of all sorts, and to have the members elect

the directors "with the intervention or approval of the secretaries" of the community. The directors were given the right to enforce the payment by members of all "they would promise or be obligated to." In many Polish communities the communal elders frequently intervened in guild affairs, because of the internal strife between various groups of artisans. The tailors' guild in Berdiczew, pushing aside the communal elders, obtained in 1732 a confirmation of its charter directly from the town's landlady. But this is an exception which confirms the general rule of strict supervision by the Jewish community. In Poznań the control of the communal elders went as far as admission of members, which was controlled jointly by the elders and the respective guild officers. Przemyśl forbade the officers of the guild to issue new regulations or to institute collections without previous consultation with the communal organs. In Lithuania, as a rule, communal representatives occupied one-half of the seats on the boards of the associations. When a guild in Minsk ventured to complain to the state authorities against the leaders of the *kahal*, the latter suppressed the "rebellion" by publicly putting in chains one of the association's elders and by excluding another from the exercise of his craft. There were other instances of such economic and political conflicts which, in the eighteenth and even more in the nineteenth century, often assumed the character of a developed class struggle. The community of Dubno in 1766 altogether suppressed artisan guilds for a time. This was not the outgrowth of any particular anti-guild movement such as had been spreading over capitalistically advanced areas of western Europe and as was to produce, within ten years, the famous decrees of Turgot. It was more in line with the sudden outbursts of impatience of some medieval cities (Paris 1305, Bremen 1322, Frankfort 1443, 1447, etc.) which suppressed their guilds. In many cases, on the other hand, the community extended financial subsidies to the individual societies. Not infrequently, however, the community, loaded with state taxes and debts, was forced to borrow money from the wealthier associations. After 1682, the community of Rome owed substantial amounts to several charitable societies (for the benefit of ladies and girls, for charity with the dead, and the Talmud Torah). As in all other organizational endeavors there was frequent friction and much politics in these intracommunal relationships, but by a remarkable combination of individual initiative and authoritarian control, these associations effectively supplemented the more rigidly controlled and legally enforceable activities of the official community.[25]

5. INTRACOMMUNAL AUTONOMY

As in the field of supercommunal relations, so also in that of group life within the community, European Jewry departed in many ways from accepted talmudic patterns. It was stimulated thereto by both the surviving traditions of the free Graeco-Roman associations and the growth of corporative trends in the European environment. Although less affected than were their Christian neighbors by feudal forces of territorial dissolution, European Jews, too, felt the effects of the weakness of the European states and their enforced delegation of responsibilities to a variety of self-governing agencies. The same forces, moreover, which fostered decentralization of Jewish communal endeavor and increasing replacement of individual regional leadership by elective bodies representative of more or less independent communities, operated also to stimulate the formation of smaller groups catering to specific religious, educational, charitable or professional needs of their members.

To be sure, primarily due to the peculiarities of Jewish economy and the minority status of the people, the professional guilds never assumed in the Jewish community that position of pre-eminence which they often held in medieval cities. Not even in Poland-Lithuania, where the Jewish guild system reached the apex of its evolution, did any guild or combination of guilds ever dominate the Jewish quarter. The relative absence of merchant guilds in a society in which commerce played an ever more preponderant role, was in itself a sufficient obstacle to such guild domination. The responsibility of the community as a whole, moreover, for taxes due the government, indeed, for nearly all services rendered by Jewish subjects to the country, likewise necessitated concentration of power in communal rather than in guild leadership. Finally, the pre-eminence of scholarship, descent and wealth in the accepted medieval Jewish scale of values also counteracted political expansion of craftsmen who, as a rule, had little of these three major types of social distinction.

None the less, the functions of these associations, especially those organized for charity, education or worship, were an invaluable supplement to the activities of the official community. They not only furnished an outlet for stored-up energies of masses who could rarely participate in the active performance of communal duties, but they also corresponded closely to the wishes of a basically egalitarian society which, often for reasons beyond its control, was forced to delegate active management to certain minority groups. The more oligarchic a community became the greater was the need for shifting its function to self-governing associations. On the other hand, this training in self-government and the loyalties and traditions which it developed proved of greatest importance wherever the official community was losing its hold on members. Especially in the countries of resettlement in western Europe and in their American colonies, where the Jewish community often had to contend with non-recognition or even direct repudiation by public law, the experiences of millennial intra-communal group endeavors paved the way for that new, rich, congregational life outside public law sanctions, which was to save the Jewish community from threatening extinction under the new regimes of a capitalist, secularized and democratic civilization.